Critical Essays on

WILLIAM BLAKE

CRITICAL ESSAYS
ON
BRITISH LITERATURE

Zack Bowen, General Editor
University of Miami

◆

Critical Essays on
WILLIAM BLAKE

◆

edited by

HAZARD ADAMS

G. K. Hall & Co.
BOSTON, MASSACHUSETTS

PR
4147
C75
1991

First published 1991.
10 9 8 7 6 5 4 3 2 1

Library of Congress Cataloging-in-Publication Data

Critical essays on William Blake / edited by Hazard Adams.
    p.   cm. — (Critical essays on British literature)
    Includes bibliographical references and index.
    ISBN 0-8161-8857-2 (alk. paper)
    1. Blake, William, 1757–1827—Criticism and interpretation.
    I. Adams, Hazard, 1926– .   II. Series.
    PR4147.C74 1991
    821.'7—dc20   90-23345

The paper used in this publication meets the minimum requirements of
American National Standard for Information Sciences—Permanence of
Paper for Printed Library Materials, ANSI Z39.48-1984.⊗™

Printed and bound in the United States of America

Contents

♦

General Editor's Note

♦

The Critical Essays on British Literature series provides a variety of approaches to both classical and contemporary writers of Britain and Ireland. The formats of the volumes in the series vary with the thematic designs of individual editors, and with the amount and nature of existing reviews—criticism augmented, where appropriate, by original essays by recognized authorities. It is hoped that each volume will be unique in developing a new overall perspective on its particular subject.

Hazard Adams's selection of essays stresses the wide disparity between the attitudes toward Blake's art and poetry in his own time and those of modern literary critics and art historians. Adams's introductory history of Blake criticism analyzes the issues involved both in the initial negative response to Blake and in the enormous growth in recent attention paid to Blake's poetry and art.

The first section of essays includes Robert Hunt's original attack on Blake's work, as well as more recent retrospective summaries of the early issues, including the accusations of madness, on which Blake's contemporaries took him to task. The second section of the book, beginning with Northrop Frye's influential study of Blake and archetype, deals with overriding themes and issues of Blake criticism, rather than criticism on specific poems. Adams's own treatment of Blake's worldview regarding art; scientific, empirical methodology; and metaphoric, symbolic meaning, as they influence both the individual and the universal, forms a brilliant conclusion to this exceptionally interesting volume.

ZACK BOWEN

University of Miami

Publisher's Note

♦

Producing a volume that contains both newly commissioned and reprinted material presents the publisher with the challenge of balancing the desire to achieve stylistic consistency with the need to preserve the integrity of works first published elsewhere. In the Critical Essays series, essays commissioned especially for a particular volume are edited to be consistent with G. K. Hall's house style; reprinted essays appear in the style in which they were first published, with only typographical errors corrected. Consequently, shifts in style from one essay to another are the result of our efforts to be faithful to each text as it was originally published.

Introduction

♦

HAZARD ADAMS

I

This collection of writings about William Blake and his work can give only a small idea of the immense amount of scholarly and critical activity that has rapidly accumulated over the past few decades. Early in this century Blake was generally regarded as an outsider to the mainstreams of English literature and English visual art. Today he is viewed as a major poet and artist of his age. His writings have been carefully edited, and a large interpretive enterprise has grown up around them. His influence has been felt among literary critics and theorists. Scholarly reproductions of his paintings and engravings now abound. Many of his major paintings are exhibited in the Tate Gallery, London, in a splendid room devoted entirely to his works.

The contrast to Blake's reputation in his own lifetime (1757–1827) and later in the nineteenth century is extreme. In his own time he was little known as a poet. Coleridge had read and commented in a letter on his *Songs of Innocence and Experience,* and we know that Wordsworth, Lamb, and Hazlitt had read at least some of them, but the longer poems were hardly known at all. Indeed, only the *Poetical Sketches* (1783) and *The French Revolution* (1791) were ever set in type, and they were not sold. Blake's later poems he published himself by his own method of relief etching, printing off copies and hand-coloring them, usually only when he had a request.

There were few requests. His masterpiece *Jerusalem: The Emanation of the Giant Albion* survives in but five complete copies, only one of which was colored. His long poem *Milton* survives in four. Though references to these and other long poems are made by a few contemporaries of Blake, his major efforts are usually treated as works of visual art, not poems, as, for example, in the newspaper obituaries on the occasion of Blake's death. Some of Blake's most important poems came to light only after his death. This was the case with the poems of Blake's notebook, known for years as the Rossetti manuscript, and those in a fair copy known as the Pickering manuscript, which contains "The Mental Traveller," to mention only the best known. It was not until 1893 that *The Four Zoas* was discovered and published by Edwin J. Ellis and W. B. Yeats. This long poem of a hundred manuscript pages, though unfinished, is now regarded as indispensable to an intelligent reading of Blake's other poems and a very important work in its own right.

Before Ellis and Yeats's three-volume edition and interpretation, little had been written about Blake's work. The most ambitious effort after Alexander Gilchrist's *Life of William Blake: "Pictor Ignotus"* (1863; rev. 1880) had been A. C. Swinburne's rhapsodic and subjective *William Blake* (1869), hampered by ignorance of *The Four Zoas*. The modern study of Blake's writings really begins with S. Foster Damon's *William Blake: His Philosophy and Symbols* (1924), a brilliant work, though somewhat hampered by an attempt to organize Blake's life and art on the theme of the traditional path of the mystic. Although several writers followed Damon with various studies—Geoffrey Keynes, Max Plowman, Joseph Wicksteed, J. Middleton Murry, Milton O. Percival, Mark Schorer, and Jacob Bronowski—the major event in Blake criticism took place in 1947, with the publication of Northrop Frye's *Fearful Symmetry: A Study of William Blake,* which paid particular attention to the way Blake read the Bible and to the symbolic structure of Blake's work. Frye's book continues today to exert a powerful influence on Blake studies, though now critics are less likely to find Blake's symbolism as systematic and self-consistent as Frye did. But Frye, of course, was attempting to combat the old tradition, originating in the myth of Blake's madness and the difficulty of his work, that Blake's longer works were chaotic and irrational. Extensive scholarship since Frye has revealed more and more the intelligibility of many parts of Blake's writings once thought hopelessly obscure. As a result, critics are no longer as anxious to systematize Blake as to work through—on the basis of better knowledge—a variety of interpretive issues, including in what ways Blake's work changed or developed and what irresolutions may be present.

The next major event was the appearance of David V. Erdman's *Blake: Prophet against Empire* (1954; 3d ed. rev. 1977). Subtitled "A Poet's Interpretation of the History of His Own Times," Erdman's book studied Blake's social and political interests in far greater detail than his predecessors in this field, Schorer and Bronowski. Erdman read the newspapers and cartoons of the period and found in Blake's work allegories of contemporary history and radical political views. He also charted Blake's writings and rewritings as the poet responded to contemporary events.

In the wake of Frye and Erdman came numerous works emphasizing various aspects of Blake's canon. Robert F. Gleckner's *The Piper and the Bard* (1959) studied the earlier lyrics and longer poems. My own *William Blake: A Reading of the Shorter Poems* followed in 1963, and in 1965 Alicia Ostriker discussed Blake's poetic techniques in *Vision and Verse in William Blake.*

Meanwhile Harold Bloom took on the task of a full-scale interpretation in his *Blake's Apocalypse* of 1963. Specialized studies have since abounded. Some of the most important are listed in the bibliography at the end of this book.

Until 1964, however, no one had written extensively on the relation of Blake's texts to his designs. Following the lead of Northrop Frye's important essay "Poetry and Design in William Blake" (1951), Jean H. Hagstrum published *William Blake: Poet and Painter* (1964). Then came *Blake's Visionary Forms Dramatic* (1970), edited by David V. Erdman and John Grant. In 1978 W. J. T. Mitchell contributed the important *Blake's Composite Art: A Study of the Illuminated Poetry*. Since that time, critics have been much more sensitive to the interrelation of poetry and design. Too, a greater interest and understanding of Blake as a visual artist has developed, hastened by the work of David Bindman (*Blake as an Artist* [1977]), Raymond Lister (*Infernal Methods* [1975]), Robert N. Essick (*William Blake, Printmaker* [1980]), and Morris Eaves (*William Blake's Theory of Art* [1982]). Reproductions of Blake's visual and composite art have steadily appeared, including the splendid Trianon Press *Jerusalem* of 1951 and complete volumes of his engravings and paintings.

II

This book has two principal parts. The first is devoted to attitudes toward Blake in his own time. It begins with a selection from Deborah Dorfman's *Blake in the Nineteenth Century* (1969), which gives an account of the knowledge and opinion of Blake when he was alive. Dorfman's selection is followed by Robert Hunt's notoriously vicious review in the *Examiner* (17 Sept. 1809) of Blake's only exhibition of his own works, which took place in the house of Blake's brother, and for which Blake himself wrote a catalog. The exhibition was not a success, though it included a number of works by Blake now highly prized. The *Descriptive Catalogue* is especially valuable for its discussion of the paintings of the Canterbury Pilgrims and the Ancient Britons, the latter now lost. Hunt's review contributed substantially to the myth of Blake's madness.

Until Alexander Gilchrist's *Life* (1863), Allan Cunningham's account of Blake (1830), the last part of which follows Hunt's diatribe, was the most influential and best-known life. Cunningham's treatment was sentimental, and his criticisms suggested that Blake suffered from a kind of schizophrenia. He was particularly hard on Blake's little-known and -appreciated later works. He saw Blake as an artist suffering from an excess of imagination resulting in pictorial extravagance, but he balanced this view with recognition that excess of imagination was a "failing uncommon in this age."

Cunningham's *Life* is followed by excerpts from the *Reminiscences* (1852) of Henry Crabb Robinson, the diarist who knew Blake and who is the source of remarks by and about many well-known artists and writers of his time. *Reminiscences* gives accounts, taken from Robinson's diary, of meetings with

Blake in 1825 and 1826. Robinson, who thought Blake suffered from mono-
mania, exhibited an amusing literal mindedness and mystification about
many of Blake's remarks to him. Others who knew Blake did not think him
quite so odd, though their accounts or mention of Blake are often not as
interesting as Robinson's.

As young men, Samuel Palmer and a group of other painters who called
themselves the "Ancients" came to know and revere Blake. When Gilchrist
was writing his *Life* he asked Palmer for a reminiscence and received the
eloquent statement, written in 1855, that follows Robinson's *Reminiscences*
here. It is to be noticed that neither Palmer nor any of the other Ancients at
any time expressed the view that Blake was mad.

Part 2, a selection of recent criticism, is meant to be read in the order in
which the selections appear. The aim is to provide a broad introductory view,
touching on issues that have been central to the modern study of Blake, with
more emphasis on his writings than on his visual art. Discussion of specific
works are included only where they contribute to the understanding of issues
of general importance to Blake's work. Space does not permit as large a
selection as would be desirable given the aim, and in some cases sections of
essays have had to be omitted. Nevertheless, the selection does, I believe,
succeed in progressively revealing major aspects of Blake's work and of the
recent history of work on Blake, beginning with Northrop Frye's account of
Blake's symbolism and moving through essays that address intellectual and
historical issues, issues of interpretation, and recent consideration of Blake's
concern with language.

The section begins with Northrop Frye's "Blake's Treatment of the
Archetype" (1950), which is one of several important articles Frye wrote
extending, and in certain ways clarifying, ideas set forth in 1947 in *Fearful
Symmetry*. In this essay Frye gives a general account of the structure of Blake's
mythology that is perhaps more schematic than some of us would accept
today, but it is valuable precisely for that schematization and for the effort to
show the importance of Blake to an understanding of "the symbolic formation of poets." More than anyone else, Frye moved Blake from the edge of
English poetic tradition to the mainstream, where he remains today.

David V. Erdman's essay "Blake's Vision of Slavery" is an earlier version
of a portion of his *Blake: Prophet against Empire* (1954). The essay, which
concentrates on *Visions of the Daughters of Albion,* is a good example of the way
in which careful historical study can bring to light Blake's response to the
political events of his own time, in this case particularly, the debate over
slavery. Erdman's work was immediately recognized and is still recognized as
the most important study to appear on the political implication of Blake's
writings and the pervasive revolutionary allegory of his longer poems.

Blake's rejection of neoclassical and Enlightenment values pervades all
that he left to us. Jean H. Hagstrum's "William Blake Rejects the Enlightenment" (1963) charts the movement of Blake's attitude from his juvenilia,

written under the influence of the so-called preromantics, through his vehement objections to the unholy trinity of "Bacon, Newton, Locke," to his attacks on deism, Voltaire, and Rousseau. Hagstrum concludes by identifying Blake's ubiquitous figure Urizen as a personification of the Enlightenment.

Blake's rejection of the abstractions of Enlightenment thought is of a piece with his opposition, directly stated in *The Marriage of Heaven and Hell*, to a cultural situation that negates the particularity of the body in favor of the abstract soul. Thomas R. Frosch, in a section of his book *The Awakening of Albion* (1974), treats what he calls "the renovation of the body" as it is presented in *The Four Zoas* and *Jerusalem*. Frosch distinguishes Blake's notion of renovation from, on the one hand, Swedenborgian views and, on the other, those views which propose a "dematerialization" of man. The Blakean resurrection, Frosch argues, is a "regathering of [man's] complete substance," not into timeless fixity but into the capacity to remake even time and space in "perpetual creative activity."

Alicia Ostriker discusses in her essay (1982) the sexuality of the Blakean body and discovers four Blakean attitudes and certain contradictions among them. Her essay effectively deals, among other things, with the complex relation between the Zoas and their emanations, Blake's early attack on sexual repression, the story Blake repeatedly tells of female entrapment of the male, and his later tendency to see female subordination to the male as the unfallen condition. Ostriker speculates on what may have caused this last phase and yet shows that to some extent it was present from the beginning in Blake's writings. Claiming that Blake himself did not think an artist could transcend historical circumstance, she concludes that the sexual contradictions in Blake should not surprise us.

The next essay introduces the matter of Blake's composite (literary and visual) art, an issue that for a long time was avoided by critics. Art historians almost completely ignored the verbal dimension of Blake's work or seemed embarrassed by it. Indeed, art criticism and history have until recently had a hard time locating Blake at all, and literary critics have usually treated Blake's texts apart from the designs. W. J. T. Mitchell's *Blake's Composite Art* (1978), of which the selection after Ostriker's essay is a part, closely studies the variety of relations to be discovered between design and text, revealing significant Blakean departures from the eighteenth-century notion of the "sister arts." (Mitchell alludes to an earlier essay he wrote with the same title. This one is a revision and extension.)

The next two essays deal with important aspects of two of Blake's longest works and have implications for understanding the whole corpus. In "Act," from *Poetic Form in Blake's "Milton"* (1976), Susan Fox offers an account of what may be regarded as the central action governing the unique structure of that poem: Milton's descent into the fallen world to redeem his emanations and thereby to redeem himself, also to inspire William Blake and to accomplish the binding of Urizen. The last is a task left unfinished by Los.

The action Fox discusses is preceded in the poem by a "Bard's Song" in which events are recorded (including an allegory of Blake's difficulties with his patron William Hayley) that impel Milton to journey through the vortex into the fallen world to be united with Ololon and Jesus. Fox's essay concentrates on issues of structure, imagery, and ethos important to an understanding of Blake.

The second of these essays focuses on *Jerusalem*. One of the extended actions of that poem involves the relation of the main figure Los to his Spectre and to his emanation Enitharmon. This relationship is a deeply troubled one, and, as Morton D. Paley studies it, one that reveals, among other things, the presence of the poet and his wife in the poem. Paley's discussion is part of the fifth chapter of his *The Continuing City: William Blake's "Jerusalem"* (1983). It carefully charts the ebb and flow of the relationship, central to Blake's whole symbolism, showing as it does the ways in which Blake's extraordinary interest in the writing of William Cowper may have been germinal in the creation of the Spectre.

The final two essays of Part 2 address issues especially current in criticism: the so-called postmodernist emphases on difference, deconstruction, Hegelian negation, and language. Postmodernist theory has had a somewhat distant relation to Blake. He seems to have been either unknown to its major founding figures or deliberately ignored, perhaps because he anticipates issues that have interested them and created works that are in some way already deconstructed or deconstructive—"open to view," as Paul de Man once remarked of him. Steven Shaviro's essay (1982) is one of the first both to recognize and write strenuously about Blake in a postmodernist perspective and, at the same time, to try to set forth Blake's differences from the main line of deconstruction as variously practiced by Jacques Derrida and Paul de Man. Shaviro's claim is that Blake's text expresses difference positively and affirmatively in a movement that yet remains always other than the will to closure and interpretive fixity.

Robert Essick's "The Return to Logos," from his *William Blake and the Language of Adam* (1989), argues in a way quite different from Shaviro's for Blake's positive creativity in language. The tendency of structuralist and subsequently deconstructionist criticism was, beginning with the notion of a Saussurean linguistic chain (which makes every signified but another signifier), to presume language a sort of prison house with no center or origin outside itself—no Logos in the traditional sense. The principle of language as a differential system emphasized absence and the negative. Essick emphasizes the creativity of Blake's wordplay, his literalization of the figurative, and the value he puts on conversation. Thus Essick sees Blake moving from a negative view of language to concern with "what men can do with it—and what it does to them."

As an afterword, my own essay on Blake and cultural policy, written for a conference on cultural policy sponsored by the University of Calgary Institute for the Humanities in 1988, attempts to take a broad view and determine what a Blakean ethical ground for a livable cultural policy might be.

Early on, Henry Crabb Robinson, unprepared for but friendly to Blake's eccentricities, found Blake hard to classify according to schools or the influence of some previous thinker. As a result he considered Blake's thought confused, as in his response to Blake's refusal to separate the "natural and spiritual worlds." Early critics seeking a purchase in slippery territory tried to establish sanction for Blake (and their readings) in everything from Plato to occultism, but Blake always confounded them with his own synthetic and creative genius. We are less likely to locate Blake today in some school or predecessor, but rather than pushing him beyond the periphery for this reason, we now see him at both the center and the circumference of literary tradition.

Blakeans continue at their scholarship, construing Blake's work and making it more available. This selection is but a small representation of several decades of intense and fruitful study. The bibliography at the back suggests further reading and looking.

Note: The abbreviation "E" in the text and notes refers to *The Complete Poetry and Prose of William Blake,* rev. ed., ed. David V. Erdman (New York: Anchor Press/Doubleday, 1982). The abbreviation "K" refers to *The Complete Writings of William Blake,* ed. Geoffrey Keynes (London: Nonesuch Press; New York; Random House, 1957).

PART 1
BLAKE IN HIS TIME

◆

Knowledge and Estimation of Blake during His Lifetime
[From *Blake in the Nineteenth Century*]

DEBORAH DORFMAN

To Gilchrist Blake seemed always to have been entirely neglected, but this was not strictly the case. Though never widely known or appreciated, Blake was not simply an obscure and solitary engraver. He was active in the London art world, especially in the 1790s, and—as twentieth-century scholars have at last convinced us, despite the tradition that Gilchrist perpetuated—he led much of his life "in this world."[1] Blake himself said (in about 1810) that his "Inventive Powers & his Scientific Knowledge of Drawing is on all hands acknowledgd" (*A Public Address,* E, p. 560, and see *A Descriptive Catalogue,* p. 529). The designs to *The Grave* were almost famous.

As a poet, and as poet and illustrator in one, Blake certainly was little known, but this was in part his own doing. Only two of his works ever appeared in letterpress, though without doubt many more could have; and of the two, the *Poetical Sketches* was privately printed and then given to Blake to distribute on his own. The other, *The French Revolution: Book One* (1791), exists in a single copy, generally supposed to be a proof, that the radical publisher Joseph Johnson suppressed when the government began to make things difficult for revolutionary sympathizers. Neither book was reviewed, listed, or advertised. The remainder of his poetry, aside from works left altogether in manuscript, Blake himself engraved (both drawings and letterpress) and printed off on demand. Sometimes he had nothing ready for a prospective buyer.[2] As for the sale and advertising of such works, Blake refused (apparently) to become implicated in the hustling and "puffing" of the booksellers' trade. He resisted and resented R. H. Cromek, the one bookseller who "puffed" his designs (for Blair's *Grave*). That Blake was too uncompromising even for his friends to help is shown by the many letters extant proposing his name for engraving jobs he never took. Cunningham's interpretation was that Blake unreasonably "thought that he had but to sing songs and draw designs, and become great and famous"—and that the world in general therefore slighted him.[3]

From *Blake in the Nineteenth Century: His Reputation as a Poet from Gilchrist to Yeats,* Yale University Press, 1969. Used by permission.

In London art circles Blake was known as an exponent of republican art and a designer of abstract and allegorical subjects, and he was attacked on these grounds. His designs to Edward Young's *Night Thoughts* (1797) were labeled absurdly "over-literal" and damned for excessive imagination. Incompatible though they seem, both reactions object to a "dangerous prevalence of imagination." Clearly imaged and outlined, Death, Time, the soul, the "torrent of a sinful life," and like abstractions circle about the printed text; their actions—past Hours listening to the soul converse, the soul mourning "along the gloom," and so forth—are rendered literally. Setting aside for a moment all question of artistic theory or merit, such unabashed exercise of vision (it remained for Yeats to see Blake as a "too literal realist of imagination") was looked on by many at that time as unwholesome, overwrought, near-hallucinatory. So began the persistent attributions of mental instability which put a seal on Blake's worldly unsuccess.[4]

B. H. Malkin in 1806 and Crabb Robinson in 1810, in an article on Blake written for a German periodical, refer to these objections against Blake.[5] Malkin speaks also of calumniators who "criticise the representation of corporeal beauty," as well as objecting to "the allegorical emblems of mental perfections" (p. xxiii). Crabb Robinson mentions the same criticisms: Blake's offenses against decency in some of the designs to *The Grave* (published in 1808) and, "most offensive," the representations of the reunion of the body and soul in which "equal clearness of form and outline" is given to both; of the soul wearing an expression of reluctance as it leaves the body; of their passionate reunion at the resurrection, and so on.

In a review of the *Grave* designs in Leigh Hunt's *Examiner* (1808), Robert Hunt coupled the "visionary" Blake with a particular target of the *Examiner's* wrath, "frantic" Henry Fuseli, who wrote the introduction to the designs. Hunt condemned as absurd and outrageous both men's attempts to connect visible and invisible worlds: "Whatever is simply natural, such as 'the death of a wicked strong man,' is powerfully conceived and expressed; nearly all the allegory is not only far fetched but absurd, inasmuch as the human body can never be mistaken in a picture for its soul, as the visible can never shadow out the invisible world, 'between which, there is a great gulph fixed' of impenetrable and therefore indescribable obscurity."[6] Hunt's comment,[7] like others directed against Blake's overnaturalistic abstractions, reflect a taste still prevalent, formed according to the principles Samuel Johnson had expressed in objecting to Milton's Sin and Death, and his angels— Milton's error in trying to embody unseen things.[8]

Hunt's second and "more serious" censure of "these most heterogeneous and serio-fantastic designs" is the objection, equally Johnsonian, of a man of Sensibility: "At the awful day of Judgment, before the throne of God himself, a male and female figure are described in most indecent attitudes . . . an appearance of libidinousness intrudes itself upon the holiness of our thoughts." Johnson had spoken of the religious feeling of his time as being more "delicate" if not more fervent than that of earlier times and disposed to find wit or lightness in sacred things "offensive." The late eighteenth and the nineteenth century was not a time for the heroic nudes either of Michelangelo or of Blake in his "Ancient Britons." (One of the *Grave* illustrations was later bowdlerized for an American edition.)[9]

Blake's continuing support of a grand republican art even after the French dictatorship and English repression was evidenced in his Exhibition of 1809, with its *Descriptive Catalogue.* "The Ancient Britons," and the "Spiritual Forms" of "Nelson Guiding Leviathan" and "Pitt Guiding Behemoth" emulate works seen in vision "on walls of Temples, Towers, Cities, Palaces . . . in the highly cultivated states of Egypt, Moab" (E, p. 522). Robert Hunt, again reviewing Blake, concluded "that Blake was whitewashing the war policy associated with Pitt and Nelson." Hunt "pronounced that Blake's reputation was a civic malady so 'pernicious' that it had become 'a duty to endeavor to arrest its progress.' " In a vicious personal attack, Hunt went on to denounce Blake as "an unfortunate lunatic, whose personal inoffensiveness secures him from confinement." The *Catalogue,* Blake's manifesto in behalf of line, imaginative vision, and national art, was a "farrago of nonsense, unintelligibleness, and egregious vanity, the wild effusions of a distempered brain."[10]

In addition to its ideological statement, the *Catalogue* contained Blake's attempt (poorly, or perhaps defiantly, calculated) at self-vindication, particularly with regard to his "Chaucer's Pilgrims": "Such are the characters that compose this Picture, which was painted in self-defence against the insolent and envious imputation of unfitness for finished and scientific art; . . . This has hitherto been his [Mr. Blake's] lot—to get patronage for others and then to be left and neglected, and his work, which gained that patronage, cried down as eccentricity and madness; as unfinished and neglected by the artist's violent temper, he is sure the works now exhibited, will give the lie to such aspersions" (E, p. 528). Blake accused Thomas Stothard, R.A., and Cromek, publisher of *The Grave,* of having plagiarized his idea for a painting and an engraving of the procession of the pilgrims to Canterbury. Stothard's oil of this subject had been exhibited in 1807 and achieved some renown. This, together with Stothard and Cromek's much advertised difficulties in completing and publishing their engraving, had given a certain notoriety to the Chaucer subject and to Blake's accusations. Since Stothard and Cromek did not finally present their engraving until about 1814, the affair was kept alive; Gilchrist in 1863 writes that the Stothard engraving "had an extraordinary sale as everybody knows" (*Life, 1,* Chap. 26). Thus even after Blake's Exhibition paintings were forgotten, echoes of the quarrel perpetuated an image of Blake the complainer and accuser, if not the paranoiac.

The Exhibition and *Catalogue,* Blake's major effort to reverse the decade-long trend of abuse and misconceived criticism, failed disastrously. Blake was confirmed a madman, a self-inflated visionary whose claims to prophetic insight were compared with the special powers assumed by religious cranks and assured lunatics. He never afterward put himself before the world.[11]

Nonetheless, a few notable individuals, although they carried away with them an unshakable conviction of Blake's insanity, were able to discern in the Exhibition something of its author's genius. On Robert Southey it produced a "melancholy impression" he never forgot: "Some of the designs were hideous, especially those which he considered as most supernatural in their conception and likenesses. In others . . . nothing but madness had prevented him from being the sublimest painter of this or any other country. . . . His madness . . . [was] evident . . . fearful."[12] In 1811 Blake read to Southey parts of *Jerusalem,* "a perfectly mad poem. Oxford Street is in Jerusalem."[13]

More fateful for Blake's eventual fame was the visit of Henry Crabb Robinson. Crabb Robinson was a student of German Romantic philosophy and psychology, an admirer of Wordsworth, and had interested himself in the revival of primitive and Elizabethan poetry. He knew the brief sketch in *A Father's Memoirs* in which Malkin had compared Blake with the Elizabethans and had spoken of his "enthusiastic and high-flown ideas on the subject of religion," his "warm imagination," and undisciplined genius. After visiting the Exhibition, Crabb Robinson induced Charles Lamb to go; he also introduced Lamb, Hazlitt, Wordsworth, and others to *Songs of Innocence and of Experience.*[14] In addition, he composed his essay for the German periodical, in which he called attention to Blake as an English genius of the sublime Shakespearean type, one of "those faces . . . in which nature has set something of greatness which she has yet left unfinished." He referred to the "union of genius and madness" and genius' affinities with the childlike and the mystical—notions not very widely allowed at this time (1810) as evidence of sublimity. The article was not reprinted before the twentieth century, nor was it known in England; nevertheless, to some among his own generation, Crabb Robinson communicated a way of valuing Blake—in particular, of coming to terms with Blake's "madness."[15]

Lamb especially had been attracted by Blake's "marvellous strange pictures . . . mystical and full of vision" and his unorthodox opinions about art. He also recalled Blake's criticism, in *A Descriptive Catalogue,* of the General Prologue to the *Canterbury Tales* as one of the most spirited commentaries he had ever read on the subject. "I must look on him as one of the most extraordinary persons of the age," Lamb wrote in 1824;[16] although Blake was living only a short distance away, in Fountain Court, Lamb did not know that he was still alive.

In his very last years, while it did not significantly widen his audience, Blake does seem to have drawn some distinguished attention. Samuel Taylor Coleridge, for one, met him in 1825 or 1826, probably at the salon of Mrs. Aders. Coleridge visited Blake at Fountain Court, and according to Crabb Robinson talked "finely about him."[17] And, perhaps not surprisingly, Blake's name is sometimes linked by critics with that of Coleridge. For the most part the comparison is superficial, but it seems likely enough if one remembers how little was known about Blake's thought. Both men were reputed to be mystical, obscure, and unstable. They appear in such groupings as Coleridge, Blake, and Edward Irving (the head of the Catholic Apostolic Church); Coleridge, Blake, and Landor; Coleridge, Flaxman, and Blake.[18] A witness to a meeting of the two reported that "Blake and Coleridge, when in company, seemed like congenial beings of another sphere, breathing for a while on our earth: which may be perceived from the similarity of thought pervading their works."[19]

Although in 1865 a reviewer of Gilchrist's *Life* speculated that "had his whole training and career been different, [Blake] might have been the Coleridge of his time," the two were seldom associated after 1830. Coleridge was outside the liberal tradition of the Blake revival.[20] His comments on Blake's poetry are, however, prophetic of the central problems Blake presented to the entire nineteenth-century sensibility, even at its most sympathetic.

Coleridge read Blake's *Songs of Innocence and of Experience* in 1818 in a copy lent him by his friend Charles Augustus Tulk, a Swedenborgian. He wrote to Reverend Henry F. Cary that Blake "is a man of Genius—and I apprehend a Swedenborgian—certainly a mystic emphatically." In a letter to Tulk he rated each poem in the *Songs* according to whether "It gave me pleasure," "great pleasure," pleasure "in the highest degree," or "not at all" (his favorites being "The Little Black Boy" and "Night").[21]

Coleridge wrote Tulk that he objected to "Infant Joy" (in *Songs of Innocence*) because "a Babe two days old does not, cannot, *smile*—and Innocence and the very works of nature must go together." Where the eighteenth-century mind's objection to the *Night Thoughts* illustrations was founded on a Johnsonian dim view of sacred poetry—that "the sanctity of the matter rejects the ornaments of figurative diction"[22]—the difficulties of a newer mentality with Blake may be seen in Coleridge's comment that "Infancy is too holy a thing to be ornamented." Coleridge's obstacle, his quarrel with Blake's "despotism of symbols" is Blake's quarrel (in reverse) with nature and the natural man. All Blake critics among the post-Romantic Victorians echo Coleridge's problem in one way or another, insofar as they share the nineteenth century's legacy from Rousseau, faith in nature and piety toward the natural heart.

Coleridge also wrote that he found himself "perplexed" by "The Little Vagabond": he was alive to a "mood of mind" which rejects the remote and repressive God of the Churches, but he could not move along with it into an over-sentimental religious humanism. This perplexity leads him to a second objection to the *Songs*—this time, paradoxically, from the side of orthodoxy—concerning the absolute existence of evil and the need to accuse or restrain the natural man. His remarks point to the last stanza; and Coleridge almost certainly takes it that Blake, if not actually speaking in his own person, agrees with his speaker. "The Little Vagabond" ends

And God like a father rejoicing to see,
His children as pleasant and happy as he:
Would have no more quarrel with the Devil or the Barrel
But kiss him & give him both drink and apparel.
—[E, p. 26]

The common error among "Scholars of Em. Sw. [Emanuel Swedenborg]," Coleridge writes, "is that of utterly demerging the Tremendous incompatibilities with an evil will that arise out of the essential Holiness of the abysmal Aseity [that is, of the unknowable Other], in the love of the eternal Person— and thus giving temptation to weaker minds to sink this Love itself into *good nature*"—an error which causes Coleridge to retreat from the poem as one he "cannot approve altogether." But, he continues, "still I disapprove the mood of mind in this wild poem so much less than I do the servile blind-worm, wrap-rascal Scurfcoat & *fear of modern Saints.* . . . Anything rather than *this* degradation of Humanity [To this Coleridge remarks in a footnote, "With which how can we utter 'Our Father'?"] and there-in of the incarnate Divinity!" Evidently, one dialectical mind is clashing with another; however, Coleridge seems not to perceive the ironies in the two poems. The critic Joseph Wicksteed observed that Coleridge failed "to realize the profound element of Blakean humour mingled with Blake's scathing tongue. It is Swedenborg who is almost humourless, not Blake, and S.T.C. reads W.B. in the misleading light of Swedenborg."[23] Taking him for a Swedenborgian may have prevented Coleridge from noting that in Blake the solution to a dualistic god is not a love of the natural man and that in "The Little Vagabond" the two alternatives, Church and Ale-house, merge—the ossifying with the stupefying. Moreover, in reading "Infant Joy," Coleridge, like other readers at the time, was not open to irony in poems on childhood. The tension, evident already in Coleridge, between a belief in nature and an ethical recognition that restraints are needed is one that Swinburne later works out very largely through his study and criticism of Blake.

After Crabb Robinson himself finally made Blake's acquaintance in 1825, also at Mrs. Aders', he visited him and brought friends (and sometimes prospective buyers) such as the young German painter Gotzenberger, whom he reported as saying that "Blake [is] the first and Flaxman . . . the second man he has seen in England." He tried, though unsuccessfully, to arrange a meeting between Blake and Wordsworth.[24] These last years are the time when the Shoreham disciples made Blake's room in Fountain Court their shrine and when his *Inventions to Job* were recognized by the Royal Academy.

In spite of this last-minute attention, Blake never overcame his obscurity, and he died in 1827 without having altered his reputation of insanity.[25] After his death, Allan Cunningham could write that "few men of taste could be ignorant" of Blake's "merits," and in 1863 an irate reviewer of Gilchrist's *Life* protested that he would like to know to whom Blake was "Ignotus."[26] However, the truth seems to have been that by the time Cunningham wrote (1830) it was mainly a small circle of personal acquaintances who still *honored* Blake. A reviewer of Cunningham's *Lives* criticized the author for his absorption with such crude personalities as Blake, Fuseli, Cosway, and Barry: Blake, he said, "the able, but, alas! insane author of some very striking and original designs" barely deserves to be named among painters. The same reviewer excludes Blake's name from a list of ten fine painters of poetical subjects.[27] One anonymous writer in 1830 did, however, indicate quite succinctly the state of Blake's reputation, as well as the simplest way of accounting for it: "We are perfectly aware of the present state of public opinion on this kind of man, but we know at the same time, that every genius has a certain end to perform, and always runs before his contemporaries, and for that reason is not generally understood,—This is our candid opinion with respect to Blake."[28]

Notes

1. See Harold Bruce, *William Blake in This World* (New York, Harcourt Brace & Co., 1925); Mona Wilson, *Life of William Blake* (rev. ed. [with additional notes] New York, 1949), Chap. 6; Ruthven Todd's notes to the Everyman edition of Gilchrist's *Life* (rev. ed. New York, 1945), cited thereafter as "*Life,* ed. Todd"; G. Keynes, *Blake Studies* (London, 1949); and especially David Erdman, *William Blake: Prophet Against Empire* (Princeton, 1954). My account of Blake's part in the issues of the London art world is based almost exclusively on Erdman, Chaps. 3 and 25. For Blake's career in the 1790s, especially the commissioning of illustrations to Young's *Night Thoughts* and its association with projects such as Boydell's Shakespeare gallery and Fuseli's Milton gallery, see Chap. 14. See, too, Gilchrist's *Life, 1,* Chaps. 22–26.

Bentley and Nurmi's (*A Blake Bibliography,* Minneapolis, 1964) short prefatory account of "Blake's Reputation and Interpreters" (pp. 3 ff.), is particularly useful for the period up to about 1810. The book was published after all my own work was finished and too late for me to use it very extensively; their work generally confirms Erdman's biographical remarks, however, and tends to support my own discussions.

2. Robert Southey recalled that when he wanted to buy a copy of *Songs of Innocence and Experience,* Blake had none ready. See his letter to Caroline Bowles, dated May 8, 1830, containing a description of Blake's Exhibition of 1809 and a recollection of the man; *The Correspondence of Robert Southey with Caroline Bowles,* ed. E. Dowden (London, 1881), pp. 193–94.

For the publishing history of *Poetical Sketches,* see *Life, 1,* Chap. 4 and Sampson (1905), Bibliographical Preface to *PS.* Sampson's important edition is described more fully in Chap. 5, n. 11. From Blake's neglect to correct proofs, and his indifference to the sale (*PS* exists in 22 extant copies, most inscribed to friends, according to Keynes, *Blake Bibliography* [see too Blake, ed. Keynes, p. 883]), it has been thought that by 1783, when he had begun to work out a more individual style, Blake saw *PS* as mere juvenilia (Harold Bloom, *Blake's Apocalypse* [New York, Doubleday, 1962], Chapt. 1).

On *The French Revolution,* see *Life, 1,* Chapt. 11; *The Poetical Works of William Blake, with*

The French Revolution . . . , ed. John Sampson (London, 1913), p. xxxi; *Life,* ed. Todd, p. 373; and Erdman. See too G. E. Bentley Jr., "William Blake as a Private Publisher," *Bulletin of the New York Public Library, 61* (1957), 539–60.

3. Cunningham, *Lives of the Most Eminent British Painters, Sculptors, and Architects* (6 vols. London, 1830), 2, p. 153. For these difficulties, see Blake's *Note-Book* epigrams on William Hayley, John Flaxman, Thomas Stothard, Cromek, et al. Also letters by George Cumberland, Flaxman, Hayley, and others, in *Letters,* ed. Keynes. See, too, letters in Russell, *Letters of Blake;* Wilson, pp. 371–76, and passim; G. Keynes, "Blake's Miniatures," *Times Literary Supplement* (Jan. 29, 1960); *Life, 1,* Chapt. 22 (for a letter from R. H. Cromek to Blake); and Joseph Sandell, *Memoranda of Art and Artists* (London, 1871), p. 31, in Bentley and Nurmi, item 1909.

4. *The Farington Diary,* by Joseph Farington, R. A., ed. J. Grieg (8 vols. London, n.d.), *1,* 141–42, entry for Feb. 19, 1796. See also *1,* 151, entry for June 24, 1796; and *1,* 151–52, entry for Jan. 11, 1797. On the diary's accuracy, see *Life,* ed. Todd, pp. 377–78, and Erdman.

As soon as his original work began to be known and recognized (by some as "works of extraordinary genius and imagination" *Farington Diary, 1,* 151), Blake was classed with extravagantly imaginative artists such as Fuseli, Flaxman, and John Hoppner. Around the time of *Illustrations to Young's Night Thoughts,* one hears of Blake's "eccentric designs" influencing Stothard to "extravagance in his art" (ibid., *1,* 151–52, Jan. 11, 1797).

For the rise and turn of Blake's reputation on the failure, commercial and aesthetic, of *NT,* see *Life,* Erdman, Bentley and Nurmi, pp. 4 ff., and Tatham's memoir (in Russell, *Letters of Blake*). For evidence of the Lambeth books being the ones most often mentioned in references to Blake, from Malkin (1806) through Cunningham's *Life* (*Songs of Innocence and Experience, The Gates of Paradise, America,* and *Europe*), see Henry Crabb Robinson, "William Blake: Künstler, Dichter und Religiöser Schwärmer," *Vaterländisches Museum* (Hamburg, Jan. 1, 1811), trans. K. A. Esdaile, in "An Early Appreciation of William Blake," *The Library, 5* (July 1914), 229–56 (the article was reprinted in German by H. G. Wright, *Modern Language Review, 22* [April 1927], 137–54) and J. Watkins and F. Shoberl, *Biographical Dictionary of the Living Authors of Great Britain and Ireland* (1816). See also G. Keynes and E. Wolf, *William Blake's Illuminated Books: A Census* (New York, 1953) for the proportionately large number of extant copies of the Lambeth books.

In 1799 Blake writes to his friend George Cumberland, "I live by Miracle. . . . Since My Young's Night Thoughts have been publish'd, Even Johnson & Fuseli have discarded my Graver" (*Letters,* ed. Keynes, p. 38).

For a reference to Blake's "depraved fancy," see a review of Stanley's *Leonora* with three designs by Blake, *The British Critic* (Sept. 1796), in Erdman, p. 265. On Yeats, see my Chap. 8, n. 41.

5. Page references for Malkin's *A Father's Memoirs* are cited in parentheses in the text. Malkin's short biographical and critical sketch of Blake (who drew the portrait of the dead child, Thomas Heath Malkin, for the edition) appears in an Introductory Letter to T. Johnes of Haford dated Jan. 4, 1806. For more on Malkin's biography of Blake see my Chap. 3. References to Crabb Robinson's article, "William Blake: Künstler, Dichter und Religiöser Schwärmer, *Vaterländisches Museum,* are from the translation by K. A. Esdaile in *The Library;* the article was written during the year 1810, and printed in Jan. 1811. For more on Crabb Robinson see below.

6. "R. H.," "Blake's Edition of Blair's *Grave,*" *Examiner,* No. 32 (Aug. 7, 1808), pp. 509–10. Robert Hunt, Leigh Hunt's brother, regularly wrote the "Fine Arts" column, in which the review appears. (Leigh Hunt had nominated Blake an "Officer of Painting" in " 'the Ancient and Redoubtable Institution of Quacks' " in "Miscellaneous Sketches Upon Temporary Subjects &c.," *Examiner* [Aug. 28, 1808], p. 558; cited in Bentley and Nurmi, item 1394.)

The *Examiner's* attack on both Blake and Fuseli had a history, which Erdman reports at greater length: In 1806 R. Hunt attacked Fuseli's painting *Count Ugolino* in *Bell's Weekly Messenger* (May 25); Blake defended Fuseli in a letter to the *Monthly Magazine, 21* (July 1, 1806), pp. 520–21. Hunt's review of *The Grave* attacks both Fuseli and Blake, and thanks the engraver Schiavonetti for redeeming Blake's absurdities and indelicacies. Blake replied to attackers indirectly in the *Descriptive Catalogue,* and was viciously attacked in turn by Hunt in his review of Blake's Exhibition of 1809, *Examiner,* No. 90 (Sept. 17, 1809). See Erdman for a full account of the context (Chap. 25); also *Letters,* ed. Keynes, pp. 156–57; *Life,* ed. Todd, p. 382.

S. Foster Damon has brought out an edition of Blake's designs to Blair's *Grave,* arranged in Blake's chosen order, and reprinting Fuseli's introductory note. See *Blake's Grave: A Prophetic Book* (Providence, Brown University Press, 1963).

7. Louis Crompton associates Hunt's criticisms with his brother Leigh Hunt's antipathy to emotional evangelicism—"sacro-sensualism" and "amatory Methodism," "Blake's Nineteenth Century Critics" (University of Chicago, diss., 1953), p. 47.

8. "John Milton," *Lives of the Poets* [1779–1781], ed. G. B. Hill (3 vols. New York, 1905), *1,* 184–85. Johnson writes, "To give [abstractions like Sin and Death] any real employment or ascribe to them any material agency is to make them allegorical no longer, but to shock the mind by ascribing effects to non-entity." Of the mixture of material and spiritual,

> Another inconvenience of Milton's design is that it requires the description of what cannot be described, the agency of spirits. He saw that immateriality supplied no images, and that he could not show angels acting but by instruments of action; he therefore invested them with form and matter. . . . [He] should have secured the consistency of his system by keeping immateriality out of sight. . . . But he has unhappily perplexed his poetry with his philosophy. . . . The confusion of spirit and matter . . . pervades the war in heaven.

9. Johnson, "Abraham Cowley," ibid., *1,* 49 ff. See Blair's *Grave* (New York, A. L. Dick, 1847), where the "Meeting of a Family in Heaven" has been "gently bowdlerized" (*Life,* ed. Todd, p. 384). On the heroic nudes, see Erdman.

10. Robert Hunt, "Mr. Blake's Exhibition," quoted and described in Erdman, pp. 419–20. Erdman writes that Blake felt his paintings carried forward the "ethical and historical tradition of Mortimer and Barry" (p. 37, and see *A Public Address, A Vision of the Last Judgment,* and *A Descriptive Catalogue* for Blake on Ideal and Republican art). In politics his antagonism to the Pitt government and hatred of its war policy should have appealed to Hunt and the *Examiner,* but Hunt failed to grasp Blake's "recondite republicanism" (in "Pitt" and "Nelson"), and thought Blake was putting "a halo" on the Pitt government (pp. 419–20).

11. Blake was classed with religious fanatics like Joanna Southcote and lunatics like Richard Brothers (Tatham's *Life,* in Russell, *Letters of Blake*). Henry Crabb Robinson observed that "Excessive pride equally denoted Blake & Barry [another seer of visions]" (journal entry for Jan. 30, 1815, *On Books and Their Writers.* All references to Crabb Robinson's diaries will be to the date of entry).

After 1810, Blake did try to get *Jerusalem* read; possibly a "puff" by T. G. Wainewright ("Janus Weathercock") in "Mr. Weathercock's Private Correspondence," *London Magazine, 1* (Sept. 1820), 300, is a friendly push (see my Chap. 3, n. 3).

More sympathetic references to Blake after 1810 speak of him as an unrecognized and little known artist (see William Carey, *Critical Description and Analytic Review of "Death on a Pale Horse"* painted by Benjamin West, R.A., with desultory references to the works of some ancient masters, and living British Artists . . . [London, 1817], p. 9 [a reference to *The Grave*] and pp. 128–36; and see pp. 18 f. below).

12. Letter to Caroline Bowles, cited above.

13. Crabb Robinson's Diary, *On Books and Their Writings,* July 24, 1811. The entry reads: "Late to C. Lamb's. . . . Southey had been with Blake & admired both his designs & his

poetic talents at the same time that he held him for a decided madman. Blake, he says, spoke of his visions with the diffidence that is usual with such people & and did not seem to expect that he shd. be believed."

14. Crabb Robinson's "Reminiscences" (collected from memory and from the diaries he began keeping in 1811), for the year 1810, record that he had visited Blake's Exhibition and bought four copies of the *Descriptive Catalogue* (*On Books and Their Writers, 1*, 15). One of the copies was for his friend Charles Lamb. His diary for Mar. 10, 1811 records his reading Blake's *Songs of Innocence and Experience* to Hazlitt. For Hazlitt's reaction, see my Chap. 5, n. 34. On May 24, 1812, he read them to Wordsworth: "He was pleased with some of them, and considered Blake as having the elements of poetry a thousand times more than either Byron or Scott." For others to whom Crabb Robinson introduced Blake's poems see entry for Jan. 12, 1813.

The most important person to whom Crabb Robinson spoke of Blake was, of course, Alexander Gilchrist. Their meeting came about through Samuel Palmer, in 1855 (*On Books and Their Writers*, June 20, 1855). For Palmer see my Chap. 3, pp. 57 ff.

15. Esdaile, "An Early Appreciation of William Blake." In his Reminiscence for "1810," Crabb Robinson writes: "I was amusing myself this spring by writing an account of the insane poet, painter, and engraver, Blake." For Crabb Robinson's other references to Blake's insanity, see journal entries for April 6, 1828 and Aug. 4, 1836; and Chap. 3, p. 35. Crabb Robinson's article is cited in a sketch of Blake that appeared in *Neues Algemeines Künstler-Lexicon . . .* Bearbeitet von Dr. G. K. Nagler (Munchen, E. A. Fleischman, 1835), *1*, 519–22. In 1830, parts of Cunningham's Life of Blake were translated for *Zeitgenossen*, and are reprinted by Nagler.

16. *The Letters of Charles and Mary Lamb*, ed. E. V. Lucas (3 vols. New Haven, 1935), *2*, 424–27 and n.; letter addressed to Bernard Barton, dated May 15, 1824 (on Barton, see my Chap. 3, pp. 29 f. and 55).

Crabb Robinson may have given one copy of the *Descriptive Catalogue* to Hazlitt, who echoes Blake on Chaucer's Pilgrims in one of his lectures on Spenser and Chaucer (1818). Hazlitt writes, "Chaucer, it has been said, numbered the classes of men, as Linnaeus numbered the plants" (*Lectures on the English Poets, Works of Hazlitt*, ed. P. P. Howe [21 vols. London, J. M. Dent & Sons, 1930–34], 5, 24).

17. See a letter to Dorothy Wordsworth, dated Feb. 1826. Henry Crabb Robinson, *Coleridge, Wordsworth, Lamb, Etc.*, p. 16.

18. *On Books and Their Writers*, Jan. 8, 1826, Jan. 27, 1811, Feb. 2, 1827.

19. "The Inventions of William Blake," *London University Magazine, 2* (Mar. 1830), 323 n. The writer of the footnote, apparently, is not the writer of the article. For more on "The Inventions . . ." see my Chap. 3, pp. 42 ff.

20. Review of Gilchrist's *Life, Quarterly Review, 107* (Jan. 1865), 11. The review, unsigned, may be by Francis T. Palgrave (*S.L.*, No. 53, *1*, 94).

C. H. Herford, *The Age of Wordsworth* (London, G. Bell and Sons, 1897 and 1916), contrasted a rare and to him unmanly strain of poetry found in "Blake and Chatterton—Coleridge and Keats" to a more robust realism. The realism of Cowper and Crabbe and the "supernatural" strain of "visionaries" like Blake converge in the *Lyrical Ballads* (pp. xi and 152). In 1894, William Macneile Dixon saw Blake as combining Wordsworth's "innocence" and Coleridge's "mystic vision" (*English Poetry from Blake to Browning* [London, 1894], p. 35; cited by Crompton, "Blake's Nineteenth Century Critics," p. 30 n.). See too Walter Pater, *Appreciations* (London, 1889), pp. 98–99.

Crompton notes that Coleridge's association with the thought of Kant, Hegel, and other German philosophers, linking him to a conservative religious and political tradition, discouraged comparison between him and Blake ("Blake's Nineteenth Century Critics," Chap. 1).

21. *Collected Letters of S. T. Coleridge*, ed. Earl Leslie Griggs (4 vols. London, 1956–59), *4*, 834; letter to Rev. H. Cary dated Feb. 6, 1818. Coleridge continues, "You perhaps smile at

my calling another poet a *Mystic;* but verily I am in the very mire of common-place common-sense compared with Mr. Blake, apo- or rather—anacalyptic Poet, and Painter!" For more on Cary and Blake, see Chap. 3, p. 52. The letter to Tulk is dated [Feb. 12, 1818], ibid., *4,* 836–38. For more on Tulk, see my Chap. 3, n. 25.

22. "Isaac Watts," *Lives of the Poets, 3,* 310. See also "Abraham Cowley," ibid., *1,* 49 ff., where Johnson writes that "sacred history" is "a subject indisposed to the reception of poetical embellishments" (p. 51).

23. G. Keynes, "Blake with Lamb and His Circle," *Blake Studies,* p. 98 n.

24. In the letter to Dorothy Wordsworth cited above, Crabb Robinson suggested a meeting between Blake and Wordsworth. But although Blake was interested, Wordsworth apparently was not. He answered Crabb Robinson's letter himself, did not allude to Blake, and the subject was dropped (*Blake, Coleridge, Wordsworth, Lamb, Etc.,* pp. 14 ff.). For Gotzenberger, see *On Books and Their Writers,* Feb. 2, 1827.

Crabb Robinson, before and after Blake's death, spoke of him, recited his poems, and interested people in his designs (ibid., Jan. 8, 1826; Feb. 18, 1826; Jan. 8, 1828; May 20 and 22, 1838; Nov. 15, 1847; Apr. 16, 1848; Apr. 27, 1848; Jan. 18, 1851). His famous verbatim records of Blake's opinions on Wordsworth, Milton, and Dante; free love, education, and so forth, date from 1825–27. In 1852, he collected his notes into a "Reminiscence of Blake" (reprinted in *Blake, Coleridge, Wordsworth, Lamb, Etc.,* pp. 18 ff.). These were used by Gilchrist, who took some liberties in transcribing.

There is a record of Blake's having attended a dinner party, given by Lady Caroline Lamb, at which Byron was present. Blake's *The Ghost of Abel,* 1822, the only book engraved after *Jer,* is addressed "To LORD BYRON in the Wilderness" (see *Diary Illustrative of the Times of George the Fourth* . . . [By Lady Charlotte Bury] . . . , ed. John Galt [4 vols. London, 1839], *3,* 345–48; entry dated Jan. 21 [1820]). There is no record of what Byron knew or thought of Blake.

25. "Mad Blake" persists into the present day. In an article on the career of Theodore Roethke, Stanley Kunitz recalled:

> Eventually he [Roethke] more than half-believed that the springs of his disorder were inseparable from the sources of his art, and he could brag of belonging to the brotherhood of mad poets that includes William Blake, John Clare, and Christopher Smart, with each of whom he was able to identify himself as "lost."
>
> —[*The New York Review of Books* (Oct. 7, 1963)]

26. Cunningham, *2,* 177 and *Athenaeum,* No. 1880 (Nov. 7, 1863), 600. For more on this review, see my Chap. 4, p. 86.

The *Athenaeum*'s reviewer was probably a man acquainted with those who had known Blake personally, and whose wife, as a child, had met Blake. On reading the review, Crabb Robinson guessed the author to be Augustus DeMorgan (*On Books and Their Writers,* Nov. 24, 1863). For the DeMorgan family's contacts with Crabb Robinson, see *William De Morgan and His Wife,* by A. M. W. Stirling (New York, 1922). For Mrs. DeMorgan's meeting with Blake (She is the beautiful little girl to whom Blake wished happiness—see *Life, 1,* 353), see *Three-score Years and Ten: Reminiscences of Sophia Elizabeth De Morgan,* ed. M. A. De Morgan (London, [1895]), pp. 66–68.

27. *Edinburgh Review* (see n. 11).

28. "The Inventions of William Blake," p. 320.

[From "Mr. Blake's Exhibition"]

ROBERT HUNT

If beside the stupid and mad-brained political project of their rulers, the sane part of the people of England required fresh proof of the alarming increase of the effects of insanity, they will be too well convinced from its having lately spread into the hitherto sober region of Art. I say hitherto, because I cannot think with many, that the vigorous genius of the present worthy Keeper of the Royal Academy [Henry Fuseli] is touched, though no one can deny that his Muse has been on the verge of insanity, since it has brought forth, with more legitimate offspring, the furious and distorted beings of an extravagant imagination. But, when the ebullitions of a distempered brain are mistaken for the sallies of genius by those whose works have exhibited the soundest thinking in art, the malady has indeed attained a pernicious height, and it becomes a duty to endeavour to arrest its progress. Such is the case with the productions and admirers of William Blake, an unfortunate lunatic, whose personal inoffensiveness secures him from confinement, and, consequently, of whom no public notice would have been taken, if he was not forced on the notice and animadversion of the *Examiner,* in having been held up to public admiration by many esteemed amateurs and professors as a genius in some respect original and legitimate. The praises which these gentlemen bestowed last year on this unfortunate man's illustrations of *Blair's Grave,* have, in feeding his vanity, stimulated him to publish his madness more largely, and thus again exposed him, if not to the derision, at least to the pity of the public. That work was a futile endeavour by bad drawings to represent immaterially [immateriality?] by bodily personifications of the soul, while its partner the body was depicted in company with it, so that the soul was confounded with the body, as the personifying figure had none of the distinguishing characteristics of allegory, presenting only substantial flesh and bones. This conceit was dignified with the character of genius, and the tasteful hand of Schiavonetti, who engraved the work, assisted to give it currency by bestowing an exterior charm on deformity and nonsense. Thus encouraged, the poor man fancies himself a great master, and has painted a few wretched pictures, some of which are unintelligible allegory, others an attempt at sober character by caricature representation, and the whole "blotted and blurred," and very badly drawn. These he calls an Exhibition, of which he has published a Catalogue, or rather a

From the *Examiner* (London), 17 September 1809, 605–6.

farrago of nonsense, unintelligibleness, and egregious vanity, the wild effusions of a distempered brain. One of the pictures represents *Chaucer's Pilgrims*, and is in every respect a striking contrast to the admirable picture of the same subject by Mr. Stothard, from which an exquisite print is forthcome from the hand of Schiavonetti. "In this Exhibition," Mr. Blake very modestly observes, "the grand style of art is restored; and in it will be seen *real* art, as left us by Raphael and Albert Durer, Michael Angelo and Julio Romano, stripped from the ignorances of Rubens and Rembrandt, Titian and Correggio." Of the engraving which he proposes to make from his picture of the *Canterbury Pilgrims,* and to finish in a year, he as justly, soberly, and modestly observes, "No work of art can take longer than a year: it may be worked backwards and forwards without end, and last a man's whole life, but he will at length only be forced to bring it back to what it was, and it will be worse than it was at the end of the first twelve months. The value of this artist's year is the *criterion of society;* and as it is valued, so does society *flourish or decay."* That insanity should elevate itself to this fancied importance, is the usual effect of the unfortunate malady; but that men of taste, in their sober senses, should mistake its unmeaning and distorted conceptions for the flashes of genius, is indeed a phenomenon.

[From *Lives of the Most Eminent British Painters, Sculptors, and Architects*]

ALLAN CUNNINGHAM

William Blake was of low stature and slender make, with a high pallid forehead, and eyes large, dark, and expressive. His temper was touchy, and when moved, he spoke with an indignant eloquence, which commanded respect. His voice, in general, was low and musical, his manners gentle and unassuming, his conversation a singular mixture of knowledge and enthusiasm. His whole life was one of labour and privation,—he had never tasted the luxury of that independence, which comes from professional profit. This untoward fortune he endured with unshaken equanimity—offering himself, in imagination, as a martyr in the great cause of poetic art;—*pitying* some of his more fortunate brethren for their inordinate love of gain; and not doubting that whatever he might have won in gold by adopting other methods, would have been a poor compensation for the ultimate loss of fame. Under this agreeable delusion, he lived all his life—he was satisfied when his graver gained him a guinea a week—the greater the present denial, the surer the glory hereafter.

Though he was the companion of Flaxman and Fuseli, and sometimes their pupil, he never attained that professional skill, without which all genius is bestowed in vain. He was his own teacher chiefly; and self-instruction, the parent occasionally of great beauties, seldom fails to produce great deformities. He was a most splendid tinter, but no colourist, and his works were all of small dimensions, and therefore confined to the cabinet and the portfolio. His happiest flights, as well as his wildest, are thus likely to remain shut up from the world. If we look at the man through his best and most intelligible works, we shall find that he who could produce the Songs of Innocence and Experience, the Gates of Paradise, and the Inventions for Job, was the possessor of very lofty faculties, with no common skill in art, and moreover that, both in thought and mode of treatment, he was a decided original. But should we, shutting our eyes to the merits of those works, determine to weigh his worth by his Urizen, his Prophecies of Europe and America, and his Jerusalem, our conclusion would be very unfavourable; we

From *Lives of the Most Eminent British Painters, Sculptors, and Architects*, vol. 2 (London: John Murray, 1830). Reprinted from Arthur Symons, *William Blake* (London: Archibald Constable, 1907), 429–33.

would say that, with much freedom of composition and boldness of posture, he was unmeaning, mystical, and extravagant, and that his original mode of working out his conceptions was little better than a brilliant way of animating absurdity. An overflow of imagination is a failing uncommon in this age, and has generally received of late little quarter from the critical portion of mankind. Yet imagination is the life and spirit of all great works of genius and taste; and, indeed, without it, the head thinks and the hand labours in vain. Ten thousand authors and artists rise to the proper, the graceful, and the beautiful, for ten who ascend into "the heaven of invention." A work— whether from poet or painter—conceived in the fiery ecstasy of imagination, lives through every limb; while one elaborated out by skill and taste only will look, in comparison, like a withered and sapless tree beside one green and flourishing. Blake's misfortune was that of possessing this precious gift in excess. His fancy overmastered him—until he at length confounded "the mind's eye" with the corporeal organ, and dreamed himself out of the sympathies of actual life.

His method of colouring was a secret which he kept to himself, or confided only to his wife; he believed that it was revealed in a vision, and that he was bound in honour to conceal it from the world. "His modes of preparing his grounds," says Smith, in his Supplement to the Life of Nollekens, "and laying them over his panels for painting, mixing his colours, and manner of working, were those which he considered to have been practised by the early fresco painters, whose productions still remain in many instances vividly and permanently fresh. His ground was a mixture of whiting and carpenter's glue, which he passed over several times in the coatings; his colours he ground himself, and also united with them the same sort of glue, but in a much weaker state. He would, in the course of painting a picture, pass a very thin transparent wash of glue-water over the whole of the parts he had worked upon, and then proceed with his finishing. He had many secret modes of working, both as a colourist and an engraver. His method of eating away the plain copper, and leaving the lines of his subjects and his words as stereotype, is, in my mind, perfectly original. Mrs. Blake is in possession of the secret, and she ought to receive something considerable for its communication, as I am quite certain it may be used to advantage, both to artists and literary characters in general. The affection and fortitude of this woman entitled her to much respect. She shared her husband's lot without a murmur, set her heart solely upon his fame, and soothed him in those hours of misgiving and despondency which are not unknown to the strongest intellects. She still lives to lament the loss of Blake—and *feel* it."

[From *Reminiscences*]

Henry Crabb Robinson

1825

23/2/52.

I had heard of him from Flaxman, and for the first time dined in his company at the Aders'. *Linnell* the painter also was there—an artist of considerable talent, and who professed to take a deep interest in Blake and his work, whether of a perfectly disinterested character may be doubtful, as will appear hereafter. This was on the 10th of December.

I was aware of his idiosyncracies and therefore to a great degree prepared for the sort of conversation which took place at and after dinner, an altogether unmethodical rhapsody on art, poetry, and religion—he saying the most strange things in the most unemphatic manner, speaking of his *Visions* as any man would of the most ordinary occurrence. He was then 68 years of age. He had a broad, pale face, a large full eye with a benignant expression—at the same time a look of languor, except when excited, and then he had an air of inspiration. But not such as without a previous acquaintance with him, or attending to *what* he said, would suggest the notion that he was insane. There was nothing *wild* about his look, and though very ready to be drawn out to the assertion of his favourite ideas, yet with no warmth as if he wanted to make proselytes. Indeed one of the peculiar features of his scheme, as far as it was consistent, was indifference and a very extraordinary degree of toler-ance and satisfaction with what had taken place. A sort of pious and humble optimism, not the scornful optimism of Candide. But at the same time that he was very ready to praise he seemed incapable of envy, as he was of discontent. He warmly praised some composition of Mrs. Aders, and having brought for Aders an engraving of his Canterbury Pilgrims, he remarked that one of the figures resembled a figure in one of the works then in Aders's room, so that he had been accused of having stolen from it. But he added that he had drawn the figure in question 20 years before he had seen the *original* picture. However, there is "no wonder in the resemblance, as in my youth I

From *Reminiscences* (1852). Published in Arthur Symons's *William Blake* (London: Archibald Constable, 1907), 285–92, 294–98, 301–5.

was always studying that class of painting." I have forgotten what it was, but his taste was in close conformity with the old German school.

This was somewhat at variance with what he said both this day and afterwards—implying that he copies his Visions. And it was on this first day that, in answer to a question from me, he said, "*The Spirits told me.*" This led me to say: Socrates used pretty much the same language. He spoke of his Genius. Now, what affinity or resemblance do you suppose was there between the *Genius* which inspired Socrates and your *Spirits?* He smiled, and for once it seemed to me as if he had a feeling of vanity gratified. "The same as in our countenances." He paused and said, "I was Socrates"—and then as if he had gone too far in that—"or a sort of brother. I must have had conversations with him. So I had with Jesus Christ. I have an obscure recollection of having been with both of them." As I had for many years been familiar with the idea that an eternity *a parte post* was inconceivable without an eternity *a parte ante,* I was naturally led to express that thought on this occasion. His eye brightened on my saying this. He eagerly assented: "To be sure. We are all coexistent with God; members of the Divine body, and partakers of the Divine nature." Blake's having adopted this Platonic idea led me on our *tête-à-tête* walk home at night to put the popular question to him, concerning the imputed Divinity of Jesus Christ. He answered: "He is the only God"—but then he added—"And so am I and so are you." He had before said—and that led me to put the question—that Christ ought not to have suffered himself to be crucified. "He should not have attacked the Government. He had no business with such matters." On my representing this to be inconsistent with the sanctity of divine qualities, he said Christ was not yet become the Father. It is hard on bringing together these fragmentary recollections to fix Blake's position in relation to Christianity, Platonism, and Spinozism.

It is one of the subtle remarks of *Hume* on the tendency of certain religious notions to reconcile us to whatever occurs, as God's will. And apply this to something Blake said, and drawing the inference that there is no use in education, he hastily rejoined: "There *is* no use in education. I hold it wrong. It is the great Sin. It is eating of the tree of knowledge of Good and Evil. That was the fault of Plato: he knew of nothing but the Virtues and Vices. There is nothing in all that. Everything is good in God's eyes." On my asking whether there is nothing absolutely evil in what man does, he answered: "I am no judge of that—perhaps not in God's eyes." Notwithstanding this, he, however, at the same time spoke of error as being in heaven; for on my asking whether Dante was pure in writing his *Vision,* "Pure," said Blake. "Is there any purity in God's eyes? No. 'He chargeth his angels with folly.' " He even extended this liability to error to the Supreme Being. "Did he not repent him that he had made Nineveh?" My journal here has the remark that it is easier to retail his personal remarks than to reconcile those which seemed to be in conformity with the most opposed abstract systems. He spoke with seeming complacency of his own life in connection with Art.

In becoming an artist he "acted by command." The Spirits said to him, "Blake, be an artist." His eye glistened while he spoke of the joy of devoting himself to *divine art* alone. "Art is inspiration. When Mich. Angelo or Raphael, in their day, or Mr. Flaxman, does any of his fine things, he does them in the Spirit." Of fame he said: "I should be sorry if I had any earthly fame, for whatever natural glory a man has is so much detracted from his spiritual glory. I wish to do nothing for profit. I want nothing—I am quite happy." This was confirmed to me on my subsequent interviews with him. His distinction between the Natural and Spiritual worlds was very confused. Incidentally, Swedenborg was mentioned—he declared him to be a Divine Teacher. He had done, and would do, much good. Yet he did wrong in endeavouring to explain to the *reason* what it could not comprehend. He seemed to consider, but that was not clear, the visions of Swedenborg and Dante as of the same kind. Dante was the greater poet. He too was wrong in occupying his mind about political objects. Yet this did not appear to affect his estimation of Dante's genius, or his opinion of the truth of Dante's visions. Indeed, when he even declared Dante to be an Atheist, it was accompanied by expression of the highest admiration; though, said he, Dante saw Devils where I saw none.

I put down in my journal the following insulated remarks. *Jacob Böhmen* was placed among the divinely inspired men. He praised also the designs to Law's translation of Böhmen. Michael Angelo could not have surpassed them.

"*Bacon, Locke,* and *Newton* are the three great teachers of Atheism, or Satan's Doctrine," he asserted.

"*Irving* is a highly gifted man—he is a *sent* man; but they who are sent sometimes go further than they ought.

Calvin. I saw nothing but good in *Calvin's* house. In *Luther's* there were *Harlots.* He declared his opinion that the earth is flat, not round, and just as I had objected the circumnavigation dinner was announced. But objections were seldom of any use. The wildest of his assertions was made with the veriest indifference of tone, as if altogether insignificant. It respected the natural and spiritual worlds. By way of example of the difference between them, he said, "*You* never saw the spiritual Sun. I have. I saw him on Primrose Hill." He said, "Do you take me for the Greek Apollo?" "No!" I said. "*That* (pointing to the sky) that is the Greek Apollo. He is Satan."

Not everything was thus absurd. There were glimpses and flashes of truth and beauty: as when he compared moral with physical evil. "Who shall say what God thinks evil? That is a wise tale of the Mahometans—of the Angel of the Lord who murdered the Infant."—The Hermit of Parnell, I suppose.—"Is not every infant that dies of a natural death in reality slain by an Angel?"

And when he joined to the assurance of his happiness, that of his having suffered, and that it was necessary, he added, "There is suffering in Heaven; for where there is the capacity of enjoyment, there is the capacity of pain."

I include among the glimpses of truth this assertion, "I know what is true by internal conviction. A doctrine is stated. My heart tells me It *must* be true." I remarked, in confirmation of it, that, to an unlearned man, what are called the *external* evidences of religion can carry no conviction with them; and this he assented to.

After my first evening with him at Aders's, I made the remark in my journal, that his observations, apart from his Visions and references to the spiritual world, were sensible and acute. In the sweetness of his countenance and gentility of his manner he added an indescribable grace to his conversation. I added my regret, which I must now repeat, at my inability to give more than incoherent thoughts. Not altogether my fault perhaps. . . .

26/2/52.

He was making designs or engravings, I forget which. Carey's Dante was before [*sic*]. He showed me some of his designs from Dante, of which I do not presume to speak. They were too much above me. But Götzenberger, whom I afterwards took to see them, expressed the highest admiration of them. They are in the hands of *Linnell* the painter, and, it has been suggested, are reserved by him for publication when Blake may have become an object of interest to a greater number than he could be at this age. *Dante* was again the subject of our conversation. And Blake declared him a mere politician and atheist, busied about this world's affairs; as Milton was till, in his (M.'s) old age, he returned back to the God he had abandoned in childhood. I in vain endeavoured to obtain from him a qualification of the term atheist, so as not to include him in the ordinary reproach. And yet he afterwards spoke of Dante's being *then* with God. I was more successful when he also called Locke an atheist, and imputed to him wilful deception, and seemed satisfied with my admission, that Locke's philosophy led to the Atheism of the French school. He reiterated his former strange notions on morals—would allow of no other education than what lies in the cultivation of the fine arts and the imagination. "What are called the Vices in the natural world, are the highest sublimities in the spiritual world." And when I supposed the case of his being the father of a vicious son and asked him how he would feel, he evaded the question by saying that in trying to think correctly he must not regard his own weaknesses any more than other people's. And he was silent to the observation that his doctrine denied evil. He seemed not unwilling to admit the Manichaean doctrine of two principles, as far as it is found in the idea of the Devil. And said expressly said [*sic*] he did not believe in the omnipotence of God. The language of the Bible is only poetical or allegorical on the subject, yet he at the same time denied the *reality* of the natural world. Satan's empire is the empire of nothing.

As he spoke of frequently seeing Milton, I ventured to ask, half ashamed at the time, which of the three or four portraits in *Hollis's* Memoirs (vols. in

4to) is the most like. He answered, "They are all like, at different ages. I have seen him as a youth and as an old man with a long flowing beard. He came lately as an old man—he said he came to ask a favour of me. He said he had committed an error in his Paradise Lost, which he wanted me to correct, in a poem or picture; but I declined. I said I had my own duties to perform." It is a presumptuous question, I replied—might I venture to ask—what that could be. "He wished me to expose the falsehood of his doctrine, taught in the Paradise Lost, that sexual intercourse arose out of the Fall. Now that cannot be, for no good can spring out of evil." But, I replied, if the consequence were evil, mixed with good, then the good might be ascribed to the common cause. To this he answered by a reference to the *androgynous* state, in which I could not possibly follow him. At the time that he asserted his own possession of this gift of Vision, he did not boast of it as peculiar to himself; all men might have it if they would.

1826

27/2/52.

On the 24th I called a second time on him. And on this occasion it was that I read to him *Wordsworth's Ode* on the supposed pre-existent State, and the subject of Wordsworth's religious character was discussed when we met on the 18th of Feb., and the 12th of May. I will here bring together Blake's declarations concerning Wordsworth, and set down his marginalia in the 8vo. edit. A.D. 1815, vol. i. I had been in the habit, when reading this marvellous Ode to friends, to omit one or two passages, especially that beginning:

> "But there's a Tree, of many one,"

lest I should be rendered ridiculous, being unable to explain precisely *what* I admired. Not that I acknowledged this to be a fair test. But with Blake I could fear nothing of the kind. And it was this very stanza which threw him almost into a hysterical rapture. His delight in Wordsworth's poetry was intense. Nor did it seem less, notwithstanding the reproaches he continually cast on Wordsworth for his imputed worship of nature; which in the mind of Blake constituted Atheism [p. 46].

28/2/52.

The combination of the warmest praise with imputations which from another would assume the most serious character, and the liberty he took to interpret as he pleased, rendered it as difficult to be offended as to reason with him. The eloquent descriptions of Nature in Wordsworth's poems were conclusive proofs of atheism, for whoever believes in Nature, said Blake, disbelieves in God. For Nature is the work of the Devil. On my obtaining from him the declaration that the Bible was the Word of God, I referred to the commencement of Genesis—In the beginning God created the Heavens and the Earth. But I gained nothing by this, for I was triumphantly told that this God was not Jehovah, but the Elohim; and the doctrine of the Gnostics repeated with sufficient consistency to silence one so unlearned as myself. . . .

1/3/52.

19*th Feb.* It was this day in connection with the assertion that the Bible is the Word of God and all truth is to be found in it, he using language concerning man's reason being opposed to grace very like that used by the Orthodox Christian, that he qualified, and as the same Orthodox would say utterly nullified all he said by declaring that he understood the Bible in a Spiritual sense. As to the natural sense, he said *Voltaire* was commissioned by God to expose that. "I have had," he said, "much intercourse with Voltaire, and he said to me, "I blasphemed the Son of Man, and it shall be forgiven me, but they (the enemies of Voltaire) blasphemed the Holy Ghost in me, and it shall not be forgiven to them." "I ask him in what language Voltaire spoke. His answer was ingenious and gave no encouragement to cross-questioning: "To my sensations it was English. It was like the touch of a musical key; he touched it probably French, but to my ear it became English." I also enquired as I had before about the form of the persons who appeared to him, and asked why he did not *draw* them. "It is not worth while," he said. "Besides there are so many that the labour would be too great. And there would be no use in it." In answer to an enquiry about Shakespeare, "he is exactly like the old engraving—which is said to be a bad one. I think it very good." I enquired about his own writings. "I have written," he answered, "more than Rousseau or Voltaire—six or seven Epic poems as long as Homer and 20 Tragedies as long as Macbeth." He shewed me his "Version of Genesis," for so it may be called, as understood by a Christian Visionary. He read a wild passage in a sort of Bible style. "I shall print no more," he said. "When I am commanded by the Spirits, then I write, and the moment I have written, I see the words fly about the room in all directions. It is then published. The Spirits can read, and my MS. is of no further use. I have been tempted to burn my MS., but my wife won't let me." She is right, I answered; you write not from yourself but from higher order. The MSS. are their property, not yours. You cannot tell what purpose they may answer. This was addressed *ad hominem.* And it indeed amounted only to a deduction from his own principles. He incidentally denied *causation,* every thing being the work of God or Devil. Every man has a Devil in himself, and the conflict between his *Self* and God is perpetually going on. I ordered of him to-day a copy of his songs for 5 guineas. My manner of receiving his mention of price pleased him. He spoke of his horror of money and of turning pale when it was offered him, and this was certainly unfeigned.

In the No. of the *Gents. Magazine* for last Jan. there is a letter by *Cromek* to Blake printed in order to convict Blake of selfishness. It cannot possibly be substantially true. I may elsewhere notice it.

13th June. I saw him again in June. He was as wild as ever, says my journal, but he was led to-day to make assertions more palpably mischievous, if capable of influencing other minds, and immoral, supposing them to express the will of a responsible agent, than anything he had said before. As, for instance, that he had learned from the Bible that Wives should be in common. And when I objected that marriage was a Divine institution, he referred to the Bible—"that from the beginning it was not so." He affirmed that he had committed many murders, and repeated his doctrine, that reason is the only sin, and that careless, gay people are better than those who think, etc. etc.

It was, I believe, on the 7th of December that I saw him last. I had just heard of the death of Flaxman, a man whom he professed to admire, and was curious to know how he would receive the intelligence. It was as I expected. He had been ill during the summer, and he said with a smile, "I thought I should have gone first." He then said, "I cannot think of death as more than the going out of one room into another." And Flaxman was no longer thought of. He relapsed into his ordinary train of thinking. Indeed I had by this time learned that there was nothing to be gained by frequent inter-course. And therefore it was that after this interview I was not anxious to be frequent in my visits. This day he said, "Men are born with an Angel and a Devil." This he himself interpreted as Soul and Body, and as I have long since said of the strange sayings of a man who enjoys a high reputation, "it is more in the language than the thought that this singularity is to be looked for." And this day he spoke of the Old Testament as if [*sic*] were the evil element. Christ, he said, took much after his mother, and in so far was one of the worst of men. On my asking him for an instance, he referred to his turning the money changers out of the Temple—he had no right to do that. He digressed into a condemnation of those who sit in judgement on others. "I have never known a very bad man who had not something very good about him."

Speaking of the Atonement in the ordinary Calvinistic sense, he said, "It is a horrible doctrine; if another pay your debt, I do not forgive it."

[Letter to Alexander Gilchrist]

Samuel Palmer

I regret that the lapse of time has made it difficult to recall many interesting particulars respecting Mr. Blake, of whom I can give you no connected account; nothing more, in fact, than the fragments of memory; but the general impression of what is great remains with us, although its details may be confused; and Blake, once known, could never be forgotten.

His knowledge was various and extensive, and his conversation so nervous and brilliant, that, if recorded at the time, it would now have thrown much light upon his character, and in no way lessened him in the estimation of those who know him only by his works.

In him you saw at once the Maker, the Inventor; one of the few in any age: a fitting companion for Dante. He was energy itself, and shed around him a kindling influence; an atmosphere of life, full of the ideal. To walk with him in the country was to perceive the soul of beauty through the forms of matter; and the high gloomy buildings between which, from his study window, a glimpse was caught of the Thames and the Surrey shore, assumed a kind of grandeur from the man dwelling near them. Those may laugh at this who never knew such an one as Blake; but of him it is the simple truth.

He was a man without a mask; his aim single, his path straightforwards, and his wants few; so he was free, noble, and happy.

His voice and manner were quiet, yet all awake with intellect. Above the tricks of littleness, or the least taint of affectation, with a natural dignity which few would have dared to affront, he was gentle and affectionate, loving to be with little children, and to talk about them. "That is heaven," he said to a friend, leading him to the window, and pointing to a group of them at play.

Declining, like Socrates, whom in many respects he resembled, the common objects of ambition, and pitying the scuffle to obtain them, he thought that no one could be truly great who had not humbled himself "even as a little child." This was a subject he loved to dwell upon, and to illustrate.

His eye was the finest I ever saw: brilliant, but not roving, clear and intent, yet susceptible; it flashed with genius, or melted in tenderness. It could also be terrible. Cunning and falsehood quailed under it, but it was never

Written in 1855. From Alexander Gilchrist, *Life of William Blake: "Pictor Ignotus"* (Macmillan: London and Cambridge, 1863).

busy with them. It pierced them, and turned away. Nor was the mouth less expressive; the lips flexible and quivering with feeling. I can yet recall it when, on one occasion, dwelling upon the exquisite beauty of the parable of the Prodigal, he began to repeat a part of it; but at the words, "When he was yet a great way off, his father saw him," could go no further; his voice faltered, and he was in tears.

I can never forget the evening when Mr. Linnell took me to Blake's house, nor the quiet hours passed with him in the examination of antique gems, choice pictures, and Italian prints of the sixteenth century. Those who may have read some strange passages in his *Catalogue,* written in irritation, and probably in haste, will be surprised to hear, that in conversation he was anything but sectarian or exclusive, finding sources of delight throughout the whole range of art; while, as a critic, he was judicious and discriminating.

No man more admired Albert Dürer; yet, after looking over a number of his designs, he would become a little angry with some of the draperies, as not governed by the forms of the limbs, nor assisting to express their action; contrasting them in this respect with the draped antique, in which it was hard to tell whether he was more delighted with the general design, or with the exquisite finish and the depth of the chiselling; in works of the highest class, no mere adjuncts, but the last development of the design itself.

He united freedom of judgment with reverence for all that is great. He did not look out for the works of the purest ages, but for the purest works of every age and country—Athens or Rhodes, Tuscany or Britain; but no authority or popular consent could influence him against his deliberate judgment. Thus he thought with Fuseli and Flaxman that the Elgin Theseus, however full of antique savour, could not, as ideal form, rank with the very finest relics of antiquity. Nor, on the other hand, did the universal neglect of Fuseli in any degree lessen his admiration of his best works.

He fervently loved the early Christian art, and dwelt with peculiar affection on the memory of Fra Angelico, often speaking of him as an inspired inventor and as a saint; but when he approached Michael Angelo, the *Last Supper* of Da Vinci, the Torso Belvidere, and some of the inventions preserved in the Antique Gems, all his powers were concentrated in admiration.

When looking at the heads of the apostles in the copy of the *Last Supper* at the Royal Academy, he remarked of all but Judas, "Every one looks as if he had conquered the natural man." He was equally ready to admire a contemporary and a rival. Fuseli's picture of *Satan building the Bridge over Chaos* he ranked with the grandest efforts of imaginative art, and said that we were two centuries behind the civilisation which would enable us to estimate his *Aegisthus.*

He was fond of the works of St. Theresa, and often quoted them with other writers on the interior life. Among his eccentricities will, no doubt, be numbered his preference for ecclesiastical governments. He used to ask how it was that we heard so much of priestcraft, and so little of soldiercraft and lawyercraft. The Bible, he said, was the book of liberty and Christianity the sole regenerator of nations. In politics a Platonist, he puts no trust in demagogues. His ideal home was with Fra Angelico: a little later he might have been a reformer, but after the fashion of Savonarola.

He loved to speak of the years spent by Michael Angelo, without earthly reward, and solely for the love of God, in the building of St. Peter's, and of the wondrous architects of our cathedrals. In Westminster Abbey were his earliest and most sacred recollections. I asked him how he would like to paint on glass, for the great west window, his "Sons of God shouting for Joy," from his designs in the *Job*. He said, after a pause, "I could do it!" kindling at the thought.

Centuries could not separate him in spirit from the artists who went about our land, pitching their tents by the morass or the forest side, to build those sanctuaries that now lie ruined amidst the fertility which they called into being.

His mind was large enough to contain, along with these things, stores of classic imagery. He delighted in Ovid, and, as a labour of love, had executed a finished picture from the *Metamorphoses,* after Giulio Romano. This design hung in his room, and, close by his engraving table, Albert Dürer's *Melancholy the Mother of Invention,* memorable as probably having been seen by Milton, and used in his *Penseroso.* There are living a few artists, then boys, who may remember the smile of welcome with which he used to rise from that table to receive them.

His poems were variously estimated. They tested rather severely the imaginative capacity of their readers. Flaxman said they were as grand as his designs, and Wordsworth delighted in his *Songs of Innocence.* To the multitude they were unintelligible. In many parts full of pastoral sweetness, and often flashing with noble thoughts or terrible imagery, we must regret that he should sometimes have suffered fancy to trespass within sacred precincts.

Thrown early among the authors who resorted to Johnson, the bookseller, he rebuked the profanity of Paine, and was no disciple of Priestley; but, too undisciplined and cast upon times and circumstances which yielded him neither guidance nor sympathy, he wanted that balance of the faculties which might have assisted him in matters extraneous to his profession. He saw everything through art, and, in matters beyond its range, exalted it from a witness into a judge.

He had great powers of argument, and on general subjects was a very patient and good-tempered disputant; but materialism was his abhorrence: and if some unhappy man called in question the world of spirits, he would answer him "according to his folly," by putting forth his own views in their most extravagant and startling aspect. This might amuse those who were in the secret, but it left his opponent angry and bewildered.

Such was Blake, as I remember him. He was one of the few to be met with in our passage through life, who are not, in some way or other, "double minded" and inconsistent with themselves; one of the very few who cannot be depressed by neglect, and to whose name rank and station could add no lustre. Moving apart, in a sphere above the attraction of worldly honours, he did not accept greatness, but confer it. He ennobled poverty, and, by his conversation and the influence of his genius, made two small rooms in Fountain Court more attractive than the threshold of princes.

PART 2
BLAKE IN OUR TIME

◆

Blake's Treatment of the Archetype

NORTHROP FRYE

The reader of Blake soon becomes familiar with the words "innocence" and "experience." The world of experience is the world that adults live in while they are awake. It is a very big world, and a lot of it seems to be dead, but still it makes its own kind of sense. When we stare at it, it stares unwinkingly back, and the changes that occur in it are, on the whole, orderly and predictable changes. This quality in the world that reassures us we call law. Sitting in the middle of the lawful world is the society of awakened adults. This society consists of individuals who apparently have agreed to put certain restraints on themselves. So we say that human society is also controlled by law. Law, then, is the basis both of reason and of society: without it there is no happiness, and our philosophers tell us that they really do not know which is more splendid, the law of the starry heavens outside us, or the moral law within. True, there was a time when we were children and took a different view of life. In childhood happiness seemed to be based, not on law and reason, but on love, protection, and peace. But we can see now that such a view of life was an illusion derived from an excess of economic security. As Isaac Watts says, in a song of innocence which is thought to have inspired Blake:

> Sleep, my babe; thy food and raiment,
> House and home, thy friends provide;
> All without thy care or payment:
> All thy wants are well supplied.

And after all, from the adult point of view, the child is not so innocent as he looks. He is actually a little bundle of anarchic will, whose desires take no account of either the social or the natural order. As he grows up and enters the world of law, his illegal desires can no longer be tolerated even by himself, and so they are driven underground into the world of the dream, to be joined there by new desires, mainly sexual in origin. In the dream, a blind, unreasoning, childish will is still at work revenging itself on experience and rearranging it in terms of desire. It is a great comfort to know that this world, in which we are compelled to spend about a third of our time, is

From *English Institute Essays, 1950,* ed. Alan S. Downer, copyright 1951, Columbia University Press. Used by permission.

unreal, and can never displace the world of experience in which reason predominates over passion, order over chaos, classical values over romantic ones, the solid over the gaseous, and the cool over the hot.

The world of law, stretching from the starry heavens to the moral conscience, is the domain of Urizen in Blake's symbolism. It sits on a volcano in which the rebellious Titan Orc, the spirit of passion, lies bound, writhing and struggling to get free. Each of these spirits is Satanic or devilish to the other. While we dream, Urizen, the principle of reality, is the censor, or, as Blake calls him, the accuser, a smug and grinning hypocrite, an impotent old man, the caricature that the child in us makes out of the adult world that thwarts him. But as long as we are awake, Orc, the lawless pleasure principle, is an evil dragon bound under the conscious world in chains, and we all hope he will stay there.

The dream world is, however, not quite securely bound: every so often it breaks loose and projects itself on society in the form of war. It seems odd that we should keep plunging with great relief into moral holidays of aggression in which robbery and murder become virtues instead of crimes. It almost suggests that keeping our desires in leash and seeing that others do likewise is a heavy and sooner or later an intolerable strain. On a still closer view, even the difference between war and law begins to blur. The social contract, which from a distance seems a reasonable effort of cooperation, looks closer up like an armed truce founded on passion, in which the real purpose of law is to defend by force what has been snatched in self-will. Plainly, we cannot settle the conflict of Orc and Urizen by siding with one against the other, still less by pretending that either of them is an illusion. We must look for a third factor in human life, one which meets the requirements of both the dream and the reality.

This third factor, called Los by Blake, might provisionally be called work, or constructive activity. All such work operates in the world of experience: it takes account of law and of our waking ideas of reality. Work takes the energy which is wasted in war or thwarted in dreams and sets it free to act in experience. And as work cultivates land and makes farms and gardens out of jungle and wilderness, as it domesticates animals and builds cities, it becomes increasingly obvious that work is the realization of a dream and that this dream is descended from the child's lost vision of a world where the environment is the home.

The worker, then, does not call the world of experience real because he perceives it out of a habit acquired from his ancestors: it is real to him only as the material cause of his work. And the world of dreams is not unreal, but the formal cause: it dictates the desirable human shape which the work assumes. Work, therefore, by realizing in experience the child's and the dreamer's worlds, indicates what there is about each that is genuinely innocent. When we say that a child is in the state of innocence, we do not mean that he is sinless or harmless, but that he is able to assume a coherence, a simplicity and a kindliness in the world that adults have lost and wish they could regain. When we dream, we are, whatever we put into the dream, revolting against experience and creating another world, usually one we like better. Whatever in childhood or the dream is delivered and realized by work is innocent; whatever is suppressed or distorted by experience becomes selfish or vicious. "He who desires but acts not, breeds pestilence."

Work begins by imposing a human form on nature, for "Where man is not, nature is barren." But in society work collides with the cycle of law and war. A few seize all its benefits and become idlers, the work of the rest is wasted in supporting them, and so work is perverted into drudgery. "God made Man happy & Rich, but the Subtil made the innocent, Poor." Neither idleness nor drudgery can be work: real work is the creative act of a free man, and wherever real work is going on it is humanizing society as well as nature. The work that, projected on nature, forms civilization, becomes, when projected on society, prophecy, a vision of complete human freedom and equality. Such a vision is a revolutionary force in human life, destroying all the social barriers founded on idleness and all the intellectual ones founded on ignorance.

So far we have spoken only of what seems naturally and humanly possible, of what can be accomplished by human nature. But if we confine the conception of work to what now seems possible, we are still judging the dream by the canons of waking reality. In other words, we have quite failed to distinguish work from law, Los from Urizen, and are back where we started. The real driving power of civilization and prophecy is not the mature mind's sophisticated and cautious adaptations of the child's or the dreamer's desires: it comes from the original and innocent form of those desires, with all their reckless disregard of the lessons of experience.

The creative root of civilization and prophecy can only be art, which deals not only with the possible, but with "probable impossibilities"—it is interesting to see Blake quoting Aristotle's phrase in one of his marginalia. And just as the controlling idea of civilization is the humanizing of nature, and the controlling idea of prophecy the emancipation of man, so the controlling idea of art, the source of them both, must be the simultaneous vision of both. This is apocalypse, the complete transformation of both nature and human nature into the same form. "Less than All cannot satisfy Man"; the child in us who cries for the moon will never stop crying until the moon is his plaything, until we are delivered from the tyranny of time, space, and death, from the remoteness of a gigantic nature and from our own weakness and selfishness. Man cannot be free until he is everywhere: at the center of the universe, like the child, and at the circumference of the universe, like the dreamer. Such an apocalypse is entirely impossible under the conditions of experience that we know, and could only take place in the eternal and infinite context that is given it by religion. In fact, Blake's view of art could almost be defined as the attempt to realize the religious vision in human society. Such religion has to be sharply distinguished from all forms of religion which have been kidnapped by the cycle of law and war, and have become capable only of reinforcing the social contract or of inspiring crusades.

When we say that the goal of human work can only be accomplished in eternity, many people would infer that this involves renouncing all practicable improvement of human status in favor of something which by hypothesis, remains forever out of man's reach. We make this inference because we confuse the eternal with the indefinite: we are so possessed by the categories of time and space that we can hardly think of eternity and infinity except as endless time and space, respectively. But the home of time, so to speak, the only part of time that man can live in, is now; and the home of space is here. In the world of experience there is no such time as now; the present never quite exists, but is hidden somewhere between a past that no longer exists and a future that does not yet exist. The mature man does not know where "here" is: he can draw a circle around himself and say that "here" is inside it, but he cannot locate anything except a "there." In both time and space man is being continually excluded from his own home. The dreamer, whose space is inside his mind, has a better notion of where "here" is, and the child, who is not yet fully conscious of the iron chain of memory that binds his ego to time and space, still has some capacity for living in the present. It is to this perspective that man returns when his conception of "reality" begins to acquire some human meaning.

> The Sky is an immortal Tent built by the Sons of Los:
> And every Space that a Man views around his dwelling-place
> Standing on his own roof or in his garden on a mount
> Of twenty-five cubits in height, such space is his Universe:
> And on its verge the Sun rises & sets, the Clouds bow
> To meet the flat Earth & the Sea in such an order'd Space:
> The Starry heavens reach no further, but here bend and set
> On all sides, & the two Poles turn on their valves of gold . . .

If the vision of innocence is taken out of its eternal and infinite context, the real here and now, and put inside time, it becomes either a myth of a Golden Age or a Paradise lost in the past, or a hope which is yet to be attained in the future, or both. If it is put inside space, it must be somewhere else, presumably in the sky. It is only these temporal and spatial perversions of the innocent vision that really do snatch it out of man's grasp. Because the innocent vision is so deep down in human consciousness and is subject to so much distortion, repression, and censorship, we naturally tend, when we project it on the outer world, to put it as far off in time and space as we can get it. But what the artist has to reveal, as a guide for the work of civilization and prophecy, is the form of the world as it would be if we could live in it here and now.

Innocence and experience are the middle two of four possible states. The state of experience Blake calls Generation, and the state of innocence, the potentially creative world of dreams and childhood, Beulah. Beyond Beulah is Eden, the world of the apocalypse in which innocence and experience have become the same thing, and below Generation is Ulro, the world as it is when no work is being done, the world where dreams are impotent and waking life haphazard. Eden and Ulro are, respectively, Blake's heaven or unfallen world and his hell or fallen world. Eden is the world of the creator and the creature, Beulah the world of the lover and the beloved, Generation the world of the subject and the object, and Ulro the world of the ego and the enemy, or the obstacle. This is, of course, one world, looked at in four different ways. The four ways represent the four moods or states in which art is created: the apocalyptic mood of Eden, the idyllic mood of Beulah, the elegiac mood of Generation, and the satiric mood of Ulro. These four moods are the tonalities of Blake's expression; every poem of his regularly resolves on one of them.

For Blake the function of art is to reveal the human or intelligible form of the world, and it sees the other three states in relation to that form. This fact is the key to Blake's conception of imagery, the pattern of which I have tried to simplify by a table.

EXPERIENCE		CATEGORY	INNOCENCE	
Individual Form	*Collective Form*		*Collective Form*	*Individual Form*
sky-god (Nobodaddy)	aristocracy of gods	(1) Divine	human powers	incarnate God (Jesus)
a) leader and high priest (Caiaphas)	tyrants and victims	(2) Human	community	*a)* one man (Albion)
b) harlot (Rahab)				*b)* bride (Jerusalem)
dragon (Covering Cherub)	beasts of prey (tiger, leviathan)	(3) Animal	flock of sheep	one lamb (Bowlahoola)
tree of mystery	forest, wilderness (Entuthon Benython)	(4) Vegetable	garden or park (Allamanda)	tree of life
a) opaque furnace or brick kilns	*a)* city of destruction (Sodom, Babylon, Egypt)	(5) Mineral	city, temple (Golgonooza)	living stone
b) "Stone of Night" (not given)	*b)* ruins, caves salt lake or dead sea (Udan Adan)	(6) Chaotic	fourfold river of life	"Globule of Blood"

Let us take the word "image" in its vulgar sense, which is good enough just now, of a verbal or pictorial replica of a physical object. For Blake the real form of the object is what he calls its "human form." In Ulro, the world with no human work in it, the mineral kingdom consists mainly of shapeless rocks lying around at random. When man comes into the world, he tries to make cities, buildings, roads, and sculptures out of this mineral kingdom. Such human artifacts therefore constitute the intelligible form of the mineral world, the mineral world as human desire would like to see it. Similarly, the "natural" or unworked form of the vegetable world is a forest, a heath or a wilderness; its human and intelligible form is that of the garden, the grove, or the park, the last being the original meaning of the word Paradise. The natural form of the animal world consists of beasts of prey: its human form is a society of domesticated animals of which the flock of sheep is the most commonly employed symbol. The city, the garden and the sheepfold are thus the human forms of the mineral, vegetable, and animal kingdoms, respectively. Blake calls these archetypes Golgonooza, Allamanda, and Bowlahoola, and identifies them with the head, heart, and bowels of the total human form. Below the world of solid substance is a chaotic or liquid world, and the human form of that is the river or circulating body of fresh water.

Each of these human forms has a contrasting counterpart in Ulro, the world of undeveloped nature and regressive humanity. To the city which is the home of the soul or City of God, the fallen world opposes the city of destruction which is doomed through the breakdown of work described by Ezekiel in a passage quoted by Blake as "pride, fullness of bread and abundance of idleness." Against the image of the sheep in the pasture, we have the image of the forest inhabited by menacing beasts like the famous tiger, the blasted heath or waste land full of monsters, or the desert with its fiery serpents. To the river which is the water of life the fallen world opposes the image of the devouring sea and the dragons and leviathans in its depths. Blake usually calls the fallen city Babylon, the forest Entuthon Benython, and the dead sea or salt lake Udan Adan. Labyrinths and mazes are the only patterns of Ulro; images of highways and paths made straight belong to the world informed with intelligence.

The essential principle of the fallen world appears to be discreteness or opacity. Whatever we see in it we see as a self-enclosed entity, unlike all others. When we say that two things are identical, we mean that they are very similar; in other words "identity" is a meaningless word in ordinary experience. Hence in Ulro, and even in Generation, all classes or societies are aggregates of similar but separate individuals. But when man builds houses out of stones, and cities out of houses, it becomes clear that the real or intelligible form of a thing includes its relation to its environment as well as its self-contained existence. This environment is its own larger "human form." The stones that make a city do not cease to be stones, but they cease to be separate stones: their purpose, shape, and function is identical with that of the city as a whole. In the human world, as in the work of art, the individual thing is there, and the total form which gives it meaning is there: what has vanished is the shapeless collection or mass of similar things. This is what Blake means when he says that in the apocalypse all human forms are "identified." The same is true of the effect of work on human society. In a completely human society man would not lose his individuality, but he would lose his separate and isolated ego, what Blake calls his Selfhood. The prophetic vision of freedom and equality thus cannot stop at the Generation level of a Utopia, which means an orderly molecular aggregate of individuals existing in some future time. Such a vision does not capture, though it may adumbrate, the real form of society, which can only be a larger human body. This means literally the body of one man, though not of a separate man.

Everywhere in the human world we find that the Ulro distinction between the singular and the plural has broken down. The real form of human society is the body of one man; the flock of sheep is the body of one lamb; the garden is the body of one tree, the so-called tree of life. The city is the body of one building or temple, a house of many mansions, and the building itself is the body of one stone, a glowing and fiery precious stone, the unfallen stone of alchemy which assimilates everything else to itself, Blake's grain of sand which contains the world.

The second great principle of Ulro is the principle of hierarchy or degree which produces the great chain of being. In the human world there is no chain of being: all aspects of existence are equal as well as identical. The one man is also the one lamb, and the body and blood of the animal form are the bread and wine which are the human forms of the vegetable world. The tree of life is the upright vertebrate form of man; the living stone, the glowing transparent furnace, is the furnace of heart and lungs and bowels in the animal body. The river of life is the blood that circulates within that body. Eden, which according to Blake was a city as well as a garden, had a fourfold river, but no sea, for the river remained inside Paradise, which was the body of one man. England is an island in the sea, like St. John's Patmos; the human form of England is Atlantis, the island which has replaced the sea. Again, where there is no longer any difference between society and the individual, there can hardly be any difference between society and marriage or between a home and a wife or child. Hence Jerusalem in Blake is "A City, yet a Woman," and at the same time the vision of innocent human society.

On the analogy of the chain of being, it is natural for man to invent an imaginary category of gods above him, and he usually locates them in what is above him in space, that is, the sky. The more developed society is, the more clearly man realizes that a society of gods would have to be, like the society of man, the body of one God. Eventually he realizes that the intelligible forms of man and of whatever is above man on the chain of being must be identical. The identity of God and man is for Blake the whole of Christianity: the adoration of a superhuman God he calls natural religion, because the source of it is remote and unconquered nature. In other words, the superhuman God is the deified accuser or censor of waking experience, whose function it is to discourage further work. Blake calls this God Nobodaddy, and curses and reviles him so much that some have inferred that he was inspired by an obscure psychological compulsion to attack the Fatherhood of God. Blake is doing nothing of the kind, as a glance at the last plate of *Jerusalem* will soon show: he is merely insisting that man cannot approach the superhuman aspect of God except through Christ, the God who is Man. If man attempts to approach the Father directly, as Milton, for instance, does in a few unlucky passages in *Paradise Lost,* all he will ever get is Nobodaddy. Theologically, the only unusual feature of Blake is not his attitude to the person of the Father, but his use of what is technically known as pre-existence: the doctrine that the humanity of Christ is coeternal with his divinity.

There is nothing in the Ulro world corresponding to the identity of the individual and the total form in the unfallen one. But natural religion, being a parody of real religion, often develops a set of individual symbols corresponding to the lamb, the tree of life, the glowing stone, and the rest. This consolidation of Ulro symbols Blake calls Druidism. Man progresses toward a free and equal community, and regresses toward tyranny; and as the human form of the community is Christ, the one God who is one Man, so the human form of tyranny is the isolated hero or inscrutable leader with his back to an aggregate of followers, or the priest of a veiled temple with an imaginary sky-god supposed to be behind the veil. The Biblical prototypes of this leader and priest are Moses and Aaron. Against the tree of life we have what Blake calls the tree of mystery, the barren fig tree, the dead tree of the cross, Adam's tree of knowledge, with its forbidden fruit corresponding to the fruits of healing on the tree of life. Against the fiery precious stone, the bodily form in which John saw God "like a jasper and a sardine stone," we have the furnace, the prison of heat without light which is the form of the opaque warm-blooded body in the world of frustration, or the stone of Druidical sacrifice like the one that Hardy associates with Tess. Against the animal body of the lamb, we have the figure that Blake calls, after Ezekiel, the Covering Cherub, who represents a great many things, the unreal world of gods, human tyranny and exploitation, and the remoteness of the sky, but whose animal form is that of the serpent or dragon wrapped around the forbidden tree. The dragon, being both monstrous and fictitious, is the best animal representative of the bogies inspired by human inertia: the Book of Revelation calls it "the beast that was, and is not, and yet is."

Once we have understood Blake's scheme of imagery, we have broken the back of one of the main obstacles to reading the prophecies: the difficulty in grasping their narrative structure. Narrative is normally the first thing we look for in trying to read a long poem, but Blake's poems are presented as a series of engraved plates, and the mental process of following a narrative sequence is, especially in the later poems, subordinated to a process of comprehending an inter-related pattern of images and ideas. The plate in Blake's epics has a function rather similar to that of the stanza with its final alexandrine in *The Faerie Queene:* it brings the narrative to a full stop and forces the reader to try to build up from the narrative his own reconstruction of the author's meaning. Blake thinks almost entirely in terms of two narrative structures. One of these is the narrative of history, the cycle of law and war, the conflict of Orc and Urizen, which in itself has no end and no point and may be called the tragic or historical vision of life. The other is the comic vision of the apocalypse or work of Los, the clarification of the mind which enables one to grasp the human form of the world. But the latter is not concerned with temporal sequence and is consequently not so much a real narrative as a dialectic.

The tragic narrative is the story of how the dream world escapes into experience and is gradually imprisoned by experience. This is the main theme of heroic or romantic poetry and is represented in Blake by Orc. Orc is first shown us, in the "Preludium" to *America,* as the libido of the dream, a boy lusting for a dim maternal figure and bitterly hating an old man who keeps him in chains. Then we see him as the conquering hero of romance, killing dragons and sea monsters, ridding the barren land of its impotent aged kings, freeing imprisoned women, and giving new hope to men. Finally we see him subside into the world of darkness again from whence he emerged, as the world of law slowly recovers its balance. His rise and decline has the rotary movement of the solar and seasonal cycles, and like them is a part of the legal machinery of nature.

Blake has a strong moral objection to all heroic poetry that does not see heroism in its proper tragic context, and even when it does, he is suspicious of it. For him the whole conception of $\varkappa\lambda\acute{\epsilon}\alpha$ $\grave{\alpha}\nu\delta\epsilon\tilde{\omega}\nu$ as being in itself, without regard to the larger consequences of brave deeds, a legitimate theme for poetry, has been completely outmoded. It has been outmoded, for one thing, by Christianity, which has brought to the theme of the heroic act a radically new conception of what a hero is and what an act is. The true hero is the man who, whether as thinker, fighter, artist, martyr, or ordinary worker, helps in achieving the apocalyptic vision of art; and an act is anything that has a real relation to that achievement. Events such as the battle of Agincourt or the retreat from Moscow are not really heroic, because they are not really acts: they are part of the purposeless warfare of the state of nature and are not progressing towards a better kind of humanity. So Blake is interested in Orc only when his heroism appears to coincide with something of potentially apocalyptic importance, like the French or American revolutions.

For the rest, he keeps Orc strictly subordinated to his main theme of the progressive work of Los, the source of which is found in prophetic scriptures, especially, of course, the Bible. Comprehensive as his view of art is, Blake does not exactly say that the Bible is a work of art: he says "The Old & New Testaments are the Great Code of Art." The Bible tells the artist what the function of art is and what his creative powers are trying to accomplish. Apart from its historical and political applications, Blake's symbolism is almost entirely Biblical in origin, and the subordination of the heroic Orc theme to the apocalyptic Los theme follows the Biblical pattern.

The tragic vision of life has the rhythm of the individual's organic cycle: it rises in the middle and declines at the end. The apocalyptic theme turns the tragic vision inside out. The tragedy comes in the middle, with the eclipse of the innocent vision, and the story ends with the re-establishment of the vision. Blake's major myth thus breaks into two parts, a Genesis and an Exodus. The first part accounts for the existence of the world of experience in terms of the myths of creation and fall. Blake sees no difference between creation and fall, between establishing the Ulro world and placing man in it. How man fell out of a city and garden is told twice in Genesis, once of Adam and once of Israel—Israel, who corresponds to Albion in Blake's symbolism, being both a community and a single man. The Book of Genesis ends with Israel in Egypt, the city of destruction. In the Book of Exodus we find the state of experience described in a comprehensive body of Ulro symbols. There is the fallen civilization of Egypt, destroyed by the plagues which its own tyranny has raised, the devouring sea, the desert with its fiery serpents, the leader and the priest, the invisible sky god who confirms their despotic power, and the labyrinthine wanderings of a people who have nothing but law and are unable to work. Society has been reduced to a frightened rabble following a leader who obviously has no notion of where he is going. In front of it is the Promised Land with its milk and honey, but all the people can see are enemies, giants, and mysterious terrors. From there on the story splits in two. The histories go on with the Orc or heroic narrative of how the Israelites conquered Canaan and proceeded to run through another cycle from bondage in Egypt to bondage in Babylon. But in the prophecies, as they advance from social criticism to apocalyptic, the Promised Land is the city and garden that all human effort is trying to reach, and its conqueror can only be the Messiah or true form of man.

The New Testament has the same structure as the Old. In the life of Jesus the story of the Exodus is repeated. Jesus is carried off to Egypt by a father whose name is Joseph, Herod corresponds to Pharaoh, and the massacre of the innocents to the attempt to exterminate the Hebrew children. The organizing of Christianity around twelve disciples corresponds to the organizing of the religion of Israel among twelve tribes, the forty days wandering of Jesus in the desert to the forty years of Israel, the crucifixion to the lifting of the brazen serpent on the pole, and the resurrection to the invasion of Canaan by Joshua, who has the same name as Jesus. From there on the New Testament splits into a historical section describing the beginning of a new Christian cycle, which is reaching its Babylonian phase in Blake's own time, and a prophetic section, the Book of Revelation, which deals with what it describes, in a phrase which has fascinated so many apocalyptic thinkers from

Joachim of Floris to Blake, as the "everlasting gospel," the story of Jesus told not historically as an event in the past, but visually as a real presence.

The characters of Blake's poems, Orc, Los, Urizen, Vala, and the rest, take shape in accordance with Blake's idea of the real act. No word in the language contains a greater etymological lie than the word "individual." The so-called undivided man is a battleground of conflicting forces, and the appearance of consistency in his behavior derives from the force that usually takes the lead. To get at the real elements of human character, one needs to get past the individual into the dramatis personae that make up his behavior. Blake's analysis of the individual shows a good many parallels with more recent analyses, especially those of Freud and Jung. The scheme of the Four Zoas is strikingly Freudian, and the contrast of the Orc and Los themes in Blake is very like the contrast between Jung's early book on the libido and his later study of the symbols of individuation. Jung's anima and persona are closely analogous to Blake's emanation and specter, and his counsellor and shadow seem to have some relation to Blake's Los and Spectre of Urthona.

But a therapeutic approach will still relate any such analysis primarily to the individual. In Blake anything that is a significant act of individual behavior is also a significant act of social behavior. Orc, the libido, produces revolution in society: Vala, the elusive anima, produces the social code of Frauendienst; Urizen, the moral censor, produces the religion of the externalized God. "We who dwell on Earth can do nothing of ourselves," says Blake: "everything is conducted by Spirits." Man performs no act as an individual: all his acts are determined by an inner force which is also a social and historical force, and they derive their significance from their relation to the total human act, the restoration of the innocent world. John Doe does nothing as John Doe: he eats and sleeps in the spirit of Orc the Polypus: he obeys laws in the spirit of Urizen the conscience; he loses his temper in the spirit of Tharmas the destroyer; and he dies in the spirit of Satan the death-impulse.

Furthermore, as the goal of life is the humanization of nature, there is a profound similarity between human and natural behavior, which in the apocalypse becomes identity. It is a glimmering of this fact that has produced the god, the personalized aspect of nature, and a belief in gods gradually builds the sense of an omnipotent personal community out of nature. As long as these gods remain on the other side of nature, they are merely the shadows of superstition: when they are seen to be the real elements of human life as well, we have discovered the key to all symbolism in art. Blake's Tharmas, the "id" of the individual and the stampeding mob of society, is also the god of the sea, Poseidon the earth-shaker. His connection with the sea is not founded on resemblance or association, but, like the storm scene in *King Lear,* on an ultimate identity of human rage and natural tempest.

In the opening plates of *Jerusalem* Blake has left us a poignant account of one such struggle of contending forces within himself, between his creative powers and his egocentric will. He saw the Industrial Revolution and the great political and cultural changes that came with it, and he realized that something profoundly new and disquieting was coming into the world, something with unlimited possibilities for good or for evil, which it would tax all his powers to interpret. And so his natural desire to make his living as an engraver and a figure in society collided with an overwhelming impulse to tell the whole poetic truth about what he saw. The latter force won, and dictated its terms accordingly. He was not allowed to worry about his audience. He revised, but was not allowed to decorate or stylize, only to say what had to be said. He was not allowed the double talk of the sophisticated poet, who can address several levels of readers at once by using familiar conceptions ambiguously. Nothing was allowed him but a terrifying concentration of his powers of utterance.

What finally emerged, out of one of the hottest poetic crucibles of modern times, was a poetry which consisted almost entirely in the articulation of archetypes. By an archetype I mean an element in a work of literature, whether a character, an image, a narrative formula, or an idea, which can be assimilated to a larger unifying category. The existence of such a category depends on the existence of a unified conception of art. Blake began his prophecies with a powerfully integrated theory of the nature, structure, function, and meaning of art, and all the symbolic units of his poetry, his moods, his images, his narratives and his characters, form archetypes of that theory. Given his premises about art, everything he does logically follows. His premises may be wrong, but there are two things which may make us hesitate to call them absurd. One is their comprehensiveness and consistency: if the Bible is the code of art, Blake seems to provide something of a code of modern art, both in his structure of symbols and in his range of ideas. The other is their relationship to earlier traditions of criticism. Theories of poetry and of archetypes seem to belong to criticism rather than to poetry itself, and when I speak of Blake's treatment of the archetype I imply that Blake is a poet of unique interest to critics like ourselves. The Biblical origin of his symbolism and his apocalyptic theory of perception have a great deal in common with the theory of anagoge which underlies the poetry of Dante, the main structure of which survived through the Renaissance at least as late as Milton. Blake had the same creative powers as other great poets, but he made a very unusual effort to drag them up to consciousness, and to do deliberately what most poets prefer to do instinctively. It is possible that what impelled him to do this was the breakdown of a tradition of criticism which could have answered a very important question. Blake did not need the answer, but we do.

The question relates to the application of Blake's archetypes to the criticism of poetry as a whole. The papers delivered to this body of scholars are supposed to deal with general issues of criticism rather than with pure research. Now pure research is, up to a point, a co-ordinated and systematic form of study, and the question arises whether general criticism could also acquire a systematic form. In other words, is criticism a mere aggregate of research and comment and generalization, or is it, considered as a whole, an intelligible structure of knowledge? If the latter, there must be a quality in literature which enables it to be so, an order of words corresponding to the order of natrue which makes the natural sciences intelligible. If criticism is more than aggregated commentary, literature must be somewhat more than an aggregate of poems and plays and novels: it must possess some kind of total form which criticism can in some measure grasp and expound.

It is on this question that the possibility of literary archetypes depends. If there is no total structure of literature, and no intelligible form to criticism as a whole, then there is no such thing as an archetype. The only organizing principle so far discovered in literature is chronology, and consequently all our larger critical categories are concerned with sources and direct transmission. But every student of literature has, whether consciously or not, picked up thousands of resemblances, analogies, and parallels in his reading where there is no question of direct transmission. If there are no archetypes, then these must be merely private associations, and the connections among them must be arbitrary and fanciful. But if criticism makes sense, and literature makes sense, then the mental processes of the cultivated reader may be found to make sense too.

The difficulty of a "private mythology" is not peculiar to Blake: every poet has a private mythology, his own formation of symbols. His mythology is a cross-section of his life, and the critic, like the biographer, has the job of making sure that what was private to the poet shall be public to everyone else. But, having no theory of archetypes, we do not know how to proceed. Blake supplies us with a few leading principles which may guide us in analyzing the symbolic formation of poets and isolating the archetypal elements in them. Out of such a study the structure of literature may slowly begin to emerge, and criticism, in interpreting that structure, may take its rightful place among the major disciplines of modern thought. There is, of course, the possibility that the study of Blake is a long and tortuous blind alley, but those who are able to use Blake's symbols as a calculus for all their criticism will not be much inclined to consider it.

The question that we have just tried to answer, however, is not the one that the student of Blake most frequently meets. The latter question runs in effect: you may show that Blake had one of the most powerful minds in the modern world, that his thought is staggeringly comprehensive and consistent, that his insight was profound, his mood exalted, and his usefulness to critics unlimited. But surely all this profits a poet nothing if he does not preserve the hieratic decorum of conventional poetic utterance. And how are we to evaluate an utterance which is now lucid epigram and now a mere clashing of symbols, now disciplined and lovely verse and now a rush of prosy gabble? Whatever it is, is it really poetry or really great and good poetry?

Well, probably not, in terms of what criticism now knows, or thinks it knows, about the canons of beauty and the form of literary expression.

Othello was merely a bloody farce in terms of what the learned and acute Thomas Rymer knew about drama. Rymer was perfectly right in his own terms; he is like the people who say that Blake was mad. One cannot refute them; one merely loses interest in their conception of sanity. And critics may be as right about Blake as Rymer was about Shakespeare, and still be just as wrong. We do not yet know whether literature and criticism are forms or aggregates: we know almost nothing about archetypes or about any of the great critical problems connected with them. In Dante's day critics did know something about the symbols of the Bible, but we have made little effort to recover that knowledge. We do not know very much even about genres: we do not know whether Blake's "prophecy" form is a real genre or not, and we certainly do not know how to treat it if it is. I leave the question of Blake's language in more competent hands, but after all, even the poets are only beginning to assimilate contemporary speech, and when the speech of *Jerusa-lem* becomes so blunt and colloquial that Blake himself calls it prosaic, do critics really know whether it is too prosaic to be poetic, or even whether such an antithesis exists at all? I may be speaking only of myself, for criticism today is full of confident value-judgments, on Blake and on everyone else, implying a complete understanding of all such mysteries. But I wonder if these are really critical judgments, or if they are merely the aberrations of the history of taste. I suspect that a long course of patient and detailed study lies ahead of us before we really know much about the critical problems which the study of Blake raises, and which have to be reckoned with in making any value-judgment on him. Then we shall understand the poets, including Blake, much better, and I am not concerned with what the results of that better understanding will be.

Blake's Vision of Slavery
[From *Prophet against Empire*]

DAVID V. ERDMAN

The fire, the fire is falling!
Look up! look up! O citizen of London enlarge thy countenance:
O Jew, leave counting gold! return to thy oil and wine. O African!
black African! (go, winged thought widen his forehead.)
—"A Song of Liberty"

I

When Blake came to believe, in the decade after Waterloo, that the revolutions in America and France had been merely bourgeois revolutions, destroying colonial and monarchic restraints only to establish the irresponsible "right" to buy and sell, he concluded that nearly everything of value in those revolutions had been lost—at least as far as his own countrymen were concerned. When he declared that most Englishmen "since the French Revolution" had become "intermeasurable by one another" like coins in a till and had reduced all values to the experiment of chance, he meant that such Englishmen had absorbed nothing of the real meaning of Republican culture, had not learned that everything that *lives* is holy and without price and that each "line or lineament" is *itself* and is "not intermeasurable by anything else."[1]

Most of his life Blake was more or less confident that the sons and daughters of Albion would learn; would enlarge their views rather than their investments, would "look up" and open their minds to the visions in the air. For "counting gold" is not abundant living; and grasping colonies and shedding blood whether in the name of royal dignity or in the name of commerce is not living at all, but killing. When Blake urges the London merchant to turn from banking to the exchange of useful commodities (Biblical "oil and wine") he is thinking on the one hand of the need to abolish hunger; on the other hand he is thinking of the gold amassed from colonial plunder, traffic in slaves, and open war. The winged thought which must inspire the African slave to revolt must also inspire the British citizen to let "the British Colonies beneath the woful Princes fade" and to desist from coveting the colonies of

From *Prophet against Empire: A Poet's Interpretation of the History of His Own Times*, copyright 1954, © 1982 renewed by Princeton University Press. Used by permission.

France. And it must also inspire the sexes to *love* and let *live* without possessive jealousy.

Blake sees all these matters as interrelated. War grows out of acquisitive-
ness and jealousy and mischanneled sexual energy, all of which grow out of
the intrusion of possessiveness into human relations. "Number weight &
measure" signify "a year of dearth."[2] The Rights of Man are not the rights of
dealers in human flesh—warriors, slavers, and whoremongers. When Fayette
was "bought & sold" in the service of the royal whore, his and other people's
happy morrow was also "bought & sold." Purchase and sale only bring the
old relationship of tyrant and slave out into the open market.

The economic side of Blake's myth is often expressed in images of
fertility and sterility, fire and frost and seasonal growth. The soul of America
who sings passionately of "lovely copulation" is a woman and also a continent
longing for fruit in her fertile valleys. To say that she wants to be loved, not
raped, is to say, economically, that she wants to be cultivated by free men,
not slaves or slave-drivers; for joy, not for profit. The revolutionary energy
which appears in history as Orcus pulling tyrants down to the pit appears in
husbandry as the plower, sower, and reaper of abundant harvests, symbolized
as ὄρχεις, the root of sexual growth in the womb of the earth. Orc as the
spirit of living that transcends the spirit of trading is the divine seed-fire that
exceeds the calculations of Urizen, god of commerce. The portrait of Urizen
with golden compasses is made in the image of Newton, the mighty spirit of
weighing and measuring who thought to reduce the prolific universe to an
orrery of farthing balls. When Newton's trump marks the end of weight and
measure, the great starry heavens prove to be as light as leaves.

In the symbolic Preludiums of *America* and subsequent poems, the rich
sexual-agrarian implications of Blake's economics are condensed into a crypti-
cally ritualized myth. But some of the reasoning behind this myth, or more
properly the questioning behind it, is available in *Visions of the Daughters of
Albion,* 1793, a dramatized treatise on the related questions of moral, economic, and sexual freedom and an indictment of the "mistaken Demon"
whose code separates bodies from souls and reduces women and children,
nations and lands, to possessions.

Superficially the *Visions* appears to be a debate on free love with passing
allusions to the rights of man, of woman, and of beasts and to the injustices
of sexual inhibition and prohibition, of life ruled by "cold floods of abstraction," and of Negro and child slavery. Yet love and slavery prove to be the
two poles of the poem's axis, and the momentum of its spinning—for it does
not progress—is supplied by the oratory of Oothoon, a female slave, free in
spirit but physically bound; Bromion, the slave-driver who owns her and has
raped her to increase her market value; and Theotormon, her jealous but
inhibited lover who fails to recognize her divine humanity. As a lament over
the possessiveness of love and the hypocrisy of moral legislators, the poem has
been widely explored in the light of Blake's notebook poems on this theme

and in the light of Mary Wollstonecraft's *Vindication of the Rights of Woman.* The other pole, equally important in the dynamics of the work, has scarcely been discovered. Yet we can understand the three symbolic persons of the myth, their triangular relationship, and their unresolved debate if we recognize them as, in part, poetic counterparts of the parliamentary and editorial debates of 1789–1793 on a bill for abolition of the British slave trade—the frustrated lover, for example, being analogous to the wavering abolitionist who cannot bring himself openly to condemn slavery although he deplores the *trade.*

Blake, in relating his discussion of freedom to the "voice of slaves beneath the sun" (*V.D.A.* 31), was directing the light of the French Revolution upon the most vulnerable flaw in the British constitution, and in doing so he was contributing to the most widely agitated reform movement of the time. The Society for the Abolition of the Slave Trade, formed in 1787, had begun at once to gather evidence, organize town meetings, and enlist the help of artists and writers. Wedgwood produced a cameo of a suppliant Negro, widely used on snuffboxes, bracelets, hairpins. William Cowper wrote a number of street ballads such as *The Negro's Complaint* and *Sweet Meat Has Sour Sauce.* And Blake's *Little Black Boy* coincided with the early phase of this campaign. But the Parliamentary phase began in 1789 and coincided with the revolution in France and the ensuing revolution of slaves in 1791 in French Santo Domingo. It reached its height in 1792–1793, and Wordsworth, returning to England early in 1793 after more than a year in France, was struck by the extent of the English movement: "little less in verity Than a whole Nation crying with one voice" against "the Traffickers in Negro blood."[8] The abolitionists nevertheless were "baffled." The bill was defeated in Parliament by the pressure of Antijacobin attacks from Burke and Lord Abingdon and various slave-agents, of whom Blake's thundering Bromion is a caricature.

This movement "had diffus'd some truths And more of virtuous feeling through the heart Of the English People," but its breadth was due partly to the fact that relatively few had any direct stake in the trade. Conservative as well as liberal humanitarians were not unwilling to dissociate British honor and British commerce from "this most rotten branch of human shame." Moreover, the slaves themselves made the trade a risky one, both for slave drivers and for ship owners. Scarcely a year went by without its quota of slave ship mutinies, battles on the African coast, and insurrections in the plantations. Military statesmen complained that merchant seamen died off twice as rapidly in the slave trade as in any other, effecting a loss of manpower for the British navy. And many active abolitionists were merchants who preferred to invest in well-behaved cargoes manufactured in Manchester and Birmingham. It is Blake's view that the movement failed because of an insufficient diffusion of "truths" and a considerable misapplication of "virtuous feeling," to use Wordsworth's terms.

In *Visions of the Daughters of Albion* the true feelings which the Heart must "know" before there can be human freedom are discussed by Oothoon, Bromion, and Theotormon for the edification of the "enslav'd" Daughters of Albion—an almost silent audience or chorus, who lament upon their mountains and in their valleys and sigh "toward America," and who may be considered the Blakean equivalent of traditional personifications of the trades and industries of Great Britain: in *The Four Zoas* some of them appear as the textile trades whose "needlework" is sold throughout the earth. They are of course, in the moral allegory, "oppressed womanhood," as Damon points out. They are shown that as long as possessive morality prevails, all daughters remain slaves; and that while the trafficker in Negro blood continues to stamp his signet on human flesh, none of the traffic on the golden Thames is untainted. In short, freedom is indivisible, and Oothoon's is a test case.[4]

II

Blake's knowledge of the cruelties of slavery came to him doubtless through many sources, but one was directly graphic. In 1791 or earlier the bookseller Joseph Johnson distributed to Blake and other engravers a sheaf of some eighty sketches of the flora and fauna and conditions of human servitude in the South American colony of Dutch Guiana during some early slave revolts. With more than his usual care Blake engraved at least sixteen plates, including nearly all those which illustrate slave conditions. We know he was working on them during the production of his *Visions of the Daughters of Albion* because he turned in most of the plates in batches dated December 1, 1792, and December 2, 1793. The two-volume work they illustrate was finally published in 1796 as *A Narrative, of a five Years' expedition, against the Revolted Negroes of Surinam, in Guiana, on the Wild Coast of South America; from the years 1772 to 1777*, by Captain J. G. Stedman. We may assume that Blake was familiar with the narrative, available in Johnson's shop—at least with the portions explanatory of the drawings.

Blake's engravings, with a force of expression absent from the others, emphasize the dignity of Negro men and women stoical under cruel torture: the wise, reproachful look of the *Negro hung alive by the Ribs to a Gallows* (pl. 11) who lived three days unmurmuring and upbraided a flogged comrade for crying; the bitter concern in the face of the Negro executioner compelled to break the bones of a crucified rebel; the warm, self-possessed look of his victim, who jested with the crowd and offered to his sentinel "my hand that was chopped off" to eat with his piece of dry bread: for how was it "that he, a *white man*, should have no meat to eat along with it?" Though Blake signed most of the plates, he shrank from signing his engraving of this bloody document, *The Execution of "Breaking on the Rack"* (pl. 71); but the image of the courageous rebel on the cruciform rack bit into his heart, and in the

Preludium of *America,* he drew Orc in the same posture to represent the spirit of human freedom defiant of tyranny.

For the *finis* page Blake engraved according to Stedman's specifications "an emblematical picture" of *Europe supported by Africa & America*—three comely nude women tenderly embracing each other, the Negro and the European clasping hands in sisterly equality. Roses bloom auspiciously on the barren ground at their feet. Yet there is a curious difference between this pictured relationship of Europe *supported* by her darker sisters, who wear slave bracelets while she wears a string of pearls, and the "ardent wish" expressed in Stedman's text, that all peoples "may henceforth and to all eternity be the props of each other" since "we only differ in colour, but are certainly all created by the same Hand." The bracelets and pearls may be said to represent the historical fact; the handclasp, the ardent wish. For one plate Blake had the ironic chore of engraving a "contented" slave—with Stedman's initials, J.G.S., stamped on his flesh with a silver signet.[5] "Stampt with my signet," says Bromion (*V.D.A.* 21).

In his *Narrative* Stedman demonstrates the dilemma, social and sexual, of the English man of sentiment entangled in the ethical code of property and propriety. A hired soldier in Guiana, Captain Stedman was apologetic about the "Fate" that caused him to be fighting bands of rebel slaves in a Dutch colony: " 'Twas *yours* to fall—but *Mine* to feel the wound," we learn from the frontispiece, engraved by Bartolozzi: *Stedman with a Rebel Negro prostrate at his feet.* The fortitude of the tortured Negroes and the "commiseration" of their Negro executioners impressed Stedman and led him to conclude that Europeans were "the greater barbarians." Yet he could repeat the myth that these same dignified people were "perfectly savage" in Africa and would only be harmed by "sudden emancipation," His "ears were stunned with the clang of the whip and the dismal yells"; yet he was reassured by the consideration that the tortures were legal punishment and were not occurring in a *British* colony.[6]

To the torture of female slaves Stedman was particularly sensitive, for he was in love with a beautiful fifteen-year-old slave, Joanna, and in a quandary similar to that of Blake's Theotormon, who loves Oothoon but cannot free her. Stedman managed "a decent wedding" with Joanna, for which he is shamefaced, and a honeymoon during which they were "free like the roes in the forest." But he was unable to purchase her freedom, and when he thought Joanna was to be sold at auction, he fancied he "saw her tortured, insulted, and bowing under the weight of her chains, calling aloud, but in vain, for my assistance." Even on their honeymoon, Stedman was harrowed by his inability to prevent the sadistic flagellation of a slave on a neighboring estate. We have Blake's engraving of this *Flagellation of a Female Samboe Slave* (pl. 37). Naked and tied "by both arms to a tree," the "beautiful Samboe girl of about eighteen" had just received two hundred lashes. Stedman's interference only prompted the overseer to order the punishment repeated. "Thus I had no other remedy but to run to my boat, and leave the detestable monster, like a beast of prey, to enjoy his bloody feast." The girl's crime had been "refusing to submit to the loathsome embraces of her detestable executioner." The captain's own Joanna, to prove the equality of her "soul" to "that of an European," insisted on enduring the conditions of slavery until she could purchase freedom with her own labor.[7] Blake's Oothoon invites vultures to prey upon her naked flesh for the same reason. Her lover, Theotormon, is also unable to interfere or to rescue her:

> Why does my Theotormon sit weeping upon the threshold;
> And Oothoon hovers by his side, perswading him in vain
>   —(V.D.A. 44–45)

The persons and problems of Stedman's *Narrative* reappear, creatively modified, in the text and illustrations of Blake's *Visions:* the rape and torture of the virgin slave, her pride in the purity and equality of her soul, and the frustrated desire of her lover and husband. Oothoon advertised as pregnant by Bromion is the slave on the auction block whose pregnancy enhances her price; Oothoon chained by an ankle in plate 4 is the *Female Negro Slave, with a Weight chained to her Ancle*[8]—or the similarly chained victim of the infamous Captain Kimber, cited in Parliament in 1792. The cold green wave enveloping the chained Oothoon is symbolic of the drowning of slaves in passage from Africa; the flame-like shape of the wave is symbolic of the liberating fires of rebellion. Her friend beside her hears her call but covers his eyes from seeing what must be done. In another picture Oothoon is fastened back-to-back to Bromion; yet the most prominent chains are on *his* leg, and she has not ceased struggling to be free.[9] Impotent beside these two squats Theotormon, the theology-tormented man,[10] inhibited by a moral code that tells him his love is impure. A caricature of paralyzed will power, he simultaneously clutches himself, buries his face in his arms, and scratches the back of his head. Despite his furtive sympathy ("secret tears") he makes no effective response to

> The voice of slaves beneath the sun, and children bought with money,
> That shiver in religious caves beneath the burning fires
> Of lust, that belch incessant from the summits of the earth.[11]

Stedman's anxieties shed light on the moral paralysis of Theotormon; yet we must also be aware of the analogous but more impersonal and political quandary of the Abolition Society, whose trimming announcement in February 1792 that they did not desire "the Emancipation of the Negroes in the British Colonies" but only sought to end "*the Trade* for Slaves" conflicted with their own humanitarian professions and involved an acceptance of the basic premises of the slavers: that slaves were legitimate commodities and that the rebellion of slaves was legally indefensible. [12] William Wilberforce, the Society's zealous but conservative spokesman in Parliament, became increasingly preoccupied in 1792 with clearing his reputation of the taint of republicanism in an attempt to carry water on both shoulders: to be known as a great friend of the slaves yet as an abhorrer of "democratical principles." Also he had obtained a "Royal Proclamation against Vice and Immorality" and was promoting what became known as the Vice Society, based on the proposition that woman's love is Sin and democracy is Blasphemy. Blake's deliberate emphasis on the delights of "happy copulation" could be expected to shock such angelic moralists, as if to say: you cannot free any portion of humanity from chains unless you recognize the close connection between the cat-o'-nine-tails and the moral code. [13]

The situation or story of Blake's poem is briefly this. Oothoon, a candid virgin, loves Theotormon and is not afraid to enter the experience of love. She puts a marigold between her breasts and flies over the ocean to take it to her lover; she is willing, that is, to give him the flower of her virginity. But on the way she is seized by Bromion, who rapes her despite her woeful outcries, and advertises her as a pregnant slave (harlot). [14] Her lover responds not by coming to her rescue but by accusing her and Bromion of adultery and secretly bemoaning his fate and hers. Oothoon and Bromion therefore remain "bound back to back" in the barren relationship of slavery, while Theotormon, failing as a lover, sits "weeping upon the threshold." The rest of the poem consists of their three-sided soliloquy. Oothoon argues that she is still pure in that she can still bring her lover flowers of joy, moments of gratified desire; but he cannot act because he accepts Bromion's definition of her as a sinner.

Interpretation of the story on this level is sometimes blurred by failure to distinguish Oothoon's offer of herself to Theotormon from her rape by Bromion. The flower-picking is mistaken for a symbol of the rape, and her later argument is mistaken for defense of an "affair" with Bromion. But in Blake's plot-source, Macpherson's *Oithona,* where the heroine is similarly raped in her lover's absence, the lover returning does what obviously Theotormon ought to do, considers her still faithful and goes to battle at once in her defense, against great odds. [15] Oothoon's argument is not that she likes Bromion or slavery but that she refuses to accept the status of a fallen woman: only if her lover lets Bromion's name-calling intimidate him will she be "a whore indeed" (line 170). She is not asking merely for toleration but for love.

The allegorical level, indicated by Oothoon's designation as "the soft soul of America" (line 3), must not be neglected. Bromion's signet brands not simply a woman but "Thy soft American plains," and Bromion is no simple rapist but the slaver whose claim to "thy north & south" is based on his possession in both North and South America of African slaves: "Stampt with my signet . . . the swarthy children of the sun" (lines 20–21). When the soul of America goes "seeking flowers to comfort her" she is looking for a further blossoming of the revolutionary spirit (compare the Preludium of Blake's *America*), and when she finds a "bright Marygold" in the "dewy bed" of "the vales of Leutha," she is apparently taking note of the Negro insurrections in Santo Domingo in the Caribbean around which the debate in Parliament raged: "Bromion rent her with his thunders."[16] The first risings did not succeed, but the flower or nymph comforts "Oothoon the mild" both with her own "glow" and with the observation that the spirit of liberty is irrepressible: "Another flower shall spring, because the soul of sweet delight Can never pass away." On this level Theotormon, to whom Oothoon wings over the Atlantic in "exulting swift delight" expecting him to rejoice at the good news of another rising republic, acts like those English abolitionists who were embarrassed by the thunders of the Antijacobins.

Blake's acquaintance with the abolition debate is evident. The Bromions in Parliament cried that the Africans were "inured to the hot climate" of the plantations and therefore necessary for "labour under a vertical sun." Under Bromion's words Blake draws a picture, stretching across the page, of a Negro worker smitten into desperate horizontality, wilted like the heat-blasted vegetation among which he has been working with a pickaxe, and barely able to hold his face out of the dirt. The apologists also argued that Negroes understood only "firmness," were "contented and happy" and superstitious, and were now "habituated to the contemplation" of slavery. Bromion utters the same arguments: that "the swarthy children of the sun . . . are obedient, they resist not, they obey the scourge; Their daughters worship terrors and obey the violent" (lines 21–23).

In Parliament Lord Abingdon accused the "abettors" of abolition of promoting the new philosophy of leveling: "Look at the state of the colony of St. Domingo, and see what liberty and equality, see what the rights of man have done there." They have dried up the rivers of *commerce* and replaced them with "fountains of human blood." Moreover the levelers are prophesying that "all being equal, blacks and whites, French and English [*sic*], wolves and lambs, shall all, 'merry companions every one,' promiscuously pig together; engendering . . . a new species of man as the product of this new philosophy."

It is this sort of argument that Blake's Oothoon turns right side up again. For, as Abingdon put it, "what does the abolition of the slave trade mean more or less in effect, than liberty and equality?" Wilberforce joined Burke in a committee for the relief of emigrant royalist priests partly, as he admitted, "to do away French citizenship"—for the French had misinterpreted his liberalism and named him an honorary French citizen along with Paine and Priestley! Yet this demonstration did not prevent Burke from attacking the Abolition Bill as "a shred of the accursed web of Jacobinism." Blake's Theotormon is tangled in the suspicion that his own desires are part of an accursed web.

The argument of Oothoon is triplex, as she herself is. Stedman's emblematical picture treats Europe, Africa, and America as three separate women: Blake makes them into one. He can do this because Oothoon is not a person but a "soul." Pictured in chains she is the female slave, but she does not have the black skin and tight ringlets of the Africa of the emblem. Only in the picture of the exhausted worker is the Negro slave directly represented. Allowing for difference in mediums, Oothoon is the American Indian of the emblem, with the same loose black hair, sad mouth, and angular limbs. See especially the illustration of the title-page, where she runs along the trough of a green wave pursued by the mistaken God of slavery.

Yet her skin is not the copper color of the engraved America either, but theoretically "snowy" white, according to the text. "I am pure," she cries "because the night is gone that clos'd me in its deadly black."[17] Speaking as America she means that the night of oppressive chivalry is gone with the dawn of freedom. As Africa she means that the time is gone when people's vision was limited to their five senses and they could see only her dark skin and not her inward purity.

Blake had explained this symbolism in his *Little Black Boy:*

> My mother bore me in the southern wild,
> And I am black, but O! my soul is white.
> White as an angel is the English child:
> But I am black as if bereav'd of light.

To avoid a chauvinistic interpretation Blake explained that any skin color is a cloud that cannot obscure the essential brotherhood of man in a fully enlightened society, such as Heaven. "These black bodies and this sunburnt face," said the little black boy, are "but a cloud." If the Negro is to be free of his black cloud, the little English boy must be likewise free from his "white cloud," which is equally opaque. "When I from black and he from white cloud free," I will "be like him and he will then love me." In the second illustrated page of this Song of Innocence the black boy appears as light-skinned as the English boy—or as Oothoon.[18]

Oothoon's reason for letting the vultures prey upon "her soft snowy limbs" is to let Theotormon, who is an adult version of the English child, *see* that beneath the skin her "pure transparent breast" really reflects the same human "image" as his—that her color is morally that of "the clear spring, mudded with feet of beasts," which again "grows pure & smiles" (line 42). As Africa she is urging the London citizen to ignore color differences. As America she is urging British law-makers to rescue her from the muddy feet of the slaver. As a woman enslaved by Marriage Act morality, she is imploring her lover to rise above accusations of adultery.

Beyond arguing her essential purity, she indicates by several analogies that there is something especially beautiful about dark skin and (she suggests both points at once) about pregnancy. Consider the dark skin of worm-ripened fruit, which is "sweetest"; or the darkness of "the soul prey'd on by woe"; or

> The new wash'd lamb ting'd with the village smoke & the bright swan
> By the red earth of our immortal river: I bathe my wings,
> And I am white and pure to hover round Theotormons breast.
>
> —(lines 78–81)

It is the soul rather than the body of the slave that is "inured," in being richer in experience. The black boy already loves the English boy and is thus better prepared than he to "bear the heat" of God's presence.

And still we have not done with the complexity of Blake's symbolism, for in one illustration, on the page of the "Argument," Oothoon appears not as an American Indian but as the European woman of the emblem. Or rather in this illustration the Stedman influence is supplanted by that of a French neo-classical painter and engraver, Vien. Here the focus is on the buying and selling of woman's love, and Blake is reversing Vien's picture (based on a Roman original) of a procuress offering "loves" for sale in a basket: *La Marchande d'Amours*. Oothoon kneels in the same posture as that of the love-merchant, and her hair is knotted at the back of her head in a similar fashion. But whereas Vien's procuress holds one of her cupids by his wings like a captive bird, Oothoon keeps her hands to herself and lightly "kisses the joy as it flies," springing not from a basket but from the stem of a marigold.

In the most general sense of the soaring joys which Oothoon offers her lover are sparks of Promethean fire or winged thoughts calculated to widen his brow. In her effort to prod him to cross the threshold of indecision—"I cry arise O Theotormon for the village dog Barks at the breaking day"—Oothoon insists that the revolutionary dawn is at hand and overdue and that the corn is ripe. But this "citizen of London" does not look up. He is not at all sure "what is the night or day"; he is nearly deaf to the cries of slaves and blind to visions of a new day: he cannot arise. The springs of rebellion are as obscure to him as those of moral purity. "Tell me what is a thought," he pleads, "and upon what mountains Wave shadows of discontent? and in what houses dwell the wretched" (lines 84–88). But he fears that the new philosophy may carry his thought to a "remote land" (America) or may bring "poison from the desart wilds" rather than "dews and honey and balm" (lines 89–97). And he grows silent when Bromion shakes the cavern with rhetorical questions, just as the Abolitionists were silenced in 1793 by the clamor of Antijacobinism.

Bromion's arguments and those of the apologists of slavery are of the same order: Dare anyone question that subordination must be maintained? Has anyone even in this land of liberty and poverty yet heard of any way to maintain order without the fear of punishment? Are not war and slavery the basis of our Empire? Is not sorrow intended for the poor, joy for the rich? Is not fear of Hell necessary to keep the laborious poor from pursuing "eternal life"? (lines 105–110)

III

If war and subordination are the basis of Empire, peace and equality must be the ground of that condition in which "The Whole Business of Man Is The Arts & All Things Common," as Blake would reiterate thirty years later in his Laocoön inscriptions. Oothoon, in a series of elliptical counter-questions to those of Bromion and Theotormon, makes a number of glancing observations on the connection of scarcity and inequality which are not immediately clear but become so when we consult the analogous but more plainly worded agrarian definitions of Mary Wollstonecraft in her early *Vindication of the Rights of Men* (1790). There, for example, the Blakean axiom that "virtue can only flourish among equals" is linked to an economic proposal for the division of large estates into small farms, and we may recall that one of Blake's myths of the fall, from Urthona to Los, implies that man was and must again become earth-owner. "In what gardens do joys grow?" asks Theotormon, dimly aware of a lost Paradise, "and upon what mountains Wave shadows of discontent?" (lines 95–97). In the *Vindication* the answer is that the polished vices of the rich and the "tremendous mountain of woe" oppressing the poor both depend upon economic inequality, without which England will be a garden more inviting than Eden, with "springs of joy" murmuring on every side and every man "contented to be the friend of man" (pp. 140–49).

Oothoon has similar notions. Surveying the delights of the rich and the woes of the poor, she contrasts the ideal form of human relations—in which each joy is "holy, eternal, infinite" and no one's joy absorbs another's—with the actual relations, in which the rich, both patron ("giver of gifts") and merchant, have "delights" while the poor, both industrious citizen and husbandman, have "pains." Since it is specious to call that joy which hinders and brings tears to others, she makes the point that the "joys" of the oppressor are really "tears." In a world of hindering and hindered it is a mockery for a Bromion to speak of joy and sorrow and "one law"—as if the tyrant could understand the feelings of the patriot: "Does he who contemns poverty [i.e., who views the poor with contempt], and he who turns with abhorrence From usury: feel the same passion, or are they moved alike?" (*V.D.A.* 115–124). Burke writing scornfully of "the swinish multitude," for instance, is hardly moved by the same indignation that moves Paine or Wollstonecraft to condemn monopolists and forestallers.

Oothoon comes finally to the two classes of men whose functions in the service of tyranny give them the most perverse views of human happiness, the recruiting officer and the tithing priest. The function of the priest is to supply the economic and ideological base of the whole superstructure of

Empire from fortresses to marriage laws, and Oothoon outlines this process in her questions:

> With what sense does the parson claim the labour of the farmer?
> What are his nets & gins & traps, & how does he surround him
> With cold floods of abstraction, and with forests of solitude,
> To build him castles and high spires, where kings & priests may dwell.
> —(lines 128–31)

The same process is alluded to in *America* (lines 85–120) when Paine and other Patriots are said to shelter the grain and the "fatness of the earth" from priest and prince who wish to subvert useful labor (plow and spade) to the building of fortresses (wall and moat) and who would bring "the stubbed oak to overgrow the hills." In both passages the issue is whether the land shall be used for peaceful farms or for castled "forests of solitude," an issue raised in Wollstonecraft's questions (p. 140): "Why cannot the large estates be divided into small farms? Why are huge forests still allowed to stretch out with idle pomp and all the indolence of Eastern grandeur?"

It is against such domination by "the idle" that the Patriots of *America* stand "with their foreheads rear'd toward the east." According to Paine, in the second part of *The Rights of Man,* "the government of the sword revolved from East to West" but a new government founded on a system of universal peace was "now revolving from West to East, by a stronger impulse. . . ." Blake wrote in his notebook:

> The sword sung on the barren heath
> The sickle in the fruitful field.
> The sword he sung a song of death
> But could not make the sickle yield.
> —(N. 105)

This image of the sword on the heath brings us around to Oothoon's description of the man who drums to war, the other of the two agents of tyranny whose occupations make "different the world to them" and "different their eye and ear!"

> How different far the fat fed hireling with hollow drum,
> Who buys whole corn fields into wastes, and sings upon the heath!
> —(V.D.A. 125–26)

His function is like that of Sennacherib, King of Assyria, who laid waste fortified cities and dismayed the inhabitants "as grain blasted before it is grown."[19] Literally he brings the flames and trampling of battle to the fields of corn and makes his camp indifferently on field or barren heath. Cognate passages in *The Four Zoas* make the picture clear. Horses "trample the corn fields in boastful neighings" when they have been compelled to "leave the plow" and become cavalry horses. Officers of mountainous girth thrive on the ruin of peaceful husbandry:

> Let us refuse the Plow & Spade, the heavy Roller & spiked
> Harrow; burn all these Corn fields: throw down all these fences!
> Fatten'd on Human blood & drunk with wine of life is better far
> Than all these labours of the harvest & the vintage.[20]

In short, the fat hireling is Blake's Falstaff, the eternal recruiting sergeant who leads men from the plow and musters "mortal men" for the slaughter.

The imagery is, for us, puzzlingly telescoped. "Buys" is misleading, for the hireling is not buyer but bought; it is the king hiring him who "buys" cornfields into wastes, purchasing war instead of peace as well as refusing to transform his forested estates into fruitful farms. But these ideas were familiar enough to Blake's contemporaries, who would hardly have made the modern critic's mistake of supposing that Oothoon is opposing enclosures (in the 1790s these were undertaken to create, not destroy, cornfields)—or even at the moment talking about them. She is dwelling on the direct effect of war on food, obviously agreeing wih the pamphleteers who argued that the continental war, by interfering with imports, devastating grain areas, and requisitioning grain to feed non-productive soldiers, was the cause of scarce bread and high prices. In an age when Luxury was still a sin and every fat man was a living comment on the inequitable distribution of a meager food supply, Blake shared the popular belief that the drone or waster *was* the wolf at the door. In the famine year 1795 his *Song of Los* directly indicts the war-making King as the villain whose policy calls "for Famine from the heath" (the heath being the place where soldiers were trained to war).

Oothoon's questions, like those of Enion later in *The Four Zoas*, hint at answers but remain unanswered short of a Last Judgment; but they define the crisis of humanity in soul-searching terms.

Notes

1. To Cumberland, Apr. 12, 1827, K p. 927. Blake says "Englishmen are *all*" etc., but excepts himself and his friend. On the opposition of Money to Art see Laocoön (K581).

2. "Proverbs of Hell," *The Marriage of Heaven and Hell*, 7 (K183); cf., the motion in The House of Commons, Feb. 5, 1790, for "a return from all cities and market towns of the different weights and measures now in use."

3. *The Prelude*, X, 202–27, here and below.

4. For documentation and illustration of this section and the next, see *Journal of the Warburg and Courtauld Institutes*, XV (1952), 242–52.

5. Pl. 68; see Stedman's text I, 206.

6. I, 109, 203, 90; II, 298.

7. I, 99–106, 208, 312, 319, 325–26; II, 83, 377.

8. Pl. 4, engraved by Bartolozzi.

9. *V.D.A.* Plate printed variously as frontispiece or tailpiece—an emblem of the *situation*.

10. The names Oothoon, Theotormon, Bromion, and Leutha have been traced to Ossian's Oithona, Tonthormod, Brumo, and Lutha. But the oo-oo doubling may come from African words in Stedman: apootoo, too-too, ooroocoocoo (snake). A *toremon* is a shiny black bird whose name means "a tale-bearer, or a spy"; and the rebels "have an invincible hatred against it." I, 367–368. If *Theo* is God, an accuser of sin might be considered God's spy, *Theotoreman*. Unquestionably Theotormon torments and is tormented.

11. *V.D.A.* 31–33.

12. *London Chronicle,* Feb. 2, 1792. Against the argument that it was simply strategic to concentrate first on abolition of the trade, consider the fact that as soon as the Slave Trade Bill was passed, in 1807, the Society dissolved. Slavery itself, and consequently the trade, continued to exist.

13. In *V.D.A.* pl. 9, Theotormon is flaying himself with a three-thonged scourge, while Oothoon runs by unaided.

14. See Stedman, I, 206.

15. Were Oothoon and Theotormon married before the story begins? Critics differ. Bromion's "Now thou maist marry" suggests they were not; Theotormon's jealousy of "the adulterate pair" suggests they were. What matters is that the affair was not consummated. Oothoon welcomes the "experience" that Thel shrank from, but her lover does not.

16. *V.D.A.* 4–15, 170. In the abolition debates attention was focussed on this eruption of "democratical principles" in the West Indies. The fact that London merchant firms held investments in Santo Domingo in the then large sum of £300,000 "helps to explain why the British government in [1793–1798] sacrificed more than £4,000,000 in an effort to conquer the French colony and maintain or restore Negro slavery. It helps to explain also why Wilberforce's abolitionist program suffered a momentary eclipse." C. L. Lokke, "London Merchant Interest in the St. Domingue Plantations of the Émigrés, 1793–1798," *Am. Hist. Rev.,* XLIII (1938), 795–802. Leutha's Vale appears to be Blake's place-name for the French colony, Leutha being the Queen of France. In *Fayette* the Queen is one whose smile spreads pestilence. In *Europe* Leutha is "the sweet smiling pestilence," a "silken Queen" who has "many daughters" (colonies?), and in a phrase which recalls Paine's remark she is called the "luring bird of Eden." In the "Thiralatha" fragment (K211) the fading of "The British Colonies" is compared to the dying of a dream, perhaps of French colonialism, which has left "obscured traces in the Vale of Leutha." After the West Indies docks were located in the Isle of Dogs. Blake took to calling it the Isle of Leutha's Dogs, *Jerusalem* 31. Leutha's Vale is "dewy" perhaps because it lies in the dewy bed of the Caribbean.

17. *V.D.A.* 35, 51–52. Blake usually employed brown inks in printing *V.D.A.* though sometimes he chose pink, purple, or yellow. In contrast, *Europe* and *America* are usually printed in green, blue or black.

18. Not quite true for all copies. In at least one a slight tint has been given to the black boy in heaven; but the contrast with the solid color of the first page is still pronounced.

19. 2 Kings 19:25–26.

20. *F.Z.* viia.199–201 (K328); ii.128–31 (K262).

William Blake Rejects the Enlightenment

JEAN H. HAGSTRUM

William Blake, the first English Romantic, was born in 1757, the year in which Emanuel Swedenborg said the last judgment took place. Although Blake himself was never able to regard that fact as merely coincidental, his interpreter is more interested in observing that in the year of his birth, neoclassic culture was still flourishing. Six months after the day on which Blake was born, Johnson began publishing the *Idler,* that attractive monument to witty common sense, and two years later he wrote *Rasselas,* that great embodiment of moral pessimisim and philosophical wisdom.

Blake must never be regarded as a cultural orphan, living out his days in solitary anger, hostile to the society in which he was bred. He was deeply involved even in what he rejected. The man who mounted the fiercest, longest, and most effective attack on the neoclassical and enlightened establishment ever made always revealed the marks of his origin in the age of Johnson. In an outburst of youthful impudence, he mockingly portrayed the Great Cham as winking and blinking like a bat in daylight,[1] but his Chaucer criticism shows the clear impress of Dr. Johnson's view of general nature. Though he regarded Reynolds as a hireling painter, he ringingly agreed with the President's attack on the fashionable picturesque—"So Says Sir Joshua, and So say I!"[2]—and finds the most unforgivable fact about the academician that he admired Blake's heroes for the wrong reasons. Blake's artistic pantheon is in fact more like than unlike official neoclassical taste—a taste represented, say, by the French Academy. Both placed Raphael and the high Renaissance at or near the top. Both preferred line to colour, Rome and Florence to Venice, Italy to the Low Countries. Blake, a kind of salty and angry Dufresnoy, considered Rembrandt a maker of blots and blurs, called Jan Steen a boor, and retched at "the Venetian and Flemish ooze."[3]

Such similarities between Blake and the culture he attacked are not merely fortuitous. They are signs that what he rejected in one of the mightiest efforts of his imagination had in fact invaded the deepest recesses of his being.

From *Studies on Voltaire and the Eighteenth Century* 25 (1963): 811–28, by permission of the Voltaire Foundation and the author.

I. BLAKE'S ATTACK ON NEOCLASSICAL
PSYCHOLOGY AND AESTHETICS (TO 1788)

Blake laid the foundations of his attack on the Enlightenment as a very young man—long before his first works of composite art appeared in 1788. The earliest and most obvious impulse to that attack arose from Blake's commitment to the literary school of the Wartons, the so-called pre-romantic writers of the English eighteenth century. Blake's juvenilia display a pre-romantic love of Gothic horror, of poetic melancholy, of ballad forms, and of Elizabethan song. The author of *Poetical Sketches* had obviously been impressed by the medievalism of Chatterton, the rhythms of Macpherson, and the blank-verse sonorities of Young. From Thomson Blake had learned the art of natural personification and from Collins the art of allegorical personification; and Gray's *Bard* must early have become one of the most potent influences on the younger poet's genius—a work he later pointed to as an example of the intellectual vision to which the sister art of painting should aspire.[4]

To the English pre-romantics Blake remained loyal until his death. As an old man he acknowledged a closer affinity to Macpherson and Chatterton than to Wordsworth and Byron, past whose prime his long life extended.[5] The influence of Thomson, Young, and their fellows was early united with the eccentric but powerful impact of Fuseli, fresh from Zurich, and from Breitinger and Bodmer, whose own attacks on the Enlightenment were inspired by the very poets that first inspired Blake. Collins and Gray, Thomson and Young put Blake in touch with the giants of English literature—Shakespeare and Spencer, whom he early imitated and later illustrated, and above all Milton, whose literary example was the most potent Blake was ever to encounter.

Important though it was, the pre-romantic influence alone can explain neither the intensity nor the content of Blake's rejection of neoclassical culture. Like Fuseli, Blake must have found pre-romanticism too weak and conventional, too artificial and cloying for sustained nourishment. It was primarily literary and aesthetic, and Blake's vision was psychological, ethical, religious. The pre-romantics alone can never explain why Blake indignantly turned his back on romantic Hellenism and found romantic naturalism a Satanic blight that weakened and ultimately obliterated the life of the imagination.

Blake's earliest attack on the neoclassical establishment, made in the late seventies or early eighties, transcends the pre-romantic form that encloses it. A shadowy Collinsian allegory that does not quite succeed in forming a train of Spenserian personifications, the piece beginning "Then she bore pale desire" strikes a body blow at neoclassical ethics and psychology (K, p.42). The speaker, a devotee of Gray's kind of Melancholy, attacks Honour (the social respectability, one supposes, of Pope's Thalestris), Hate and Slander (the satires and journalistic polemics of both Swift and Grub Street), and Policy (the Baconian ethic that dominated the literary periodical, the coffee house, and the school). But the most memorable action—almost imperceptible in the riot of personification—is the dethronement by his own children of Father Reason, whose long beard and tyrannous habits must surely adumbrate Urizen. Young Blake has thus anticipated himself and unmistakably foreshadowed one of the central acts of his revolutionary and prophetic myth. In the *Gates of Paradise* of 1793, on a plate that bears as its motto the lament of David over Absalom, "My Son! My Son!" a young man stands poised to plunge a feathered spear in his father's breast. In Blake's mythology the meaning is that the red Orc of change is about to attack Urizen—revolutionary youth is about to destroy Aged Ignorance. On the sixteenth plate of *Milton* the heroic poet in a climactic action strides up to a venerable and enfeebled tyrant leaning on the tablets of legalistic religion and pulls him down from his stony seat as young men and women dance and sing in the scene above.

More precisely stated, though no more central to Blake's thought, is the psychological attack on empirical rationalism that Blake made unrelentingly in the aphorisms that constitute his first works of engraved art (1788).[6] The twenty-five or so tiny engravings—each containing a proverb and a spare but appropriate linear design—all either attack sensationist psychology or praise the liberating imagination and thus establish the most fundamental and irreconcilable polarities of Blake's thought—between the "Poetic or Prophetic character" and the "Philosophical & Experimental." Let there be no mistake about the seriousness and profundity of young Blake's attack. Hume had written, "But though our thought seems to possess this unbounded liberty, we shall find . . . that it is really confined within very narrow limits, and that all this creative power of the mind amounts to no more than the faculty of compounding, transposing, augmenting, or diminishing the materials afforded us by the senses and experience."[7] Blake wrote, "Man's perceptions are not bounded by organs of perception; he perceives more than sense (tho' ever so acute) can discover." Locke had said, "All those sublime thoughts which . . . reach as high as heaven itself take their rise and footing here: in all that great extent wherein the mind wanders, . . . it stirs not one jot beyond those ideas which sense or reflection have offered for its contemplation."[8] Blake said, "The desires & perceptions of many untaught by anything but organs of sense, must be limited to objects of sense. If it were not for the Poetic or Prophetic character the Philosophic & Experimental would soon be at the ratio of all things & stand still, unable to do other than repeat the same dull round over again."

Before he was thirty Blake had already come to recognize as his chief enemy that school of thought that engaged the deepest loyalties of both the English and the continental eighteenth century—what David Mallet called "the Baconian succession"[9] and Voltaire called "the new philosophy." Later Blake will form an unholy trinity of Bacon, Newton, and Locke, but now his chief villain seems to be Locke, whom he mentions only once but who, more than any one else, had created the hell of "meer nature," the inferno of being "shut up in corporeal desires."[10] Locke's epistemological chain, that links sense to nature, mind to sense, idea to mind, Blake was determined to break. As he himself said, science (the knowledge of the outside world) and intellect (the imagination that constitutes the only true man) are absolutely discrete and separate. Knowledge cannot teach us how to think any more than thought can teach us how or what to love.[11]

In his "mental fight" Blake engages the generals and only tilts with the lieutenants. He does now and then feint at Dryden, Pope, Chesterfield, and Johnson—in a scurrilous doggerel, an insulting parody, or an angry ejaculation ("I hate scarce smiles: I love laughing").[12] Blake's real quarry are the philosophical creators of the enlightened establishment—its psychologists, scientists, and thinkers. In attacking Locke on the mind he shows a true instinct for the jugular, since Lockean psychology had insinuated itself into the work of virtually every neoclassical writer. In *A Tale of a Tub*, Swift in a bitter irony had called the memory the "grave" of things and had seemed to praise the imagination as "the womb of things"—whose "artificial mediums, false lights, refracted angles, varnish, and tinsel" minister to "the felicity and enjoyments of mortal men." Blake's life-long attack on the life-denying Daughters of Memory, without ever naming Swift, mocks his mockery. For Blake did in fact regard the memory as a grave and the imagination as a teeming, creating womb, from which spring the values that will save us all. Only the despicable "plagiary" works from the memory—the timid painter of paltry blots, the hireling of the establishment. The true artist possesses "that greatest of all blessings, a strong imagination"—the faculty that is religion, psychology, philosophy, ethics, and art all wrapped in one.[13]

II. Revolution: The Decade of the Nineties

A bad culture results from bad thought. If London's streets and London's river are "chartered" and if every face bears "marks of weakness, marks of woe," it is only because the manacles are "mind-forg'd"—because men are what their thinkers have made them. The last judgment is the casting out of bad thought by good thought, of bad art by good art; and it is prepared for by mental fight, in which the tear is an intellectual thing.

Blake had early characterized the philosophy of "demonstration by the Senses" as "Wordly Wisdom."[14] Such wisdom was not only worldly; it was official, established, and was bound to have profound artistic, political, and social consequences. A culture dominated by a passive psychology in which the mind is believed to accept data automatically from nature and then run them like water through the mill of the five senses is hardly calculated to produce visionaries, saints, or revolutionists. A society that believes, more or less officially, that the mind of its artists can do no more than reshuffle or recombine natural phenomena is one that inquires "not whether a Man has Talents & Genius, but whether he is Passive & Polite & a Virtuous Ass & obedient to Noblemen's Opinions in Arts & Science."[15] Such a culture is incapable of creating greatness and is also tragically incapable of making itself capable. For inert psychology leads to inert personalities and lukewarm art. Locke had bound Englishmen to dead nature and imprisoned them in the cavern of their material bodies.

Even stronger than his indictment of Locke—at least more direct and overt in expression—was Blake's indictment of Bacon, whose philosophy, he said in 1808, "has Ruin'd England" (K, p.456). Blake as a revolutionary was deeply concerned with mending England's ruined state, and it is not surprising that toward the end of the revolutionary decade, two years or so before he went to his retreat at Felpham by the sea and some eight years after the *Marriage of Heaven and Hell* and the *French Revolution,* Blake wrote his annotations to Bacon's essays (K, pp.396–410). The poet's indictment arises from profound hatred. Bacon was a hireling writer, guilty of "Contemptible Knavery & Folly," a Pilate who opposed Christ, a villain, a liar, a falsifier of values, an ugly embodiment of his own ugly prudential ethic, a man not really interested in the useful arts but only in himself. "His Business and Bosom was to be Lord Chancellor."

Blake's rage at the Man of Measured Merriment and at his large progeny—the elegant poetaster Haley or the "creeping Jesus" of the established church, for example—was not merely personal and moral. It was also an intellectual indignation. Blake had early in life read the *Advancement of Learning* and would have agreed with Voltaire and most other thinkers of the age of reason that Bacon was the father of empirical philosophy. The legalistic, naturalistic, and utilitarian Bacon entered Blake's revolutionary myth as a Urizenic force that had to be destroyed, just as later he figured in the Christian epics as a Satanic figure that had to be melted down in the apocalyptic fires before he could be redeemed in the New Jerusalem. "Bacon calls Intellectual Arts Unmanly, Poetry, Painting, Music are in his opinion Useless & so they are for Kings & Wars & shall in the End Annihilate them" (K, p.407). The sense is uncertain, but Blake seems to say, not that kings will annihilate art, but that art will annihilate kings. Men of imagination like Blake and Paine will drive kings and their Baconian hirelings from their lairs and burn them root and branch—to the redemption of humanity. Revolution will destroy the "Philosophy of the Five Senses," which Urizen had delivered into the hands of Locke and Newton.

Bacon figures only indirectly in Blake's revolutionary myth. But Newton, on one occasion at least, is a *dramatis persona.* When, in the revolutionary prophecy *Europe* (xiii. 1–9), the red Orc of revolution seizes the "Trump of the last doom" but fails to blow it—an act that must refer to the frustration of revolutionary energy in France—a "mighty Spirit . . . nam'd Newton" seizes the trump and blows a mighty blast. Thereupon the myriads of angels who had been ready for a triumph fall like yellow leaves to the ground, seeking their graves in howling and lamentation. Newton's action is counter-revolutionary. The establishment has won a temporary victory.

For the revolutionary Blake all angels were "counter-revolutionary cads," and it was inevitable that in his inversion of all neoclassic value Blake should have transformed the divine Newton of English song and story to his own reprehensible "St. Isaac," another Urizenic oppressor of the human mind and spirit. "Art is the Tree of Life," and Newton was no artist. "Science is the Tree of Death," and Newton was, according to Voltaire, the greatest scientist mankind had ever produced.[16]

James Thomson praised Newton for having "untwisted all the shining robe of day," presenting to the charmed eye of the poet "the gorgeous train / Of parent colours"—an "infinite source / Of beauty, ever flushing, ever new."[17] But Blake treated Newton's colours with deep irony:

> That God is Colouring Newton does shew,
> And the devil is Black Outline, all of us know.[18]

Blake, the lover of line and denigrator of colour, is obviously of the devil's party.

Voltaire said that Descartes was "the greatest geometrician of his age" but that "geometry leaves the mind where it finds it."[19] Blake made an even graver charge against Newton, whose fluxions (that is, the differential calculus) had weakened the authority of the line in art and helped to destroy human individuality. Newton's geometry subdivided the line—infinitely, to non-existence—dissolving it into the dots and points loved by the chiaroscuro colourists and tonalists, whom Blake loathed.[20] For Blake the quarrel between the line artist like Dürer and Raphael and the colourists and tonalists like the Venetians or his fashionable contemporaries was not merely a conflict of styles. Chiaroscuro he called "that infernal machine" propelled by the hands of "Venetian and Flemish Demons"[21] to the destruction of true art and of human individuality. Because of Newton Englishmen love the "Indefinite" in art and reject the wiry, bounding line that creates true artistic character and have themselves become conventional, conformist, tame, and flat—"all Intermeasurable One by Another, Certainly a happy state of Agreement to which I for One do not Agree."[22]

In his first work of composite art, the stereotyped engravings of 1788 already referred to, Blake inscribed two sentences that can serve as an epigraph for his entire philosophy: "He who sees the Infinite in all things, sees God. He who sees the Ratio only, sees only himself." The first of these Blake illustrated again and again—as when his Apollo, Los, leaps into the sun, or his Poet bounds upward from the Earth, or his Risen Man lifts fallen and enslaved woman from earth to carry her upward to the New Jerusalem. The second sentence ("He who sees the Ratio only, sees only himself") Blake also rendered often in line and word—but never more cogently than in two engravings that involve Newtonian values. Blake illustrates a phrase from Edward Young's *Night Thoughts*—"Ye searching, ye Newtonian Angels!"—by a female figure who kneels on the floor and stares at a triangle which she has drawn with her geometer's compass. In a more famous work, the colour print in the Tate gallery entitled "Newton," the scientist sits on a rock in the kind of stony and desolate landscape Blake elsewhere described as "the Barren Waste of Locke and Newton."[23] Although in some respects he resembles a Blakean hero, the young, blond, curly headed nude does not aspire upward but bends his back in a geometrical curve, applies his compasses to a scroll on the ground to create a semi-circle in a triangle, and stares at the geometrical "ratio" he has made—and also, if Blake's full meaning is allowable here, at himself. "He who sees the Ratio only, sees only himself."

III. Blake's Attack on Deism: The Period of the Great Epics

Sometime before writing his two great epics, *Milton* and *Jerusalem,* Blake shifted the emphasis of his philosophy. Without ever destroying its integrity, he altered its proportions. From being a revolutionary willing to unleash the tigers of wrath upon a decadent society, Blake became an unorthodox, undogmatic Christian, dedicated to the forgiveness of sin, the law of love, and the ways of peace. He transformed Satan from a healthy, energetic demon, capable of contributing to our salvation, to a youth of leering evil. Jehovah ceases to be an Old Testament tyrant and becomes a forgiving father. The revolutionists of America and France are replaced as guides and mentors by quietistic mystics: madame Guyon, whose *Opuscules Spirituels* were published in revolutionary Paris in 1790; Fénelon (not as author of the popular Télémaque but as the disciple and friend of Madame Guyon, who wrote the *Maxims of the Saints*); James Hervey, whose *Meditations among the Tombs* Blake epitomized in one of his greatest works of Christian art; and Wesley and Whitefield, who, with the simple medieval monk, become representatives of free, uninstitutionalized Christianity. Blake's new loyalties may not be intellectually exciting—or even respectable—but they do not quite reveal the "utter indiscrimination" that Mr. Schorer has found.[24] Blake has returned to his earliest self—to Innocence, to the simple love of the lamb, to a nature impregnated with the spirit of Christ, and to the quiet ecstasy of the pastoral life.

Blake's Tolstoyan philosophy is never sentimental or flaccid. Although love has swallowed up violence, revolutionary energy and sexual impulse remain active, and the attack on aged evil and institutional repression continues unabated. Locke, Newton, and Bacon continue to be a triad of evil—attacked unrelentingly on page after page of the major prophecies. The psychology of the senses that had succeeded only in starving the senses;

mathematical form that in depriving life of its exuberance had distorted its shape; general aesthetic law that weakens individuality and destroys Blake's "little ones"—the minute but holy life of nature—all these dessicating philosophies remain the object of Blake's withering anger.

To his pantheon of evil Blake has now added Voltaire and Rousseau, English deism and doubt, and the Greek and Roman classics. Rome now stands for war, Greece for stultifying mathematical form. The poet-painter, who had been under the spell of classicizing artists (his personal friends Cumberland and Flaxman), who had once said that he hoped to "revive the Greek workmanship,"[25] and who had himself created under classical influence, now makes ancient civilization the symbol of violence, tyranny, state religion, rationalism, the loss of imagination, and the degradation of prophetic truth to priestcraft and allegory. "The Classics! It is the Classics, & not the Goths nor Monks, that Desolate Europe with Wars."[26]

Everything that Blake came to say of the ancient classics he also came to say of what he regarded as their spiritual descendant—deism or natural religion, the faith of the European Enlightenment. Blake must always have disliked it, but during the revolutionary period he was willing to close an eye to its deficiencies, because so many of its adherents were attackers of the establishment and forerunners of revolution. Thus, ignoring Paine's religion—or lack of it—Blake put him on the side of Christ as an arouser of men to intellectual battle. He even compared Paine's achievement to the miracles of Jesus. "Is it a greater miracle to feed five thousand men with five loaves than to overthrow all the armies of Europe with a small pamphlet."[27]

But though Blake had, in the decade of the nineties, made common cause with deists against the princes of the state and church, he now regards deism as an evil closely related to and fully as mischievous as established religion, the monarchy, Jewish legalism, and utilitarian ethics. "He never can be a Friend to the Human Race who is the preacher of Natural Morality or Natural Religion" (*Jerusalem,* plate 52). Blake was prepared to find in the deist all the Urizenic and Satanic traits he had always found in Locke, Bacon, and Newton. The deist was a flatterer, a proud tyrant, a Druid, a Greek, a Pharisee, a war-like perpetuator of the talonic law of revenge. It was inevitable that Voltaire and Rousseau—and also in less degree Gibbon and Paine—should now enter Blake's hierarchy of intellectual evil.

But it had not always been so. In Blake's vision of revolutionary France he had seen pale religious spectres, weeping, shivering, driven out of their abbeys by Voltaire and Rousseau.[28] La Fayette, while still on the side of revolution and still a lover of human liberty, Blake saw as being inspired by the fiery cloud of Voltaire and the white cloud of Rousseau—Moses's pillar of the fire by night and pillar of cloud by day transformed to revolutionary symbols. In the *Song of Los* (v) Voltaire and Rousseau, melting the Urizenic snows of Europe, are engaged in direct conflict with Urizen and his servants, Newton and Locke.

It must therefore have cost Blake a considerable expense of spirit to dethrone these French thinkers and place them in his inferno. Rousseau, probably through the translation of Fuseli, may have influenced Blake in *America* and *Tiriel* and in those featurs of his myth that are concerned with luxury, agriculture, and the fall of man from natural innocence to social experience.[29] But in *Jerusalem,* Blake's last prophecy, Rousseau is viewed as a Pharisee, a hypocrite, a pretender to virtue, and one who, whatever his theory of natural goodness in actual life, discovered only evil in man and who in a long life found no friend. A kind of pseudo-Christian, Rousseau's *Confessions* do not really confess, since the author had no notion of real evil, true good, or the forgiveness of sin. The *Confessions* are a monument of apologetic self-pleading; they cloak the evil of the heart.

Blake once said that "To defend the Bible in this year 1798 would cost a man his life."[30] To have made a hero of Voltaire during the revolution was also a danger to life and limb. For the old Son of the Morning smelled of sulphur to pious Englishmen, and to the ruling Tories looked like the veriest anti-Christ. When Blake was of the devil's party, Voltaire's infernal wisdom was irresistible. The creator of Urizen could hardly have been displeased by the Frenchman who exposed the wrack and wheel of the Inquisition and the murderous practices of the Druids. Even the author of *Innocence* could make common cause with the liberal thinker. Voltaire wrote in his *Treatise on Tolerance* (chap. xxii): "What! call a Turk, a Jew and a Siamese, my brother? Yes, of course; for are we not all children of the same father, and the creatures of the same God?" One of Blake's finest lyrics proclaims that

> all must love the human form,
> In heathen, turk or jew.

In spite of the powerful affinities of the revolutionary decade, the later Blake could hardly have avoided a break with his great French contemporary. Voltaire's life and influence were in some respects anything but revolutionary. Blake's smiling, unctuous patron Hayley found it possible to admire Voltaire—and Rousseau and Gibbon, too—without altering his views. Voltaire himself, that prosperous heretic, consorted with royalty, was flattered by the first two Georges, lived intimately with the Prussian Frederick, flattered the age of Louis XIV, praised its rationalism, and lauded benevolent monarchy. The surly and impoverished Englishman's republican blood must have boiled. And when he reflected that Voltaire's deepest intellectual commitment was to deist and neoclassical England, that he regarded Bacon, Locke, and Newton as culture-heroes, that he was the world's greatest popularizer of the "new philosophy," and that to him Shakespeare was a barbarian, a fall from grace was inevitable.

Voltaire ends as a cold-hearted mocker; an ally of cruel virtue, war, glory; an enemy of prophecy, vision, and forgiveness. Blake throws in Voltaire's teeth the very epithets the Frenchman had himself hurled at the establishment. Blake calls him an intolerant "Inquisitor," a "Pharisee," and a "Hypocrite" who turns "a wracking wheel."[31]

IV. BLAKE'S ARTISTIC ACHIEVEMENT

Blake's rejection of enlightened Europe is expressed in poem, design, fiery epigram, and angry comments on the margins of books by Lavater, Swedenborg, bishop Watson, Bacon, Reynolds. Though it is nowhere reasoned out, it is not therefore intellectually despicable. Quite the contrary, Blake's position has living nerve and muscle, that bind all its members together in organic unity. Even his altered views have a living bloom on them; they are natural growths, not unnatural or unsuccessful grafts.

But though Blake's rejection of the Enlightenment is conceptually firm and consistent, it is his artistic embodiment of meaning that ought to command the attention of the twentieth century. For even though we may reject Blake's rejection on philosophical grounds, his achievement as poet-painter is inescapable.

As one would expect, that achievement is both verbal and visual. The triumph in words comes at the climax of the epic *Milton* (plates 41–43), when the poet-hero, bearing the evils of neoclassical culture in his own body and being, moves to the climactic immolation. In action, dialogue, and tableau Milton the hero destroys this "thing," as Blake calls it, that has itself ruined his country and his people (xl.2–13)—

> this Newtonian Phantasm,
> This Voltaire & Rousseau, this Hume & Gibbon & Bolingbroke,
> This Natural Religion, this impossible absurdity.

Blake's epic has its faults; but its climax persuades, as Milton enters death, strikes terror into the beholders, restores Blake and his wife to their high rôle, and causes all creatures to approach the "Great Harvest and Vintage of the Nations," when all social, philosophical, and artistic evil will be "annihilated away." The "Not Human" will be washed away—along with Rational Demonstration; the rotten rags of Memory; Bacon, Locke, & Newton; uninspired poetry and paltry rhymes; and the caterpillars of the church and state. The idiot questioner who has no answer, the despairing scientist, the imitator of nature's images drawn only from memory—all in fact who have built their faith on empirical demonstration— will be swallowed up in the fires of regeneration, and a new age of inspiration, imagination, and humanistic faith will arise out of the ashes of the neoclassical Phoenix.

Blake's other notable embodiment of the ideas discussed in this paper is the figure of Urizen, who haunts the words, borders, and designs of almost every Blakean page—from the adumbrations of him in the natural personifications of the juvenile poetry to the last sapphire-studded apocalypses. Urizen is vastly more than an allegorical personification of the faculty Reason. He is a natural force—storm, winter, snow, ice, water, rock, sand—natural death itself. He lies in a desolate landscape, his hand rests on a skull. He sits as a skeleton without flesh in the fire, he struggles in water, he emerges from a vegetable cave, he sits under blasted trees with a poisonous serpent, he weaves a frosty net. He is in part Blake's vision of Newtonian nature—cold, remote, mathematical, empty.

Urizen is also an active force. Dividing, partitioning, dropping the plummet line, applying Newton's compasses to the world, he creates abstract, mathematical forms. Like Locke, he shrinks the senses, narrows the perceptions, binds man to natural fact. Like Bacon he creates the laws of prudence and crucifies passion. He is the man neoclassical psychology and ethics have delivered into our hands—a passivity, a receptacle, a "soul-shuddering vacuum," an "abominable void," an "unknown, abstracted, brooding, secret" power of dark negation.

Urizen has Greek, Roman, and Hebrew as well as English blood in his veins. His face recalls the sightless, bearded classical statues of iron, war-like men, and the God of Sinai. He conveys powerful social meaning because, as a father-figure compounded of Zeus, Jehovah, and Dr. Johnson, he bears lineaments of traditional dignity, suggesting that the cruelty, ignorance, and repression he represents are perversions of the good. Fathers are good, but Urizen is an unnatural tyrant. Language is a great gift, but Urizen has perverted books and writing to repressive legal tablets. Religion is created by man's imagination and can produce freedom, but Urizen has rationalized it into the whip and wheel of church and state. It is the institutional Urizen who as primeval priest squats on a book bearing mystical letters, the tablets of the law at his back like stony wings. Tears of pious and conventional pity ooze from his compressed lids and drop into his frozen beard. He is that worst of all negations of living humanity—the human abstract that grows in the human brain and spreads over society.

This hoary being is more and other than a personification of the Enlightenment. But he will not achieve his full imaginative force unless we see that, besides being a symbol of social and political repression, he is also an intellectual tyrant, motivated by the *esprit de système*. He is the Geometer God of deism, the general nature of Reynolds and Locke, who sleeps the slumbers of abstraction.

He must have been conceived when Blake—"very Young," as he said when he was about fifty years old—first read the philosophers of the Enlightenment.[32] For it is Urizen who, weeping, delivers the Philosophy of the Five Senses into the hands of Newton and Locke.[33]

Notes

1. "An Island in the Moon" (*circa* 1784–1785), K, p.54.

2. Letter to Butts, 22 November 1802 (K, p.814).

3. Annotations to Reynolds (*circa* 1808, K, p.472); ms Notebook 1808–1811 (K, p.547).

4. "A Descriptive Catalogue" (1809), item no.iv (K, p.576).

5. Annotations to Wordsworth (1820), K, p.783.

6. "There is no natural religion" and "All religions are one" (K, pp.97–98).

7. "Of the Origin of ideas," *Enquiry Concerning Human Understanding, sect.*II.

8. *An Essay Concerning Human Understanding,* II.i.24.

9. "A New Life of the Author," *Works of Bacon* (London 1741), vol.i,p.li. Mallet calls Bacon "the father of the only valuable philosophy, that of fact and observation."

10. Annotations to Swedenborg (*circa* 1788), K, p.93; annotations to Lavater (*circa* 1788), K, p.74. *Corporeal* means, not sexual, which Blake regarded as energetic and wholesome, but merely physical or material.

11. "Yet science cannot teach intellect. Much less can intellect teach Affection . . . science will not open intellect . . . they are discrete and not continuous" (annotations to Swedenborg, K, p.93).

12. Annotations to Lavater (K, p.67); "Imitation of Pope" in MS Notebook 1808–1811 (K, p.545); Public address (*circa* 1810) (K, pp.595–596).

13. Remarks on Malkin's drawings (1805), K, p.439; annotations to Reynolds, K, p.452, and *passim.*

14. Annotations to Swedenborg (*circa* 1788), K, p.90.

15. Annotations to Reynolds (K, pp. 452–453).

16. "The Laocoon" (*circa* 1820), K, p.777.

17. "To the memory of sir Isaac Newton" (1727), ll.99, 101–102, 117–118.

18. Ms Notebook 1808–1811 (K, p.554).

19. "The Age of Louis XIV," chap.xxxi.

20. "I know too well that a great majority of Englishmen are fond of The Indefinite which they Measure by Newton's Doctrine of the Fluxions of an Atom, A Thing that does not Exist. . . . For a line or a lineament is not formed by chance: a Line is a Line in its Minutest Subdivisions." Letter to Cumberland, April 12, 1827 (K, p.878). Cp. Voltaire's comment on the line in Newton's geometry (*The Elements of . . . Newton's Philosophy* [London 1738], pp. 112–113). See also Martin K. Nurmi, "Blake's 'Ancient of Days' and Motte's frontispiece to Newton's Principia" in *The Divine Vision,* ed. Vivian de Sola Pinto (London 1957), pp. 208–210.

21. "A Descriptive Catalogue," item no.ix (K, p.582).

22. Letter to Cumberland, 12 April 1827 (K, p.878).

23. A Descriptive Catalogue, no.vi (K, p.581).

24. *William Blake: the Politics of Vision* (New York, 1959), p.50.

25. Letter to Cumberland, 26 August 1799 (K, p.795).

26. "On Homer's poetry" (*circa* 1820), K, p.778.

27. Annotations to Watson (1798), K, p.391.

28. *The French Revolution,* ll.274–276.

29. David V. Erdman, *Blake Prophet against Empire* (Princeton 1954), pp.118n, 399n, 229–230, 232.

30. Annotations to Watson (1798), K, p.383.

31. "A Vision of the last judgment" (1810), K, p.615; Poems from the notebook 1800–1803 (K, pp.418, 420; *Jerusalem,* plate 52 (K, p.682).

32. Annotations to Reynolds (K, p.476).

33. *The Song of Los,* iv.16–17 (K, p.246).

The Risen Body
[From *The Awakening of Albion*]

Thomas R. Frosch

The belief in a resurrection of the body is a fundamental tenet in Sweden-borg, and its articulation in his work, as well as in other mystical writings of Blake's experience, might well have stimulated Blake's own interest in the theme. Swedenborg describes the risen, or "angelic," body chiefly as a magni-fication of the natural organism. The senses are retained in their present structure, but they are sharpened: when outer sight is brought into align-ment with spiritual sight, seeing becomes understanding, and the light of heaven enables angelic vision to distinguish the minutiae on which the perception of the Divine Humanity depends.[1] Occasionally, Swedenborg indicates, ambiguously, that "an angel has every sense that a man has, and far more exquisite senses."[2] But in these matters he never goes beyond assertion. Where he is descriptive, he deals with the perfection of the five senses, and, although he integrates them to the extent that each becomes a faculty for perceiving a certain aspect of the unific Divine Humanity (for example, the eye corresponds to wisdom, the ear to obedience), ultimately he keeps them independent of one another. And sometimes he splits them in valuations which in Blake would amount to another fall:

> But the rest of the senses with the angels are less exquisite than the senses of seeing and hearing, for the reason that seeing and hearing serve their intelli-gence and wisdom, and the rest do not; and if the other senses were equally exquisite they would detract from the light and joy of their wisdom, and would let in the delight of pleasures pertaining to various appetites and to the body; and so far as these prevail they obscure and weaken the understanding. This is seen in the world, where men become gross and stupid in regard to spiritual truths so far as they indulge in the sense of taste and yield to the allurements of the sense of touch.[3]

What resemblances there are to Blake are very general, and the treat-ment of the angelic body does not help us a great deal with the intricacies of Blake's verse; it is best regarded as source material, which the poet's imagina-

From *The Awakening of Albion: The Renovation of the Body in the Poetry of William Blake,* © 1974, Cornell University Press. Used by permission of the publisher, Cornell University Press.

tion ransaked for what it could use. Blake's most direct influences in the portrayal of a risen body are Ezekiel, Isaiah, St. John of Patmos, and Milton; and the closet parallels in our own century are to be found in Rilke and Lawrence. But the most immediate context of the Blakean resurrection is the titanism of his age, the revolutionary enthusiasm that, in the last pages of the *Enquiry Concerning Political Justice,* drove Godwin to the edges of the Enlightenment when he suggested that man could evolve a human body such as he had never known, one liberated from disease and suited to the power and the freedom of an unshackled consciousness, one able for the first time to truly live. The myth of a new body, possible here and now, haunts the imagery of Wordsworth, Coleridge, Shelley, and Keats; and, outside Blake, it receives its most explicit elaboration in *Prometheus Unbound,* with its description of the transfiguration of Asia, the reintegration of both the sole self and the formerly inanimate into a joyous and personal universal body, and the regeneration of substance into radiance, music, dance, and the "perpetual Orphic song" of renovated communication.

In Night IX of *The Four Zoas,* Blake describes the resurrection of Albion through the successive renewals of each of his members and their reintegration into a community of creative work. The final movement of the apocalypse begins with Urizen's confession of ultimate failure:

Seeking the Eternal which is always present to the wise
Seeking for pleasure which unsought falls round the infants path
And on the fleeces of mild flocks who neither care nor labour. [121: 10–12, E375]

Albion by this time has been redeemed to the point of recalling his members, and the first to be regathered is the Prince of Light. It is strange at first glance that Urizen is the hero of the last book; but in the terms of Blake's myth this irony has compelling justification. The action of Night IX pivots on Urizen's surrender of self-consciousness and of his Faustian quest to carve out futurity with an imperial reason and will, and its theme is the reintegration of consciousness into the complete body of man. Thus, in a reversal that is as striking conceptually as it is dramatically, a redeemed Nobodaddy takes the lead in the work of renovation. He recognizes now that the world of nature is not an end in itself but a seedbed, and, in the sustained figure of the apocalyptic harvest that dominates the book, it is he who sows the human seed and reaps the "wide Universe."

In the joyful work of creating a new human condition and in the sensuous richness of the Dionysiac banquet with which the first phase of the apocalypse culminates, the beginnings of a reintegrated and enlarged human experience are manifest. At the same time, this "rural work" is felt among men as the revolutionary "pangs of Eternal Birth," and as the labors progress the spectres are consumed in the fires of Urizen's renovated consciousness, to re-emerge in new bodies. The emanations return to the Zoas, and the Zoas to their proper places. Luvah and Vala leave the brain and heart and return to the loins, and as Luvah gathers back his emanation the Golden Age begins anew: "Come forth O Vala from the grass & from the silent Dew / Rise from the dews of death for the Eternal Man is Risen" (126: 31–32, E380). Tharmas and Enion are renewed as children of a reorganized Innocence:

> And when Morning began to dawn upon the distant hills
> A whirlwind rose up in the Center & in the Whirlwind a shriek
> And in the Shriek a rattling of bones & in the rattling of bones
> A dolorous groan & from the dolorous groan in tears
> Rose Enion like a gentle light. [132: 13–17, E385]

As the Zoas return, the possibilities of the human body gradually expand. At the harvest feast in Urizen's once desolate South, they celebrate their reunion and, embracing the "New Born Man," commit themselves to a new faith:

> Not for ourselves but for the Eternal family we live
> Man liveth not by Self alone but in his brothers face
> Each shall behold the Eternal Father & love & joy abound.
> —[133: 24–26, E387]

The parts of Albion's body no longer work against each other but are now "Cooperating in the bliss of Man obeying his Will" (126: 16, E380).

Thus far the Zoas have risen to the State of Upper Beulah, where they are first refreshed on couches of "sweet repose" and then rise to enjoy the furious revels of Luvah's vintage, which are experienced among men both as a sudden release of pleasure and as the agonies of revolutionary change. The intoxications of Beulah are such, however, that for a moment it seems as if the renovation is to be drowned in its newly discovered fulfillments. As the revels develop, they turn destructive: the children of Luvah "catch the Shrieks in cups of gold they hand them to one another / These are the sports of love & these the sweet delights of amorous play" (137: 1–2, E390).

It is clear that man is not yet ready for a final celebration. The festival, when taken as an end in itself, is a false dawn, in which the apocalypse is in danger of being deflected back into the world of Tirzah. But at this juncture Albion urges the Zoas to further labor, and they work together in a second harvest, this one of grain. Since the triumph of Luvah needs to be regarded as a beginning of the rise from Beulah to Eden, he is "put for dung on the ground" (24); the corn is stored by Urizen and sifted by Tharmas; and the fourth Zoa, the maker Urthona, rises in "all his regenerate power" to bake the "Bread of Ages." The bread and wine of a new human substance are now prepared, even as the world beneath reaches its wintry nadir of sorrow. The new joys force the contrast between oppression and liberation to a breaking point, and a new universe at last bursts forth:

The Sun has left his blackness & has found a fresher morning
And the mild noon rejoices in the clear & cloudless night
And Man walks forth from midst of the fires the evil is all consumd
His eyes behold the Angelic spheres arising night & day
The stars consumd like a lamp blown out & in their stead behold
The Expanding Eyes of Man behold the depths of wondrous worlds

One Earth one sea beneath nor Erring Globes wander but Stars
Of fire rise up nightly from the Ocean & one Sun
Each morning like a New born Man issues with songs & Joy
Calling the Plowman to his Labour & the Shepherd to his rest
He walks upon the Eternal Mountains raising his heavenly voice
Conversing with the Animal forms of wisdom night & day
That risen from the Sea of fire renewd walk oer the Earth.
                                        —[138: 20–32, E391]

Man's marvelous powers of speech and vision indicate that he is qualita-
tively beyond the joyful body of Beulah. But Blake suggests that even this is
only a beginning. The poem closes with a triumphant Urthona preparing the
arms of intellect, which, now that war and the "dark Religions" have departed,
will take man into the day for a full and human consciousness, one that Blake
calls a "sweet Science." Blake is here not so much at odds with the Enlightenment as surpassing it in comprehensiveness. Night IX shows us an expansion
of consciousness beyond the limits of the self and of orthodox rationality, its
commitment to the discovery and the building of a new age for all men, and
the restoration of its connections with loins, emotions, what we would call the
unconscious (Blake's animal world, his water world of Tharmas, and his
Beulah dream world) and the body as a whole. The development is one from
reason to "intellect," or imagination, from a dark science of abstractionism and
a "Stern Philosophy" of good and evil[4] to the sweet science of the last line.
    The resurrection in *The Four Zoas* is thus based on a reorganization of
action, rather than a final repose from it; on the renascence of an integrated
sensibility beyond self-consciousness; and on a far-reaching myth of brotherhood that includes a brotherhood of the faculties and senses. The closing
plates of *Jerusalem* reaffirm these motifs but go far beyond them. In the new
treatment, the apocalypse is at once more embattled in its accomplishment
and more radical in its propositions. The pervasiveness and the recalcitrance
of the natural self appear substantially greater, and the sense of struggle and
affliction is more immediate because it is attributed not to the "human
grapes," or society at large, but directly to the central characters, Albion and
his Zoas. Thus the renewal is given the narrative structure not of a harvest
but of a battle against the embodiment of the Satanic selfhood, the Covering
Cherub; and the dynamics of brotherhood are extended in the themes of self-
sacrifice and forgiveness, on which a human resurrection now pivots. Los-
Jesus is now the sole agent of regeneration, for Blake seems convinced that no

mode of consciousness other than artistic can free itself sufficiently from the restrictions of the spectre to experience a Divine Vision.[5]

When Albion awakes, he compels the Zoas to return to their original places of work: Tharmas to the sheepfold, Urizen to the plow, and Luvah to the Loom; Urthona is already at his anvil in the form of the "Great Spectre Los." However, once Albion arises from the fires of self-sacrifice, we see the Zoas no longer in a community but in a fourfold oneness. When the Eternal Man reaches for his bow, the Zoas reach for their own bows; but there is a single "horned Bow Fourfold." In his description of the risen man Blake emphasizes the unison of the body's functioning and the actual process of the cooperation:

And every Man stood Fourfold. each Four Faces had. One to the West
One toward the East One to the South One to the North. the Horses Fourfold
And the dim Chaos brightened beneath, above, around! Eyed as the Peacock
According to the Human Nerves of Sensation, the Four Rivers of the Water of Life.
    [IV: 98: 12–15, E254]

The senses, as we conceive them, drop out to be replaced by faculties, which, as separate entities, themselves drop out to be replaced by a fourfold organ of imagination, the body of Albion. In their renewed unity the faculties are imaged as Albion's bow, his chariots, the Four Rivers of Paradise, and the circumference of Paradise, comprehending at once, then, his activity, his life processes, and his bodily form.

The five natural organs of perception, functioning in separation, are one-dimensional contractions of the four-dimensional risen body. This much is clear from Blake's doctrinal statements, but what begins to become clear only in the imagery of these closing plates is the problem of "numerous senses." The Four Eternal Senses are Four Faces, each commanding a cardinal point, and yet each fourfold in itself. Albion can thus see in all directions at the same time. He has no set physical position *vis-à-vis* an object and is not limited to the directional fragmentation of natural vision. Similarly, there is no longer a distinction between center and circumference, because his faculties define the changing outline of his perceptual field. In accordance with this infinite flexibility of vision, the four faculties are described as "Eyed as the Peacock." The risen man has innumerable eyes, which collectively compose his faculty of vision. There is, then, no contradiction or ambiguity when Blake refers sometimes to four paradisaical faculties and sometimes to numerous or multiplied eternal senses. In Eden man has both infinite eyes and four senses.

The imagery of Albion's new body is dynamic to the extent that it is more accurate to describe it as a risen activity than as a risen body. Its fourfoldness is difficult, deliberately, to imagine in static, naturalistic terms; but it appears instead in the constant activity of the bow and arrow, the expansion and contraction of the faculties, and the chariots always "going forward forward irresistible from Eternity to Eternity" (98: 27, E255). A body, as we tend to think of it, is a set, basically pictorial form; but the body Blake describes subsists in its activity and its motion. The only actual visual image of the risen body Blake gives us, the four fourfold chariots in motion, is one which defies the powers of the natural eye. Like the chariot of Ezekiel, on which Blake bases it, it is unconditioned and self-impelled and moves through no spatiality external to itself:

> Whithersoever the spirit was to go, they went,
> thither *was their* spirit to go; and the wheels
> were lifted up over against them: for the spirit
> of the living creatures *was* in the wheels. [1 : 20]

The following passage offers Blake's fullest portrayal of the renovated body:

And they conversed together in Visionary forms dramatic which bright
Redounded from their Tongues in thunderous majesty, in Visions
In new Expanses, creating exemplars of Memory and of Intellect
Creating Space, Creating Time according to the wonders Divine
Of Human Imagination, throughout all the Three Regions immense
Of Childhood, Manhood & Old Age[;] & the all tremendous unfathomable Non
    Ens
Of Death was seen in regenerations terrific or complacent varying
According to the subject of discourse & every Word & Every Character
Was Human according to the Expansion or Contraction, the Translucence or
Opakeness of Nervous fibres such was the variation of Time & Space
Which vary according as the Organs of Perception vary & they walked
To & fro in Eternity as One Man reflecting each in each & clearly seen
And seeing: according to fitness & order. [28–40]

There is no distinction here between perception and creation, activity and receptivity, imagination and sensation. The body has become the soul; the senses have been improved until they can perceive everything that the Poetical Genius can imagine; and the form of the risen body is like the form of fire in its continuous changes of contour, according to changes in impulse and desire.

Through the passage, images of voice, vision, sound, light, discourse, and creative power develop a radically synesthetic effect. As Ernest Tuveson has noted, "Abstraction is only one sense impression isolated from the others";[6] and the risen body reveals the antithetical condition, more than an extraordinary modification of one sense by another, but a complete and normative interplay. Merleau-Ponty writes that perception is prereflectively a total sensory response, not a sum of visual, tactile, and audible givens,[7] but in Blake the final actualization of the synesthetic character of perception is a metamorphosis, giving us a body far different from the one we know. At this point, however, the concept of synesthesia requires some exact definition. What Blake implies is not a fusion of the faculties into one undifferentiated organic sense. The effect of synesthesia here, just as, for example, in Coleridge's "sound-like power in light" ("The Eolian Harp," 28) and Shelley's music "felt like an odour within the sense" ("The Sensitive Plant," I: 28), is not to erase distinctions between kinds of sensation but to play them off against one another, setting up a rich and mutually heightening interaction. Blake's risen body is founded not on a return to nonindividuation but on the individuality of minute particulars, and its character, in all respects, is dialectical. Suggestive at this point is a dialectic of the senses that Wordsworth regards as Nature's means of opposing the despotism of the eye; Nature

> summons all the senses each
> To counteract the other, and themselves
> And makes them all, and the objects with which all
> Are conversant, subservient in their turn
> To the great ends of Liberty and Power.
> —[*The Prelude*, XII: 135–39]

And the relationship among the flowers in "The Sensitive Plant" is also similar to the kind of multifold unification that Blake's faculties display:

> For each one was interpenetrated
> With the light and the odour its neighbours shed,
> Like young lovers whom youth and love make dear
> Wrapped and filled by their mutual atmosphere. [I: 66–69][8]

The format assumed by sensory interrelationship in Blake is illuminated by the following verse from Ezekiel's description of the chariot:

> And when they went, I heard the noise of their
> wings, like the noise of great waters, as the
> voice of the Almighty, the voice of speech, as the
> noise of an host. (1 : 24)

The activity of Albion's fully awakened body is a kind of speech, presented as the mode of the Zoas' interplay; and in this Edenic conversation, the action of all the faculties at once, the tongue creates thundering, visionary forms. It is a speech like poetry, with the difference that it is poetry actualized and the universe is directly created by the tongue. In this new language the improvement of the body and the improvement of human communication converge, as they also do, in a smaller way, in the paradise imagined by Keats in "I Stood Tip-Toe," where the lovers are joined to one another through a new efficacy of speech:

> Young men, and maidens at each other gaz'd
> With hands held back, and motionless, amaz'd
> To see the brightness in each other's eyes;
> And so they stood, fill'd with a sweet surprise,
> Until their tongues were loos'd in poesy.
> Therefore no lover did of anguish die:
> But the soft numbers, in that moment spoken,
> Made silken ties, that never may be broken. [231–38]

As the description of Blake's Eden develops, more and more of existence is reclaimed by the new arts of vocalization, and forms regain their humanity as they join in the ever-expanding conversation of the risen body. Albion, now perceived as Jehovah, speaks "terrific from his Holy Place" (which is co-extensive with the body and the universe), in visible words of the Mutual Covenant Divine, the mutual humanity of perceiver and percept. This covenant is conveyed

> On Chariots of gold & jewels with Living Creatures starry & flaming
> With every Colour, Lion, Tyger, Horse, Elephant, Eagle Dove, Fly, Worm,
> And the all wondrous Serpent clothed in gems & rich array Humanize
> In the Forgiveness of Sins according to the Covenant of Jehovah . . . [42–45][9]

The new covenant, Albion's perceptible attitude toward his objects, is the forgiveness that allows all things to realize their human status, a divine accord that everything is holy, everything a man; it is, indeed, a call for lion and tiger to assume human form. In answer they vocalize their awareness of the sudden disappearance of their generative state:

> Where is the Covenant of Priam, the Moral Virtues of the Heathen
> Where is the Tree of Good & Evil that rooted beneath the cruel heel
> Of Albions Spectre the Patriarch Druid! where are all his Human Sacrifices
> For Sin in War & in the Druid Temples of the Accuser of Sin: beneath
> The Oak Groves of Albion that coverd the whole Earth beneath his Spectre
> Where are the Kingdoms of the World & all their glory that grew on Desolation
> The Fruit of Albions Poverty Tree when the Triple Headed Gog-Magog Giant
> Of Albion Taxed the Nations into Desolation & then gave the Spectrous Oath
>
> Such is the Cry from all the Earth from the Living Creatures of the Earth
> And from the great City of Golgonooza in the Shadowy Generation
> And from the Thirty-two Nations of the Earth among the Living Creatures. [46–
>   56, E256]

At last, beyond the redemption of animals, the inanimate—tree, metal, earth, and stone—is returned to humanity; and the landscape is consumed as the lost vocal power of objects is recovered. Now the speech of the risen body is answered as the human forms cry out the name of their emanations, which in their unison are called Jerusalem, as the risen speakers are in their interplay Albion.

The reorganization of the body includes a transformation of man's substance, as well as his faculties and their percepts. Judging from Blake's normal usage of the four elements, we might expect fire—the renovative medium of Orc and, in the late work, of Los at his forge, as well as the most malevolent of the elements in the form of the Cherub's sword—to be the prime material of Eden, and it does remain the redemptive substance until Plate 96. But when Albion himself, sacrificing his natural selfhood to save Los, plunges into the fires, then: "the Furnaces became / Fountains of Living Waters flowing from the Humanity Divine" (36–37, E253). In the description that follows of the re-entry of all life into Eden, fire is at first the predominant material, particularly in the flaming arrows of mental warfare. Yet when Blake describes the weapons of the Zoas—Urizen's "breathing Bow of carved Gold," Luvah's "Silver Bow bright shining," Tharmas' "Bow of Brass pure flaming richly wrought," and Urthona's "Bow of Iron terrible thundering" (97: 7–11)—the sense is not of fire, but of a comprehensive fiery matter, including such properties as silvery brightness, breathing, and thundering, as well as the attributes of specific metals. The final annihilation of the Druid Spectre is surrounded with aerial images: breath, clouds, wind, the illumination of "dim Chaos." Next, water returns in the figure of the reintegrated Zoas as the "Four Rivers of the Water of Life"; and this materiality drops out, in turn, to be replaced by gems, "gold and jewels," the precious substances of the earth which adorn the humanized forms. And in the last plate, tree, metal, earth, and stone are gathered into Eden. All four elements enter paradise; and there is finally a sense in the passage as a whole, although Blake is not explicit about this, of not one predominant element in Eden, nor even of air, earth, and water assuming the characteristics of fire, but of a new fourfold substance made from the reintegration of air, earth, water, and fire.

Blake describes the fall as a division of the elements: the Zoas collapse toward a center, which is now surrounded by four abandoned spheres: to the South, Urizen's world of burning fire; to the East, Luvah's void; to the West, Tharmas' world of raging waters; to the North, Urthona's "solid Darkness / Unfathomable without end" (J. III: 59: 19–20, E206). The implication is that the four elements in which our existence appears to us are divided portions of ourself. In the closing passage of *Jerusalem* there is no sense of a materiality distinct from human substance: fire, earth, air, and water are humanized, and together they compose the Edenic matter of man, who in his new body is fiery and fountain-like at the same time. Thus, what Blake describes, far from a dematerialization of man, is a regathering of his complete substance.

A further theme in the passage is that everything in Eden is directly available to perception and is of such closeness that it is impossible to abstract inside and outside from Blake's lines. J. H. van den Berg provides an effective analogue to this apocalyptic illumination when he writes that the visibility of God "is the nearness between man and man. When God is with us, He does not appear as a transparent ghost in the realm of the dead. He stands, face to face with us as an acquaintance, a friend, a wife, a husband, or a child."[10] Everything now is human and can be conversed with. There are no levels or orders of being, and everything is opened and revealed: Chaos brightens, the "Non Ens / Of Death was seen in regenerations." There are no dark and remote places, no spots of unconsciousness, and all is translucent, as once only the world within the center was. The discovery of a total presence and manifestation is an important tradition in the literature of apocalypse. In Ezekiel, for instance, God promises, "Neither will I hide my face any more from them" (39:29). In Blake's literal treatment, matter becomes radiant, as it is in the new world of *Prometheus Unbound* and in the lost, original landscape of Wordsworth's "Intimations of Immortality." A characteristic Blakean touch is that the illumination is not actually a property of Eden, for this is not a world of established qualities. Instead, the relative translucency or opacity of substance is under the perceiver's control. He can see up to or through, as he wishes, so determining his own horizons.

In the same way, time and space now have their being in the impulses of the risen body. They are originally, Blake tells us, "Real Beings A Male & a Female Time is a Man Space is a Woman & her Masculine Portion is death" (V.L.J., E553), or Los, Enitharmon, and the Spectre of Urthona. In nature they assume dehumanized form: spectral time is the mere accumulation of seconds and spectral space, the aggregation of inches. In Ulro there is, properly, no space or time at all, but feelings of void and of unending repetition. Man is contained by a rigid destiny and a limitless, meaningless extension. Blake's irony is that this is the immortality of the eye, in which sounds and inches are extended indefinitely, and it applies to our common imaginings of both the static monotony of heaven and the endless torments of hell. Los works to personalize time and space, to base them not on the atomistic units of their abstraction from activity but in the human time of a pulsation of an artery and in the human space of a globule of blood. His efforts begin to bear fruit in Beulah with its "watery delusions" of unification; there, space becomes intimate and qualitative, and moments of dream, play, and sexual love are experienced as "timeless." They are timeless, however, in the sense that activity takes primacy over its duration; the perceiver is not aware of a time or a space that is abstracted from his senses, feelings, and actions. But the delights of Beulah are chiefly personal; they offer relaxation from the pressures of positive time and space without finally consuming them. In Eden, time and space are reintegrated in what Frye identifies as the fourth dimension,[11] and they are fully returned to man, who now creates them in the rhythmic expansions and contractions of his risen body. For Blake, eternity and infinity involve not an emancipation from, but a reorganization of the sense of space and time. They signify the liberty to invent space and time, in the way that art does, and so to be alive in an immediate present that is delineated by the perceiver's imagination.

The visionary conversation is thus the making of life, now analogous to the making of a work of art, and in these plates Blake describes the achievement of a particular Edenic moment, in which desire finds its form and in which the natural world is replaced by a world of emanation. In the poem's final line, the moment is consummated as the enamation is joyfully recognized: a poem is completed, a world is made, Albion rejoins his bridge. But there is no finality in this accomplishment, for Blake's paradise is not the end-point of a linear development, but a state of perpetual creative activity. Eden itself moves, going from Eternity to Eternity, creation to creation. "The discovery itself," writes Merleau-Ponty, "calls forth still further quests. . . . For painters the world will always be yet to be painted."[12]

Notes

1. *Heaven and Its Wonders, and Hell,* trans. J. C. Ager, (New York: Swedenborg Foundation, 1952), p. 399.
2. Ibid., p. 126.
3. Ibid., pp. 399–400.
4. See 133: 14–15; and 138: 15, E391.
5. It is worth noting that Albion's awakening still involves political upheavel: he rises "in direful / Revolutions of Action & Passion" (IV: 95: 9–10, E252).
6. Ernest Tuveson, *The Imagination as a Means of Grace* (Berkeley: University of California Press, 1960), p. 73.
7. "The Film and the New Psychology," in *Sense and Non-Sense,* by Maurice Merleau-Ponty, trans. Hubert L. Dreyful and Patricia Allen Dreyfus, Northwestern University Studies in Phenomenology and Existential Philosophy (Evanston, Illinois: Northwestern University Press, 1964), pp. 49–50.
8. Relevant, as well, is the fourfold body described by Lawrence in his attempt to return consciousness and the body to each other. The "coming to perfection of each single individual" depends upon a dynamic interchange among the four poles of "the first, basic field of consciousness" (which are located in the solar plexus, lumbar ganglion, cardiac plexus, and thoracic ganglion) and a "passionate flux" among their various sympathetic and separatist currents. See his two responses to Freud, *Psychoanalysis and the Unconscious* and *Fantasia of the Unconscious* (New York: Viking, 1960), p. 41 et passim.
9. Percival accounts for the surprising use of the name Jehovah as a signifying the imagination as an "outward image" in Eden (*William Blake's Circle of Destiny* [1938; rpt. New York: Octagon, 1964], p. 142). But Blake's chief intention, one would think, would be to indicate Albion's replacement of the position occupied at present by Jehovah, the re-establishment of renovated man as the creator of his own universe. What the name signifies is that there is no other Jehovah.
10. J. H. van den Berg, *The Changing Nature of Man: Introduction to a Historical Psychology,* trans. H. F. Croes (New York: Dell, 1964), p. 198.
11. Frye, *Fearful Symmetry* (Princeton: Princeton University Press, 1947), p. 138.
12. Merleau-Ponty, "Eye and Mind," in *The Primacy of Perception* trans. and ed. James M. Edie (Evanston: Northwestern University Press, 1964), p. 189.

Desire Gratified and Ungratified:
William Blake and Sexuality

ALICIA OSTRIKER

To examine Blake on sexuality is to deal with a many-layered thing. Although we like to suppose that everything in the canon "not only belongs in a unified scheme but is in accord with a permanent structure of ideas,"[1] some of Blake's ideas clearly change during the course of his career, and some others may constitute internal inconsistencies powerfully at work in, and not resolved by, the poet and his poetry. What I will sketch here is four sets of Blakean attitudes toward sexual experience and gender relations, each of them coherent and persuasive if not ultimately "systematic;" for convenience, and in emulation of the poet's own method of personifying ideas and feelings, I will call them four Blakes. First, the Blake who celebrates sexuality and attacks repression, whom we may associate with Freud and even more with Reich. Second, a corollary Blake whom we may associate with Jung, whose idea of the emanation—the feminine element with man—parallels Jung's concept of the anima, and who depicts sexual life as a complex web of gender complementarities and inter-dependencies. Third, a Blake apparently inconsistent with Blake number one, who sees sexuality as a tender trap rather than a force of liberation. Fourth, and corollary to that, the Blake to whom it was necessary, as it was to his patriarchal precursor Milton, to see the female principle as subordinate to the male.

Blake number one is perhaps the most familiar to the common reader, although professional Blakeans have paid little attention to him lately. He is the vigorous, self-confident, exuberant advocate of gratified desire, writing in his early and middle thirties (that is, between the fall of the Bastille and the execution of Louis and the declaration of war between England and France) the early *Notebook* poems, the *Songs, The Marriage of Heaven and Hell* and the *Visions of the Daughters of Albion*. A few texts will refresh the memory. Among the *Notebook* epigrams we are told that

> Love to faults is always blind
> Always is to joy inclind
> Lawless wingd and unconfind
> And breaks all chains from every mind
> —(E463)[2]

From *Blake: An Illustrated Quarterly*, 16 (Winter 1982–83), 156–65. Used by permission.

Abstinence sows sand all over
The ruddy limbs & flaming hair
But Desire Gratified
Plants fruits of life & beauty there
—(E465)

What is it men in women do require?
The lineaments of Gratified Desire
What is it Women do in men require?
The lineaments of Gratified Desire
—(E466)

It was probably these lines that converted me to Blake when I was twenty. They seemed obviously true, splendidly symmetrical, charmingly cheeky—and nothing else I had read approached them, although I thought Yeats must have picked up a brave tone or two here. Only later did I notice that the epigrams were tiny manifestoes announcing an identity of interest between sexuality and the human imagination.

During these years Blake wrote numerous minidramas illustrating how possessiveness and jealousy, prudery and hypocrisy poison the lives of lovers. He pities the chaste ("The Sunflower") and depicts the pathos of chastity relinquished too late ("The Angel"), looks forward to a "future Age" when "Love! sweet Love!" will no longer be thought a crime, while protesting its repression by Church and State in his own time. One of his two major statements about sexual repression in *Songs of Experience* is the deceptively simple "The Garden of Love," in which the speaker discovers a Chapel built where he "used to play on the green." The Garden has a long scriptural and literary ancestry. "A garden shut up, a fountain sealed, is my sister, my bride," in the Song of Solomon. It is the site of the *Roman de la Rose.* It is where Dante meets Beatrice, it is Spenser's garden of Adonis and Milton's Paradise—"In narrow room, Nature's whole wealth." The garden is, in brief, at once the earthly paradise and the body of a woman. Probably Blake saw it so. Later he would draw the nude torso of a woman with a cathedral where her genitals should be. The briars at the poem's close half-suggest that the speaker is being crowned with something like thorns, somewhere about the anatomy, and it anticipates Blake's outraged demand, near the close of his life, in the *Everlasting Gospel:* "Was Jesus chaste? or did he/ Give any lessons of chastity?" Since the design for "The Garden of Love" depicts a priest and two children kneeling at an open grave beside a church, the forbidden love may be a parent as well as a peer, and the speaker might be of either sex: all repression is one. It is important that the tone here is neither angry nor self-righteous, but pathetic and passive—indeed, pathetically passive, for after the opening "I went," the governing verb is "saw." That the speaker only "saw . . . my joys and desires" being bound with briars and did not "feel" anything, should shock us into realizing that this speaker, at least by the poem's last line, has been effectively self-alienated. Repression has worked not merely from without, but from within.[3]

The other major statement is "London," where Blake hears the clanking of the mind-forg'd manacles (chains such as "Love . . . breaks from every mind") he will later associate with Urizen. Economic exploitation sanctioned by blackening churches and political exploitation sanctioned by bleeding palace walls are grievous, but "most" grievous is sexual exploitation, perhaps because it is a denial of humanity's greatest virtue, charity, as sweep's cry and soldiers' sign are denials of faith and hope; or perhaps because, to Blake, sexual malaise precedes and produces all other ills:

> But most thro' midnight streets I hear
> How the youthful Harlots curse
> Blasts the newborn Infants tear
> And blights with plagues the Marriage hearse
> —(E27)

That final stanza is Blake's most condensed indictment of the gender arrangements in a society where Love is ruled by Law and consequently dies; where virtuous females are pure, modest, and programmed for frigidity, so that healthy males require whores; where whores have ample cause to curse; and where their curses have the practical effect of infecting young families with venereal disease as well as with the more metaphoric plague of unacknowledged guilt.[4] Through his hissing, spitting and explosive alliteration Blake creates an ejaculatory harlot who is (and there are analogues to her in Spenser, Shakespeare, Milton) not the garden but the snake. That a syntactic ambivalence common in Blake makes her one who is cursed by others as well as one who curses, does not diminish the point.

The point recurs polemically in *The Marriage of Heaven and Hell*, where, according to Auden, "the whole of Freud's teachings may be found."[5] Here "Prisons are built with stones of Law, brothels with bricks of Religion," "Prudence is a rich ugly old maid courted by Incapacity," and we are exhorted: "Sooner murder an infant in its cradle than nurse unacted desires" (E36–37). Here too is the famous pre-Freudian précis of Freud's theories on suppression: "Those who restrain desire, do so because theirs is weak enough to be restrained; and the restrainer or reason usurps its place and governs the unwilling. And being restrained it by degrees becomes passive till it is only the shadow of desire" (E 34). For Freud, this process was always in some degree necessary and irreversible, as *Civilization and its Discontents* and "Analysis Terminable and Interminable" ultimately confess. But Blake—and this is what makes him more Reichian than Freudian—joyfully forsees the end of discontent and civilization too: "For the cherub with his flaming brand is hereby commanded to leave his guard at tree of life, and when he does, the whole creation will be consumed, and appear infinite, and holy where it now appears finite & corrupt. This will come to pass by an improvement of sensual enjoyment" (E 38).[6]

In all such texts Blake is not only attacking the powers of repression, particularly institutional religion, which in the name of reason and holiness attempt to subdue desire. He is also asserting that gratified desire *does* what religion *pretends* to do; gives access to vision, the discovery of the infinite. Moreover—and this is a point to which I will return—Blake in these texts does not stress the distinction between male and female, or assign conspicuously different roles to the two sexes. Youth and virgin suffer alike under chastity, man and woman have identical desires, and the "ruddy limbs and flaming hair" of which an ardent imagination makes a garden, and an abstinent imagination makes a desert, may belong interchangeably to a lover or a beloved, a male or a female.

The poem in which Blake most extensively elaborates his celebration of love and his critique of repression is *Visions of the Daughters of Albion,* printed in 1793. *Visions* is also the poem most clearly delineating male sexual aggressiveness as a component of Urizenic patriarchy, and illustrating the kinds of damage it does to both males and females. First of all, Bromion is a number of things which to Blake are one thing. He is the slaveowner who converts humans into private property and confirms his possession by impregnating the females, the racist who rationalizes racism by insisting that the subordinate race is sexually promiscuous, the rapist who honestly believes that his victim was asking for it; and, withal, he does not actually experience "sensual enjoyment." But if Bromion represents the social and psychological pathology of sexual violence, Theotormon represents its pitiable underside, sexual impotence. "Oerflowd with woe," asking unanswerable questions, weeping incessantly, Theotormon does not respond to Bromion's insult to his masculinity ("Now thou maist marry Bromion's harlot" [pl. 2.1]). Playing the hesitant Hamlet to Bromion's rough Claudius, intimidated slave to coarse slave-master, Theotormon has been victimized by an ideology that glorifes male aggressiveness, as much as by that ideology's requirement of feminine purity. Dejected and self-flagellant (design, pl. 6), he cannot look Oothoon in her intellectual and erotic eye as she maintains her spiritual virginity and offers him her love, not only because she is damaged goods but because she is taking sexual initiative instead of being "modest." Only with incredulity and grief does Oothoon realize this (pl. 6.4–20).

Most of *Visions* is Oothoon's opera. Raped, enslaved, imprisoned, rejected, the heroine's agonized rhapsody of self-offering rushes from insight to insight. Though she begins by focusing on her individual condition, her vision rapidly expands outward. She analyzes the enchainment of loveless marriage and the unhappy children it must produce, she praises the value of infant sexuality and attacks the ethos which brands joy whoredom and sublimates its sexuality in twisted religiosity. She also bewails other ramifications of the tyranny of reason over desire, such as the abuse of peasant by landlord, of worker by factory owner, of the faithful by their churches. For Oothoon life means being "open to joy and to delight where ever beauty appears," and the perception of any beauty is an erotic activity in which eye and object join "in happy copulation." Made desperate by her lover's unresponsiveness, she cries out for "Love! Love! Love! happy happy Love! free as the mountain wind! / Can that be Love, that drinks another as a sponge drinks water?" Though remaining herself "bound" to Bromion, she nevertheless concludes with a vision of the vitality of all free things:

> Arise you little glancing wings, and sing your infant joy!
> Arise and drink your bliss, for every thing that lives is holy!
> —(VDA 8.9–10)

Blake in *Visions* has created a heroine unequalled in English poetry before or since. Oothoon not only defines and defends her own sexuality rather than waiting for Prince Charming to interrupt her nap, and not only attacks patriarchal ideology root and branch, but outflanks everyone in her poem for intellectuality and spirituality, and is intellectual and spiritual precisely because she is erotic. Shakespeare's comic heroines, though witty and sexy, are of course not intellectuals, much less revolutionaries. The Wife of Bath strongly resembles Oothoon as a voice of "experience, though noon auctoritee" who "spekes of wo that is in marriage," celebrates sexuality as such and female sexuality in particular, and lectures to the Apollyon of Judeo-Christian misogyny from his own texts. Yet she lacks Oothoon's generosity, and has been locked by men's contempt into a perpetuation of the war of the sexes. (If, though, we amend the portrait of the Wife as she appears in the Prologue by that "imaginative portion" of her which is her Tale, we have something different. Here perhaps is the Wife as she would be—neither offensively-defensively bawdy, nor angrily polemical, but lively and charming—telling the wish-fulfilling story of a rapist enlightened and reformed, of male violence, ignorance and pride transformed by the "sovereyntee" of feminine wisdom and love.) Hawthorne's Hester Prynne comes close to being what Oothoon is, even to the point of foreseeing that "in Heaven's own time, a new truth would . . . establish the whole relation between man and woman on a surer ground of mutual happiness."[7] But Hawthorne cannot sustain or elaborate the vision he glimpses, and sends Hester back in the end to her knitting, her works of charity, and a lifelong celibacy which—unlike Oothoon's—is supposed to be voluntary.

Blake number two appears later than Blake number one, and shifts his psychological principles from an essentially socio-political to an essentially mythic base. Beginning with *The Book of Urizen*, engraved in 1794, and throughout his major prophecies, the poet relies on an idea of humanity as originally and ultimately androgynous, attributing the fall of man and what John Milton called "all our woe" not to female narcissism but to specifically male pride, male competitiveness, or male refusal to surrender the self, and depicting a fallen state in which sexual division—lapse of unity between male and female as one being—is the prototype of every division within the self, between self and other, and between humanity and God.

The mythology of these poems posits a hero who is both Great Britain and all mankind, and who lives in Eternity or Eden as one of a family of Eternals who collectively compose One Man, Christ. Albion's "Human Brain," the equivalent of Jung's collective unconscious, houses four energetic Jungian Zoas, each of whom has a feminine counterpart or emanation. At Man's Fall, precipitated in *Urizen* by Urizen's pride, in *The Four Zoas* and *Milton* by rivalry between Urizen and Luvah, and in *Jerusalem* by Albion's selfish refusal to maintain erotic union with his saviour and his insistence on mortal virtue, Albion lapses into what Blake variously calls sleep, death and disease, and what the rest of us call human history. The Zoas simultaneously lapse into lower forms and mutual conflict instead of harmony, and are disastrously divided from their emanations. As the late Blake formulaically puts it, "The Feminine separates from the Masculine & both from Man." Bodies grow around them, inimical "To the embrace of love":

> that no more the Masculine mingles
> With the Feminine, but the Sublime is shut out from the Pathos
> In howling torment, to build stone walls of separation, compelling
> The Pathos, to weave curtains of hiding secresy from the torment.
> —(*J* 90.10–13)

At the close of his three longest poems Blake imagines an apocalypse in which selfhood is relinquished and male and female are reunified:

> And the Bow is a Male & Female & the Quiver of the Arrows of Love
> Are the Children of this Bow: a Bow of Mercy & Loving-Kindness: laying
> Open the hidden Heart in Wars of mutual Benevolence Wars of Love
> And the Hand of Man grasps firm between the Male & Female Loves.
> —(*J* 97.12–15)

To say that Blake's emanations resemble what Jung calls the anima is to say that they represent a man's interior "female part," the "life-giving aspect of the psyche" and the "a priori element in his moods, reactions and impulses, and whatever else is spontaneous in psychic life."[8] As a positive figure the Blakean emanation like the Jungian anima is a benevolent guide to the unconscious life. As a negative figure she is seductive and destructive. She seems also to represent a man's emotionality, sensuousness, sensitivity, receptivity—all that makes him potentially effeminate—which in a fallen state he rejects or believes to be separated from himself, and must recover if he is to gain psychic wholeness. According to Jung, of course, an individual man changes and develops during the course of his lifetime but "his" anima does not. She remains static, and his only problem is to accept her existence as a portion of himself. What is particularly fascinating about Blake, then, is that he invents not one but a set of female beings, each appropriate to the Zoa she belongs to, each with her own personality and history of transformations, not radically different from the personalities in highly symbolic fiction and drama, and able to shed light very often on characters we thought we knew as well as on larger issues of sexual complementarity.

The first figures we encounter in *The Four Zoas,* for example, are Tharmas and Enion—humanity's Sensation—in the midst of a marital quarrel. Tharmas and Enion are bucolic characters of the sort that the wheels of history run over: good but not too bright, easily confused. We may recognize their like in mythic pairs like Baucis and Philemon, Deucalion and Pyrrha, and the Wakefield Noah with his farcically shrewish wife. Fictionally, and especially when a sentimental English novelist needs a pair of innocent parent-figures, they are legion: they are Sterne's Shandies, Goldsmith's Vicar and Mrs. Wakefield, and a troop of Dickensian folk like the Micawbers and Pockets, Casby (nicknamed "The Patriarch") and Flora, and perhaps most interestingly, the Gargeries of *Great Expectations.*[9] Across the Atlantic, they stumble through the fiction of writers like W. D. Howells and John Steinbeck. What Tharmas lacks when he loses Enion is his own sense of coherence. Without her he is a frantic and suicidal "flood" of feelings. What she lacks without him is resistance to pain. In her fallen form she becomes a grieving Demeter-figure who laments the sufferings of all earthly creatures,[10] and Blake gives her some of his best lines:

Why does the Raven cry aloud and no eye pities her?
Why fall the Sparrow & the Robin in the foodless winter?

—(FZ I.17.2–3)

It is an easy thing to triumph in the summers sun
And in the vintage & to sing on the waggon loaded with corn
It is an easy thing to talk of patience to the afflicted
To speak the laws of prudence to the houseless wanderer

. . . .

It is an easy thing to laugh at wrathful elements
To hear the dog howl at the wintry door, the ox in the slaughter house moan . . .
While our olive & vine sing & laugh round our door & our children bring fruit &
    flowers
Then the groan & the dolor are quite forgotten & the slave grinding at the mill
And the captive in chains & the poor in the prison & the soldier in the field
When the shattered bone hath laid him groaning among the happier dead.
It is an easy thing to rejoice in the tents of prosperity
Thus could I sing & thus rejoice, but it is not so with me.

—(FZ II.35.16–36.13)

Enion gives birth to Los and Enitharmon, the Eternal Prophet and his Muse, who from the start are as arrogant and self-absorbed as their parents are humble and selfless. Enitharmon espouses parent-abuse:

> To make us happy let them weary their immortal powers
> While we draw in their sweet delights while we return them scorn
> On scorn to feed our discontent; for if we grateful prove
> They will withhold sweet love, whose food is thorns & bitter roots.
> —(FZ I.10.3–6)

Soon she turns these arts on her twin and consort, becoming a seductive and maddening tease. She is the muse who won't come across, taunting the poet with failure and giving her alliance to Reason (Neoclassicism, let us say) instead of Prophecy, while forbidding the poet to love anyone but herself. As a couple, the Los and Enitharmon who are united "in discontent and scorn" uncannily resemble the self-destructive, sullen, jealous, incestuous or quasi-incestuous couples in novels like *Wuthering Heights, Women in Love,* and *The Sound and the Fury:* novels which in the light of Blake we can read as visions of a primitive creative energy thwarted by the impossibility of creativity in a culturally collapsed world they never made. Enitharmon is also La Belle Dame Sans Merci, she is Pip's Estella, or Lady Brett, or Marlene Dietrich in *The Blue Angel;* which is to say that she is the feminine agent of male sexual humiliation, who is herself governed by *ennui.*

A third couple is Urizen and Ahania: Reason and the Faith or Idealism necessary to it. Early in *The Four Zoas,* Urizen as cosmic architect places Ahania in a zodiacal shrine and burns incense to her. Here we have Blake's version of the "pedestal," and of that neo-Platonically inspired sexual reverence which prefers ladies pure, exalted and static rather than adjacent and active. When Ahania is uncomfortable in her shrine and tries to give her spouse some advice about returning to Eternity, he seizes her by the hair, calling her "Thou little diminutive portion that darst be a counterpart," and throws her out of heaven, declaring "Am I not God? Who is equal to me?" (FZ III.42.21–43.9). Without Ahania, Urizen is Doubt instead of Faith, and degenerates in the course of *The Four Zoas* from Prince of Light, to tyrannic parody of Milton's God, to William Pitt opposing the Bread Bill of 1800, to the Dragon Form of Antichrist. Ahania falls from being a sky goddess who opened her mouth once too often to "the silent woman" about whom feminist critics are presently writing a good deal.[11] Until just before the end of *The Four Zoas* Ahania has nothing further to say. As "the furrowed field" she is a figure of complete submission. We should compare her possibly to those other victims of exacerbated and anxious male intellect, Hamlet's Ophelia and Faust's Gretchen.[12]

Luvah and Vala, last of the Zoas and Emanations, are in their unfallen form lover and beloved, the Eros and Psyche of Man. Fallen, Luvah is born into this world as the revolutionary babe and flaming youth who must become a sacrificed god in epoch after epoch, while Vala is the *dolorosa* who, believing she loves him, always sacrifices him.

As all Blake readers know, Vala is one of Blake's most complicated characters. Her name means "vale" as in "valley," and as Nature she is the valley of the shadow of death, the declivity of the female genitals, and the membranous "veil" which preserves virginity, as well as the "veil" covering the tabernacle of the Old Testament. Like the chapel in "The Garden of Love" and the "chapel all of gold," she stands at the intersection between corrupt sexuality and institutional religion; thus she is also the veil of the temple which was rent when Jesus died, for Vala is the Nature we worship when we should worship Christ, she is Fortuna, Babylon, the Great Whore, enemy of Jerusalem. Where Enitharmon is a tease and a betrayer, Vala is the "Female Will" incarnate as killer. She is the chaste mistress who withholds favors so that her lovers will become warriors, and she is the blood-spattered priestess who with a knife of flint cuts the hearts out of men—all the while protesting that she craves nothing but Love. So powerful a figure is she that I expect we see at least as much of her in popular culture—where she is the voluptuous pinup on barracks walls, and she is the lady in black leather who will punish you—as in conventional fiction and drama. Pornography magazines offer us endless reproductions of Vala-Babylon, and, in the most high-chic phases of fashion design, the ideal fashion model is "cruel" Vala.

If we judge by Mario Praz' exploration of the "tormented, contaminated beauty" and "femme fatale" in western literature, this type of female seems— at least prior to Swinburne—to have been more extensively treated by French than by English writers.[13] Ste.-Beuve, Gautier, Baudelaire adore her. For Swinburne, she becomes the Venus of "Laus Veneris," Faustine, and Mary Stuart. But if we look earlier, she certainly figures in Jacobean drama, and in at least one play of Shakespeare's.

Late in *Jerusalem,* one of Vala's avatars has a warrior-lover whom she craves to possess completely. "O that I could live in his sight," she says; "O that I could bind him to my arm" (*J* 82.44). Concealing him under her veil, she wishes him to become "an infant love" at her breast. When she opens the veil, revealing "her own perfect beauty," her lover has become "a winding worm." Blake hopes at this moment to show that Female Will is ultimately self-defeating. The winding worm is a further degeneration of helpless infancy, so that her wish has come true beyond her intention, as in folktales. The worm is also the phallic worm (cf. Yeats' "Chambermaid's Song," where "Pleasure has made him / Weak as a worm") and the devouring worm of the grave. The parallel story is of course *Antony and Cleopatra*. There, too, Woman reduces Warrior to absurd infantile dependency, out of pure erotic possessiveness. She then dies by the instrument of a worm that she describes as an infant—"the baby at my breast / That sucks the nurse asleep (V.ii.308–309) and that she croons to as lover. Without the aid of Blake, we might not think to identify the asp in *Antony and Cleopatra* as the last essence of Antony himself. With Blake, the identification seems compelling. At the same time, with the aid of Shake-speare, we may see Vala more clearly as the fallen form of female desire.

As the individual characters of Zoas and Emanations differ, so do the plots of their reconciliations. Los-Enitharmon's begins earliest in *The Four Zoas,* and involves a channeling of their arrogant energy through suffering. Following the binding of Urizen they have sunk, exhausted, to their nadir, "shrunk into fixed space . . . Their senses unexpansive" (V.57.12–18). Re-demption starts with the painful birth of Orc, and the grief that follows the Los-Enitharmon-Orc Family Romance. Though repentance and sorrow over their mutual failure to free Orc are apparently useless, Enitharmon's heart-break (V.63.10–14) triggers a process of imaginative re-expansion and re-unification that continues through the complex episodes of Spectre-Shadow and Spectre-Los reunions (VIIa.81.7–86.14) and the "six thousand years of self denial and of bitter contrition" during which Los builds Golgonooza and Los and Enitharmon finally labor together as partners in the Art which gives regenerate form to all of life (VIIa.90.2–57). At the opening of Night IX "Los and Enitharmon builded Jerusalem weeping" and at no point thereafter are separated. In the final two pages the regenerate "dark Urthona" has reclaimed them both.

Reunion of the other Zoas and Emanations completes the Eternal Man's awakening and resumption of control over his warring "members." Ahania revives at the moment of Urizen's rejuvenation. She bursts with excess of joy, sleeps a winter and returns in spring as Kore, and finally takes her seat "by Urizen" (i.e., not enshrined) "in songs & joy." Next, when Orc's passion burns itself out, Albion takes the somewhat-charred Luvah and Vala in hand and admonishes them: "Luvah & Vala henceforth you are Servants obey & live" (IX.126.6). They enact their obedience first in the ensuing pastoral episode, with its idyllic evocation of a new Golden Age, and then in the Last Vintage, where human grapes are orgiastically crushed in the winepresses of Luvah. The episode concludes with Luvah and Vala described as a couple linked to the seasons; together they sleep, wake, and are "cast . . . thro the air till winter is over & gone" while the "Human Wine" they have made "stood wondering in all their delightful expanses" (IX.137.30–32). Finally Tharmas and Enion, first pair to be seen in collapse and last to be seen regenerate, also undergo a double transformation. They are initially reborn into Vala's garden as naive and wayward children, as befits their innocent character. But a fully renewed and humanized Enion and Tharmas embrace and are welcomed by the Eternal Man (IX.132.10–133.1) to the final feast.

For the Blake who conceived of humanity as androgynous, the division of Zoas from Emanations signified human disorder and disaster. His poetry describing sexual division is some of the most anguished in the language. By the same token, re-couplings precipitate and are accompanied by all the images for joy and order Blake knew: a seasonal cycle culminating in harvest, vintage and communal feast; a painful bread-making and wine-making which issues in happiness; music and "vocal harmony" concluding in human "conversing"; and a beaming morning sun.

To trace the lineaments of Blake number three, we must return to the very outset of the poet's career, and the extraordinary lyric "How sweet I roamed from field to field," where an unidentified winged speaker is lured and trapped by "the prince of love." The poem is in a quasi-Elizabethan diction, but with the swoon of eroticism and ecstatic surrender we associate with Keats. Keatsian too are the lushness and fertility of the natural setting, and the painful close:

> With sweet May dews my wings were wet,
>   And Phoebus fir'd my vocal rage;
> He caught me in his silken net,
>   And shut me in his golden cage.
> He loves to sit and hear me sing,
>   Then laughing, sports and plays with me;
> Then stretches out my golden wing,
>   And mocks my loss of liberty.

Un-Keatsian is the ambivalent gender of the speaker and the personification power of love as male not female. Although the theme of romantic enthrall-ment of a woman by a man is relatively unusual in English poetry, Irene H. Chayes argues convincingly that the speaker is Psyche and the manipulator of "silken net" and "golden cage" is Eros. [14]

But in later versions of this scenario, the instruments of entrapment and enclosure—net, cage, locked box—will be the sexually symbolic props of females who imprison males. "The Crystal Cabinet," "The Golden Net" and "The Mental Traveller" are all versions of this theme, and the "Woman Old" of the last of these is a brillant portrayal of the *vagina dentata* in action, for she torments male vitality simultaneously by nailing and piercing, and by bind-ing and catching. As if correcting his own earlier naiveté, one of Blake's *Notebook* poems asks rhetorically "Why was Cupid a Boy?" and answers that the illusion of a male Cupid who inflicts sexual suffering "was the Cupid Girls mocking plan," part of a scheme to keep real boys who "cant interpret the thing" unsuspecting while she shot them full of darts (E 470). Along similar lines, "My Spectre Around Me" envisages a war between the sexes dominated by female pride, scorn, jealousy and lust for "Victory" imaged as possession and enclosure: "Living thee alone Ill have / And when dead Ill be thy Grave." The solution is a Spectral threat of rejection and retaliation:

> Till I turn from Female Love
> And root up the Infernal Grove
> I shall never worthy be
> To step into Eternity

> And to end thy cruel mocks
> Annihilate thee on the rocks
> And another form create
> To be subservient to my fate.
> —(E 468)

This brings the Emanation round, for it is either she, or Emanation and Spectre in duet, who "agree to give up Love" for "the world of happy Eternity."

Among the engraved poems, "To Tirzah" is a furious repudiation of female sexuality in its maternal aspect as that which encloses and divides man from Eternity. To appreciate the impact of "To Tirzah" in its original context we should probably see it as the contrary poem to "A Cradle Song" in *Innocence*. Where in *Innocence* a mother sings lullingly to a sleeping infant of the "sweet" smiles and tears that Jesus as "an infant small" sheds and shares with herself and the child, in *Experience* the child responds, ironically using Jesus' adolescent rejection of Mary (John 2.4) for his punch line:

> Thou Mother of my mortal part
> With cruelty didst mould my Heart,
> And with false self-deceiving tears
> Didst bind my Nostrils Eyes & Ears.

> Didst close my Tongue in senseless clay
> And me to Mortal Life betray:
> The Death of Jesus set me free,
> Then what have I to do with thee?

A second strong repudiation is *Europe,* where erotic entrapment both maternal and sexual, the former expressing itself as possessive, the latter as seductive manipulation of male desire, takes place so that "Woman, lovely Woman! may have dominion" during the corrupt centuries of Enitharmon's reign. Here Enitharmon's "crystal house" is analogous to the crystal cabinet, and within it there is a constant claustrophobic movement of nocturnal binding, circling, cycling, broken only by the dawn of European revolution.

How well do these poems fit the Blake who praises "gratified Desire" and insists that "Energy is the only life and is from the body"? Rather poorly, I think. However allegorically we interpret the thing, sexual love in these poems is neither gratifying nor capable of gratification, and the poet consistently associates "sensual enjoyment" with cruelty, imprisonment, illusion and mortality instead of liberation, vision and immortality. Morton Paley has pointed out that Blake's Lambeth books involve "a sort of involuntary dualism, a myth with implications that in some ways conflicted with his own beliefs. Blake's intuition of the goodness of the body in general and of sexual love in particular had not weakened . . . but . . . the Lambeth myth seems to imply that physical life is inherently evil."[15] If, in other words, we have one Blake for whom physical life is type and symbol of spiritual life and fulfilled joy in one leads us to the other, there is also a Blake for whom body and spirit are as irreconcilably opposed as they are for any Church Father. But the contradiction is exacerbated rather than resolved in the later books, where the anatomical image of the enclosure vastly expands to become a whole world, the realm of Beulah, a dreamy moony place presided over by tender females, which is both comfort and trap.

To a fallen and depleted consciousness, Beulah is the source of poetry and our one hope of returning to Eden. The "Daughters of Beulah" are reliably compliant "Muses who inspire the Poets Song" or nurse-figures who comfort and protect the weary and distressed. That "Contrarieties are equally true" in Beulah makes it seem an obvious advance over single vision and Newton's sleep. Yet as another Crystal Cabinet writ large, Beulah inevitably means confinement, limitation, illusion. It can never mean Infinity. Where Eden is fourfold and human, Beulah is merely threefold and sexual, the vacation spot for beings who cannot sustain the strenuous mental excitement of Eden and need "repose":

> Into this pleasant shadow all the weak & weary
> Like Women & Children were taken away as on wings
> Of dovelike softness, & shadowy habitations prepared for them
> But every Man returnd & went still going forward thro'
> The Bosom of the Father in Eternity on Eternity.
> —(*M* 31.1–5)

Of the double potentialities of Beulah, benign yields to malign in successive works. In *The Four Zoas,* Beulah is purely protective. *Milton* begins to emphasize not only its pleasantness but also its delusiveness. In *Jerusalem,* where the Daughters of Beulah have been replaced as muses by a single male muse and lover, "the Saviour . . . dictating the words of his mild song," Blake firmly identifies "the lovely delusions of Beulah" (*J* 17.27) with the terrors of sexuality. Thus Vala, claiming precedence over the Savior, hypnotizes Albion with her concave allure and her usurped phallic power:

> The Imaginative Human Form is but a breathing of Vala
> I breathe him forth into the Heaven from my secret Cave
> Born of the Woman to obey the Woman O Albion the mighty
> For the Divine appearance is Brotherhood, but I am Love
> Elevate into the Region of Brotherhood with my red fires
> —(*J* 29.48–30.1)

Responding to Vala's triumph, Los laments:

> What may Man be? Who can tell! But what may Woman be?
> To have power over Man from Cradle to corruptible Grave.

> There is a Throne in every Man, it is the Throne of God
> This Woman has claim'd as her own & Man is no more! . . .
> O Albion why wilt thou Create a Female Will?
> To hide the most evident God in a hidden covert, even
> In the Shadows of a Woman & a secluded Holy Place
> —(*J* 30.25–33)

Beulah itself seems at fault, in Los's agonized cry:

> Humanity knows not of Sex: wherefore are sexes in Beulah?
> —(*J* 44.3)

And again, anticipating Keats's yearning description of a work of art "all breathing human passion far above," redeemed

> Humanity is far above
> Sexual organization; & the Visions of the Night of Beulah
> —(*J* 79.73–4)

For, as Blake in his own persona tells us, however tender and pleasant and full of "ever varying delights" the "time of love" passed in Beulah may be, where "every Female delights to give her maiden to her husband" and

> The Female searches sea & land for gratification to the
> Male Genius: who in return clothes her in gems & gold
> And feeds her with the food of Eden, hence all her beauty beams
> —(*J* 69.17–19)

Love in Beulah inevitably brings a depletion of energy and the advent of jealousies, murders, moral law, revenge, and the whole panoply of inhuman cruelties the poet has taught us to struggle against. In visionary contrast, Blake imagines a love that transcends sexuality because it is a mingling of male with male:

> I am in you & you in me, mutual in love divine:
> Fibres of love from man to man thro Albions pleasant land . . .
> I am not a God afar off, I am brother and friend;
> Within your bosoms I reside, and you reside in me.
> —(*J* 4.7–19)

Such is the opening promise of the Saviour, and if in Eternity "Embraces are Cominglings from the Head even to the Feet" (*J* 69.43), we well may wonder whether such embraces can ever occur between male and female. For if the Blake who celebrates desire sees it as equally distributed between genders, the Blake who fears desire sees sexuality in general and sexual threat in particular as a female phenomenon. This third Blake gives us an array, culminating in *Jerusalem,* of passive males subject to females who seduce, reject, betray, bind, lacerate, mock and deceive them. After *Visions of the Daughters of Albion,* though Blake continues strenuously to oppose the idea that woman's love is *sin,* he increasingly describes it as *snare.* There is no comparable depiction of males seducing and betraying females.

This brings me to Blake number four, who is perhaps not quite a classic misogynist—though he sometimes sounds like one—but someone who believes that the proper study of woman is the happiness of her man, and who cannot conceive of a true woman in any but a supportive, subordinate role. In the margin of his 1789 edition of Lavater's *Aphorisms on Man,* Blake wrote, "Let the men do their duty & the women will be such wonders, the female life lives from the light of the male, see a mans female dependents, you know the man" (E 585). Females, in other words, may be wonders, but only if men are: and to be female is to be dependent.

Examining Blake from this point of view, and returning to *Visions,* we notice that Oothoon is good, and she is wise, but she is completely powerless. So long as her menfolk refuse enlightenment, she will be bound hand and foot, imprisoned in a passivity which she does not desire but to which she must submit. Looking at *The Four Zoas,* we see that Enion and Ahania are likewise good—indeed, they represent precisely the goodness of selfless love and compassion—but passive, while Enitharmon and Vala are active and evil. In *Milton* and *Jerusalem* the story is the same: female figures are either powerful or good; never both. The late prophecies may even constitute a retreat from the point Blake arrived at in *Visions,* for the better the late females are, the more passive, the more submissive and obedient they also are.[16] When Ololon finds Milton, she tearfully apologizes for being the cause of Natural Religion. And when Milton concludes his splendid final speech on "Self-annihilation and the grandeur of Inspiration" with a peroration against the "Sexual Garments, the Abomination of Desolation," Ololon responds by dividing into the sixfold Virgin who dives "into the depths / Of Miltons Shadow as a Dove upon the stormy sea" and a "moony Ark" who enters into the fires of intellect

> Around the Starry Eight: with one accord the Starry Eight became
> One Man Jesus the Saviour. Wonderful! round his limbs
> The Clouds of Ololon folded as a Garment dipped in blood
> —(M 42.9–11)

At the climax of *Jerusalem* there is a similar self-immolative plunge when "England" awakes on Albion's bosom. Having blamed herself for being "the Jealous Wife" who has caused all the troubles of the poem:

England who is Brittania enterd Albions bosom rejoicing
Rejoicing in his indignation! adoring his wrathful rebuke.
She who adores not your frowns will only loathe your smiles
—(*J* 95.22–4)

But this somewhat gratuitous-seeming passage lacks—since we have not met "England" until now—the systematic quality of Blake's treatment of his chief heroine.

The poet's final and most fully-idealized heroine "is named Liberty among the sons of Albion" (*J* 26.3–4), yet we seriously mistake Blake's intention if we think Jerusalem is herself a free being, or even a being capable of volition. She is the City of God, bride of Christ, and man's Christian Liberty, to be sure, but that is only in Eden, and even there she does not act; she simply is. What happens to Jerusalem within the body of the poem at no point involves her in action or in protest. At its outset she is withheld by Albion from "the vision & fruition of the Holy-one" (*J* 4.17) and is accused of sin by Albion and Vala. Unlike Oothoon she does not deny the accusation, nor does she defend her own vision with anything like Oothoon's exuberance. Patiently, meekly, she explains and begs Love and Forgiveness from her enemies. That is her last initiative. Subsequently she is rejected as a whore, cast out, imprisoned, driven finally to insanity, and becomes wholly incapable even of remembering her original self without being reminded of her origins by the voice of her pitying and merciful God. Even this comfort does not help; for at the poem's darkest moment, just before the advent of the Covering Cherub, Jerusalem passively receives a cup of poison from the conquering Vala (*J* 88.56).

The final movement of *Jerusalem* evokes its heroine twice, when "the Universal Father" speaking through "the vision of Albion" echoes the Song of Solomon:

Awake! Awake Jerusalem! O lovely Emanation of Albion
Awake and overspread all Nations as in Ancient Time
For lo! the Night of Death is past and the Eternal Day
Appears upon our hills: Awake Jerusalem, and come away
—(*J* 97.1–4)

and when the poet's vision of "All Human Forms" is complete:

And I heard the Name of their Emanations they are named Jerusalem
—(*J* 99.5)

Yet however amorous, however reverential our attitude toward this "persecuted maiden"[17] redeemed, we do not and cannot encounter the "awakened" Jerusalem directly. As *A Vision of the Last Judgment* explicitly tells us, and as the whole of *Jerusalem* implies, "In Eternity Woman is the Emanation of Man; she has no Will of her own. There is no such thing in Eternity as a Female Will" (E 552). If we wonder what the Emanative role in Eternity is, Blake has already told us:

> When in Eternity Man converses with Man, they enter
> Into each other's Bosom (which are universes of delight)
> In mutual interchange, and first their Emanations meet . . .
> For Man cannot unite with Man but by their Emanations . . .
> —(*J* 88.3–9)

Is femaleness, then, ideally a kind of social glue? Susan Fox argues that although "in his prophetic poems Blake conceives of a perfection of humanity defined by the complete mutuality of its interdependent genders," he nevertheless in these same poems "represents one of these equal genders as inferior and dependent . . . or as unnaturally and disastrously dominant," so that females come to represent either "weakness" or "power-hunger."[18] Anne Mellor has observed that Blake's ideal males throughout the major prophecies are creative and independent while his ideal females "at their best are nurturing . . . generous . . . compassionate . . . all welcoming and never-critical emotional supporters," and that "in Blake's metaphoric system, the masculine is both logically and physically prior to the feminine."[19] But at its most extreme, Blake's vision goes beyond proposing an ideal of dominance-submission or priority-inferiority between the genders. As a counter-image to the intolerable idea of female power, female containment and "binding" of man to mortal life, Blake wishfully imagines that the female can be reabsorbed by the male, be contained within him, and exist Edenically not as a substantial being but as an attribute. Beyond the wildest dreams of Lévi-Strauss, the ideal female functions as a medium of interchange among real, that is to say male, beings.

And what are we as readers to make of Blake's contradictions?[20] Morris Dickstein, noting the shift from the "feminism" of *Visions* to his later stress on "female Will," calls it "a stunning change that seems rooted less in politics than in the nearly unknown terrain of Blake's personal life."[21] Diana George believes that Blake became entrapped in a culturally mandated sexual typology which he initially intended to "redeem."[22] Although all our anecdotal material about the Blakes indicates that Catherine adored her visionary husband even when he was not bringing home the bacon, much less adorning her in gems and gold, marital friction looks like a reasonable source for many *Notebook* and other poems. Perhaps, too, Blake had a model for Oothoon in Mary Wollstonecraft, whose vigorous equal may not have been encountered in his other female acquaintances after Wollstonecraft's death.[23] At the same time, we should recognize that the shift in Blake's sexual views coincides with other ideological and doctrinal transformations: from a faith in political revolution perhaps assisted or exemplified by Art to a faith in Imagination as that which alone could prepare humanity for its harvest and vintage; for what looks like a love of nature that makes him one of the great pastoral poets in the English language and extends as far as *Milton,* to a growing and finally absolute rejection of nature and all fleshly things; and from an immanent to a transcendent God.

Yet to say that Blake's views moved from X to Y would be an absurd oversimplification. It would be truer to say that X and Y were with him always—like his Saviour—in varying proportions, and that the antagonism between them is the life of his poetry. One of the idols of our tribe is System, a Blakean term signifying a set of ideas bounded by an adhesive inflexible consistency, cognate of the "bounded" which its possessor soon loathes, the "Circle" that any sensible God or Man should avoid, and the "mill with complicated wheels." If "Unity is the cloke of Folly" in a work of art, we might make it our business as critics not only to discover, but also to admire, a large poet's large inconsistencies—particularly in an area like the meaning of sex, where the entire culture, and probably each of us, in the shadows of our chambers, feels profound ambivalence.

If "without contraries is no progression," I think we should be neither surprised nor dismayed to find in Blake both a richly developed anti-patriarchal and proto-feminist semsibility, in which love between the sexes serves as a metaphor for psychic wholeness, integrity, and more abundant life, and its opposite, a homocentric gynophobia in which heterosexual love means human destruction.[24] "If the doors of perception were cleansed every-thing would appear to man as it is, infinite." What then if we concede that Blake's vision, at least part of the time, was fogged to the degree that he could perceive Man as infinite but could not perceive Woman as equally so? Blake understood that it is impossible for any prophet finally to transcend historical time. He understood so of Isaiah and Ezekiel, he understood the same of John Milton. "To give a Body to Error" was, he believed, an essential service performed by mighty intellects for posterity. We might, with grati-tude for this way of comprehending great poetry, see him as he saw his precursors. To paraphrase Emerson and the *Gita,* when him we fly, he is our wings.

Notes

1. Northrop Frye, *Fearful Symmetry* (Princeton: Princeton Univ. Press, 1947), p. 14.

2. Quotations are from David V. Erdman, ed., *The Poetry and Prose of William Blake* (New York: Doubleday, 1970).

3. I am disagreeing at this point with Morris Dickstein's otherwise excellent essay, "The Price of Experience: Blake's Reading of Freud" in *The Literary Freud,* ed. Joseph Smith (New Haven: Yale Univ. Press, 1980), pp. 67–111. Dickstein (pp. 95–96) sees "The Garden of Love" as "angry polemical simplification," arguing that the speaker "thinks of repression in

terms of a very simple etiology: *They* have done it to him," and that there is no question of "delusion or projection" here. A persuasive reading of the poem's Oedipal dimension is in Diana George, *Blake and Freud* (Ithaca: Cornell Univ. Press, 1980), pp. 104–106.

4. For a harrowing account of the phenomenon of the youthful harlot in nineteenth-century England, see Florence Rush, *The Best-Kept Secret: Sexual Abuse of Children* (Englewood Cliffs, N.J.: Prentice-Hall, 1980), ch. 5.

5. W. H. Auden, "Psychoanalysis and Art To-day" (1935), in *The English Auden*, ed. Edward Mendelson (New York: Random House, 1977), p. 339.

6. Analysis of Freud's rationalist and scientific pessimism, versus Blake's imaginative and artistic optimism, is a primary theme in *Blake and Freud*, which argues that in other respects the two men's diagnoses of western man's psychosexual ills were close to identical. Politically of course Freud remained conservative; the close parallels between Blake and Reich as radical psycho-political thinkers are discussed in Eliot Katz, "Blake, Reich and *Visions of the Daughters of Albion*," unpub.

7. *The Centenary Edition of the Works of Nathaniel Hawthorne*, vol. 1 (Ohio State Univ. Press, 1962), p. 263.

8. C. G. June, "Archetypes of the Collective Unconscious," *Collected Works*, ed. Herbert Read, Michael Fordham, Gerhard Adler and W. McGuire, trans. R. F. C. Hull, Bollingen Series (Princeton: Princeton Univ. Press, Bollingen Series XX, 1967–78), vol. 9, part 1, p. 27. Jung also discusses the anima and the anima-animus "sacred marriage" in "Two Essays on Analytical Psychology" (vol. 7) and "Aion: Researches into the Phenomenology of the Self" (vol. 9, part 2). Among his less predictable parallels to Blake is Jung's idea that the anima-animus marriage is always accompanied and completed by the figure of a Wise Old Man— who I am ready to presume is "Old" in the same sense that Albion is an "Ancient" Man; i.e., he is Urmensch, not elderly. Among the critics who identify anima with emanation are June Singer, *The Unholy Bible: A Psychological Interpretation of William Blake* (New York: Putnam, 1970), p. 212, and W. P. Witcutt, *Blake: A Psychological Study* (Port Washington, N.Y.: Kennikat Press, 1946), pp. 43ff. Christine Gallant, in *Blake and the Assimilation of Chaos* (Princeton: Princeton Univ. Press, 1978) disagrees, arguing that although "the anima in Jungian psychology is a personification in a symbol, or in an actual human being, of those aspects of his unconscious of which a man is most ignorant, usually his emotional, irrational qualities," Blake's emanations are not animae because "if they were . . . they would have characteristics as differentiated as those of their Zoas" (pp. 53–54). It is my contention that they do. Although Jung in general diverges from both Freud and Blake in uncoupling psychological issues from socio-historic ones, he departs from Freud and coincides with Blake in at least three major respects: his insistence on the validity of spirituality in human life, his belief in a collective unconscious, and his relatively non-phallocentric exploration of female identity.

9. That Deucalion-Pyrrha and the Noahs are flood-survivors who renew the human race, and that the fallen Tharmas-Enion are identified with water and Tharmas in Night III struggles to take on Man's form, is a coincidence I do not pretend to understand but feel obliged to notice. My *primary* point here is that these couples are all parental, and all naive. The relation of Dickens' Gargeries to Tharmas and Enion seems to me particularly charming in that Joe Gargery is rather a perfect Tharmas throughout, but is given two wives by Dickens—as it were to parallel the quarrelsome and the redeemed Enion.

10. Gallant (p. 54) notes the Poseidon-Demeter/Tharmas-Enion parallel (another coincidence) and points out that the questing Demeter disguised herself as an old woman.

11. See, for example, Mary Daly, *Beyond God the Father* (Boston: Beacon Press, 1973), Marcia Landy, "The Silent Woman," in *The Authority of Experience*, ed. Arlyn Diamond and Lee Edwards (Amherst: Univ. of Massachusetts Press, 1977), Susan Griffin, *Woman and Nature: The Roaring Inside Her* (New York: Harper and Row, 1978), Sandra M. Gilbert and Susan Gubar, *The Madwoman in the Attic* (New Haven: Yale Univ. Press, 1980), chaps. 1 and 2. The

contention of these and other feminist writers in America, England and France is that western religion and philosophy, by consistently associating power and authority with masculinity, have deprived women of access to authoritative speech and muted their ability to "voice" female experience authentically. The critique of rationalism in such works for the most part tallies very well with Blake's.

12. Ophelia's selfless "O what a noble mind is here o'erthrown" speech nicely resembles Ahania's memory of "those sweet fields of bliss / Where liberty was justice & eternal science was mercy" (*FZ* III.39.12–13). Later, when Hamlet has rejected her and slain her father (cf. Urizen's rejection of Ahania and his defiance of Albion), Ophelia's "speech is nothing." Both Ophelia and Gretchen, of course, express profound admiration for their lovers' intellects.

13. Mario Praz, *The Romantic Agony* (1933; rpt. Cleveland: World Publishing Co., 1956) pp. 28ff, 189ff. Among Praz' many valuable observations is a remark on Ste.-Beuve which is particularly relevant to the Vala-Jerusalem relationship: "Whenever it happens that a writer feels admiration for [female] passionate energy—particularly if this energy have fatal results . . . it is always the diabolical . . . who ends by occupying the whole stage and causing her angelic rival . . . to appear a mere shadow" (p. 191).

14. Irene H. Chayes, "The Presence of Cupid and Psyche," in *Blake's Visionary Forms Dramatic,* ed. David V. Erdman and John E. Grant (Princeton: Princeton Univ. Press, 1970), pp. 214–43.

15. Morton D. Paley, *Energy and the Imagination: A Study of the Development of Blake's Thought* (Oxford: Clarendon Press, 1970), p. 90.

16. A partial exception is the prophetic figure of Erin in *Jerusalem,* yet in a sense Erin is an exception that proves the rule; for though her voice is inspirational without passivity or subordination, she remains undeveloped as a character, lacking the internal struggles and self-transformations of the other major figures in the poem.

17. The term is from Praz, who suggests Clarissa and Sade's Justine as two examples of the type.

18. Susan Fox, "The Female as Metaphor in William Blake's Poetry," *Critical Inquiry* 5 (Spring 1977), 507.

19. Anne K. Mellor, "Blake's Portrayal of Women," in *Blake/An Illustrated Quarterly* 16.3 (Winter 1982–83), pp. 148–155.

20. For some readers, of course, no contradiction worth noticing exists. Consider, for example, the following: "Some modern women may have much to object to in Blake's latest thought about the relations between the sexes. But it is hard to believe that *l'homme moyen sensuel* would reject the hearty bread and fullbodied wine the late Blake is offering him. Or his wife either, for that matter: 'let men do their duty & the women will be such wonders.' " Such is Jean Hagstrum's pleasant conclusion in "Babylon Revisited, or the Story of Luvah and Vala," in *Blake's Sublime Allegory: Essays on The Four Zoas, Milton and Jerusalem,* ed. Stuart Curran and Joseph Anthony Wittreich, Jr., (Madison: Univ. of Wisconsin Press, 1973), p. 118. David Aers, in "William Blake and the Dialectic of Sex," *ELH* 44 (1977), 500–14, feels that in *Visions* Blake "may have slipped toward an optimistic, idealistic illusion in his handling of Oothoon's consciousness. The illusion lies in assuming that revolutionary consciousness can ever be as uncontaminated by dominant structures and ideologies as Oothoon's appears to be" (p. 505). By stressing female will in later poems, Blake "is casting out the vestiges of optimistic delusions," having discovered that "it is utopian and undialectical to imagine a female consciousness like Oothoon's" (p. 507). Since Aers does not seem to reflect that Oothoon's inventor himself must have been as "uncontaminated" as his invention, and that Los in *Jerusalem* seems likewise, I take Aers' position to be that we can believe in a male uncontaminated consciousness but that it is undialectical to believe in a female one.

21. Dickstein, pp. 77–78.

22. *Blake and Freud,* chap. 6, includes this argument in a larger discussion of Blake's treatment of "the feminine."

23. See Alicia Ostriker, "Todd, *Wollstonecraft Anthology*," *Blake/An Illustrated Quarterly* 14 (1980–81), 129–31.

24. The mirror image of this view appears in a number of contemporary lesbian feminist works. See, for example, Griffin, pp. 207–27.

[From *Blake's Composite Art*]

W. J. T. MITCHELL

[*Ed. note:* In the illustrations following this essay, referred to by bracketed numbers in Mitchell's text, copies of illuminated books are identified by the letter assigned to them in the Erdman-Keynes *Census*. Plate numbers follow Erdman, *The Illuminated Blake.*]

It has become superfluous to argue that Blake's poems need to be read with their accompanying illustrations. Almost everyone would now agree with Northrop Frye's remark that Blake perfected a "radical form of mixed art," a "composite art" which must be read as a unity.[1] It is not superfluous, however, to ask in what precise sense Blake's poems "need" their illustrations, and vice versa. Neither element of Blake's illuminated books is unintelligible or uninteresting without the support of the other. Indeed, a notable feature of the history of Blake's reputation has been the extraordinary success which his paintings and poems have enjoyed without the mutual support of one another. For over a century Blake's admirers had a truncated view of his art, some admiring the bust, others the torso, all finding a sufficient aesthetic unity in the fragment they beheld. This suggests that Blake's poems do not need their illustrations in the same sense that Wagner's libretti need their musical settings to be aesthetically successful. It suggests that his composite art is, to some extent, *not* an indissoluble unity, but an interaction between two vigorously independent modes of expression. "When a Work has Unity," Blake reminds us, "it is as much in a Part as in the Whole. the Torso is as much a Unity as the Laocoon" ("On Homer's Poetry," E 267).

Suzanne Langer has argued that this sort of composite art is impossible, that "there are no happy marriages in art—only successful rape."[2] Her argument must be borne in mind by anyone who would ravish one of Blake's art forms for the sake of elucidating the other. Langer suggests that the juxtaposition of two art forms always results in the absorption of one form into the other, poetry being subordinated to musical values in song, musical values subordinated to visual considerations in ballet. A picture hanging on the wall in a set for *Man and Superman* is not seen as an aesthetic object in its own right, but is absorbed into the dramatic illusion. Similarly, an illustrated book tends to become either a portable picture gallery with running captions or a literary text with attendant illustrations. The historical fact that Blake's illuminated books have been read in *both* of these ways strongly suggests that his composite art is an exception to Langer's rule, a successful marriage of two aesthetically independent art forms.

This is not to say that the partnership is equal or harmonious on every plate of Blake's illuminated books. There are many individual instances of the subordination of one mode to the demands of the other. Many of Blake's visual images move toward the realm of language, operating as arbitrary signs, emblems, or hieroglyphics which denote the unseeable, rather than as "natural" representations: an eagle is "a portion of Genius" and a serpent may symbolize nature as a whole.[3] Similarly, the text sometimes derives its coherence not primarily from its verbal order, but from the series of pictures for which it provides titles, as in *The Gates of Paradise* series. In general, however, neither the graphic nor the poetic aspect of Blake's composite art assumes consistent predominance: their relationship is more like an energetic rivalry, a dialogue or dialectic between vigorously independent modes of expression.

I. VISUAL-VERBAL DIALECTICS

The most obvious manifestation of the independence of design from text is the presence of illustrations which do not illustrate. The figure of a young man carrying a winged child on his head in the frontispiece to *Songs of Experience* [1], for instance, is mentioned nowhere in the *Songs,* nor for that matter anywhere else in Blake's writings. In the absence of explicit textual associations we are forced, I would suggest, to concentrate on the picture *as a picture in the world of pictures,* rather than seeing it as a visual translation of matters already dealt with in words. We have to look at the picture's expressive content, "reading" facial expressions, bodily gestures, and details for their innate significance, and we tend to see it not in relation to words but in the context of other, similar compositions both in and out of Blake's *œuvre.* It is inevitable, of course, that this concentration on the picture as picture will move over into the world of verbal language at some point—the moment, in fact, that we begin to articulate an interpretation, or the moment that we encounter a related composition that *does* have an explicit verbal equivalent.[4] The mysterious figure carrying the cherub has an obvious pictorial relative, the figure looking up at a child on a cloud in the frontispiece to *Songs of Innocence* [2]. And this latter composition *does* have an explicit verbal equivalent: it serves as an illustration to the song of the Piper "piping down the valleys wild" and seeing a child on a cloud, the introductory poem to *Songs of Innocence.* We cannot, however, make a direct verbal translation of the frontispiece to *Experience* from the Piper's song by way of the intermediate association of the picture of the Piper. It is clear that the two frontispieces function not just as companion pieces with similar compositions but as "contraries" whose differences are as important as their similarities. Any words we find to describe the frontispiece to *Experience* will have to involve transformations and reversals of the language discovered in the poem and illustration which introduce *Songs of Innocence*.

This process of transformation goes on quite unobtrusively and perhaps unconsciously whenever we interpret a problematic illustration in Blake's illuminated books. It is generally assumed without question that since the frontispiece to *Innocence* clearly depicts the Piper, the frontispiece to *Experience* must depict the analogous figure in the latter group of poems, the Bard whose voice is heard in the opening poems to *Songs of Experience*. This assumption seems wholly justified, but it is important for us to remember that it is not directly "given" by the text or its illustrations, but must be arrived at by a series of associations transformations, and creative inferences. And once this initial inference has been made, the problem of interpretation has only begun. We must then account for other transformations suggested by a comparison of the two frontispieces: in one the child floats without the aid of wings on a cloud above the Piper; in the other the child has wings and yet must be carried by the Bard. The Piper looks up at the child, his setting an enclosed grove of trees; the Bard looks straight ahead, backed by a vista of open fields. The significance of these contrasts may not strike us as terribly complex, but the process by which we arrive at that significance is rather involved and it entails a good deal more than simple matching or translating of visual signs into verbal.

The creative inferences involved in reading this sort of picture are multiplied when we make associations in pictorial realms outside of Blake's own art. The Bard carrying the child is rather similar, for instance, to representations of St. Christopher carrying the Christ-child across the river, a theme which Blake and his readers could have seen in many English churches and in the works of European masters such as Dürer [3].[5] The implication that the child on the Bard's head is Christ is certainly consistent with the symbolism of *Songs of Innocence and Experience,* and it introduces a whole new set of verbal associations to be found in the legends of St. Christopher, the saint who, according to Jacobus de Voragine, is not only the "Christ-bearer," but "hast . . . borne all the world" upon his shoulders.[6] For some readers the allusion might evoke the popular image of the patron of travelers (English folk belief had it that anyone who saw St. Christopher's image in a church could not die that day),[7] giving the Bard a kind of protective significance, as guide and guardian in the approaching journey through the dangerous world of Experience. The allusion would thus reinforce the contrast with the carefree, wandering figure of the Piper, who is blissfully unaware of the road ahead and need not carry his Christ-child muse as a burden.

For readers more deeply versed in the lore of St. Christopher more complex intersections with Blake's imagery would emerge. St. Christopher was called "reprobus" (reprobate or outcast) before his conversion, a striking analogue to Blake's later description of the prophetic Bard as an angry

"Reprobate" crying in the wilderness.[8] Disparities between Blake's frontis-piece and the saint's iconography also invite transformational inferences: Blake's Bard carries his child on his head rather than in the traditional place, on the shoulders, perhaps a way of stressing the suggestion in *The Golden Legend* that the burden of Christ's weight is mental rather than physical.[9] The presence of wings on the child (something that never occurs in traditional representations of the Christ-child), and the ironic contrast between this weighty cherub and the weightless but unwinged child of the Piper may suggest sinister overtones: Geoffrey Keynes sees the winged child as a "Covering Cherub," an image of what Blake called the Selfhood, that burden of alienated consciousness which emerges in the state of Experience.[10] In this reading, our Bard/St. Christopher may begin to resemble Christian of *Pilgrim's Progress,* whose burden is his own sense of guilt, depicted in Blake's illustrations to Bunyan as a childlike form swaddled in a fleshy bundle that grows from Christian's back and shoulders [4]. This darker reading of the winged child is not really incompatible with our earlier association of the child with Christ; it serves rather as a way of complicating the image, and rendering what Blake saw as the ambiguity of the poet's relation to his own inspiration in the state of Experience. Unlike the Piper, the Bard must carry the weight of his inspiration (or perhaps hold it down to prevent it from flying away), and he has to watch where he is going. The burden of Christian prophecy is, for Blake, inseparable from the burden of the Selfhood, and its weight, as he was to suggest in a later sketch in the pages of *The Four Zoas* [5], is equivalent to the weight of the world, the burden of Atlas.

The absence of direct illustrative function in the frontispiece to *Experience* allows the picture to be experienced as the focus for an invisible text compounded from a wide range of verbal and visual associations. While these associations involve creative inferences and transformations, they are any-thing but "free" in the sense of random, arbitrary, or capricious: the test of their validity is their coherence and adequacy in returning us to our point of departure, the picture itself, with a more precise and comprehensive sense of its significance. A more discriminating and lengthy analysis would differenti-ate between historically probable "meanings" and the more open realm of "significance" (Blake could not have "meant" in 1794 to link his Bard figure with his later drawing of Atlas in *The Four Zoas,* but the figure could have assumed that significance for him at a later date).[11] The crucial element in either kind of reading is the demand for creative participation. It is almost as if there were a missing poem that Blake could have written to go with this picture. By refusing to supply this poem, he challenges us to fill the void, and places us in a position analogous to that of his Bard/St. Christopher, making us work for our meanings rather than passively receive them as we do in the frontispiece to *Innocence.* The Bard is thus an emblem not only of the poet but of the reader in the state of Experience, and a full encounter with the picture is not just a glimpse through the window into Blake's world, but a look at ourselves in the mirror he provides.

The wealth of independent, nonillustrative pictorial significance which Blake can deposit in a given design is, of course, most obvious in "illustrations which do not illustrate," and the frontispiece to *Experience* is a kind of limiting example of how far this process can go. But other, subtler kinds of visual-verbal independence and interplay occur—as, for instance, when Blake plays text and design off against one another, an effect rather like counterpoint in music, or, more precisely, like the interaction of image and sound in cinema. In plate 8 of *America* [6], for example, the text begins with the words "The terror answered: I am Orc, wreath'd round the accursed tree" (8:I, E 52), printed on a cloud bank which hangs over the sea. Seated on this cloud bank, however, we find not the youthful Orc but the aged Urizen, or his political equivalent, Albion's Angel. For a moment Orc's voice seems to emerge from the figure of his aged antagonist. This effect lasts only a moment, however, for Orc's voice goes on to describe how "Urizen perverted to ten commands" the "fiery joy" of human energy (8:3), and we begin to see the design at the top of the page as an image not of the speaker but of the speaker's *vision*. We are invited, in other words, to see Urizen through Orc's eyes by his presence as an invisible narrator-commentator on the image before us.

Two plates later in *America* [7] a similar effect occurs: the text, printed among flames which wash up the page, begins, "Thus wept the Angel voice & as he wept the terrible blasts / Of trumpets, blew a loud alarm across the Atlantic deep"—lines which evoke the seascape of *America* 8 with its "angelic" aged Urizen on the bank of clouds. But the picture now shows Orc, not Urizen or Albion's Angel, and the accompanying voice belongs not to one of the characters but to the omniscient narrator of the poem, Blake himself, describing the "perturbation" of Albion's Thirteen Angels as they sit in their Atlantic kingdom. Why does Blake couple his vision of Orc with a verbal description of Orc's apparent opposites, Albion's Angels? The answer comes at the top of the very next plate: "Fiery the Angels rose, & as they rose deep thunder roll'd / Around their shores: indignant burning with the fires of Orc" (*A* II: 1–2). What we have witnessed in the orchestration of this series of texts and designs is a kind of cinematic transformation or conversion. The angel has become a devil (a conversion that Blake presents in a narrative fashion in plate 24 of *The Marriage of Heaven and Hell*). The cold, oppressive, aged figure of plate 8 has become the flaming youth of plate 10, a transformation which can be seen even more dramatically if one superimposes mentally (or with film transparencies) the "lineaments" of one figure over the other. The aged figure can then be made to "dissolve" into his youthful counterpart, and vice versa. The effect is a kind of counterpoint in which each medium proceeds with its own independent formal integrity, while interacting with the other to form a complex, unified whole.

In Blake's longer books he employs a technique of maintaining the independence of design from text which Northrop Frye has called "syncopation"—the placement of a design at a considerable distance from its best textual reference point. [12] In general, however, this sort of syncopation is achieved not by physical distance but by the introduction of iconographic disparities which complicate and attenuate our equations of text and design. Blake invites us, for instance, to see the title page of *The Marriage of Heaven and Hell* [8] as an "illustration" of the textual episode on plate 24 near the end of the book, the conversion of the angel into a devil. And yet he complicates this equation with a number of disparities: (1) the textual devil and angel seem to be males, while the pictured figures look female, or (in some copies) sexually ambiguous; (2) the text describes a single conversation followed by a self-immolation, while the design depicts a sexual encounter followed by a flight (if we can infer that the couple in the foreground will soon join the others floating up the center of the page); (3) none of the other details in the design refers directly to the scene of conversion related in plate 24, particularly the figures arranged along the "ground line" at the top of the page. These disparities produce a metaphorical richness which multiplies the independent complexities of text and design: conversation becomes copulation, immolation becomes flight, single conversion becomes catalyst for mass resurrection. [13]

The most interesting feature of the title page to the *Marriage* is that Blake manages to play upon all these metaphoric lines while keeping the design a simple and direct evocation of the book's central theme, the interaction of contraries. Every aspect of the composition—the strong contrasts of color and shape of flames and clouds, the thrust and recoil of the opposed trees at the top of the page, the aggressive inward thrust of the devil versus the receptive outward pose of the angel—is designed to embody the encounter of active and passive contraries. These contraries are seen not as they are perceived by the religious, as categories of good and evil (Blake employs none of the conventional imagery of horns, tails, wings, or halos to distinguish devil from angel), but as mutually "necessary to Human existence" (*MHH* 3). This does not mean that they are presented in an absolutely symmetrical balance, however. Blake clearly sides with the devils in the text because he sees the history of his culture as the deification of the angelic virtues of rational passivity and self-restraint. Thus, despite the theoretical and representational equality of devils and angels, the thrust of the design cuts diagonally across the page rather than vertically down the middle, tipping the balance of the composition in favor of the devil's party. And in one detail at least, this implicit preference verges on overt satire: on the ground line, the left (devil's) side shows a harmonious vision of the sexes, a couple walking beneath the trees, while the right side displays an inharmonious "di-vision" in the figure of a young man playing a musical instrument, apparently unable to stir a reclining female out of her bored passivity. [14]

The independence of Blake's text and designs, then, allows him to introduce independent symbolic statements, to suggest ironic contrasts and transformations, and to multiply metaphorical complexities. The most important kind of independence to watch for, however, is found not where the picture clearly departs from or contradicts the text, but in cases where the design seems nothing more than a literal illustration. The second illustration to "The Little Black Boy" in *Songs of Innocence,* for instance, seems to be a merely literal rendering of the concluding stanzas:

> When I from black and he from white cloud free,
> And round the tent of God like lambs we joy:
>
> Ill shade him from the heat till he can bear,
> To lean in joy upon our fathers knee.
> And then I'll stand and stroke his silver hair,
> And be like him and he will then love me.

The design shows a white boy leaning on the knee of a shepherd Christ, the black boy standing behind him to "stroke his silver hair" [9]. The details not mentioned in the text, such as the flock of sheep in the background or the willow tree (emblem of paradise), do not introduce complications, but are predictable features of the heavenly state which the black boy envisions. And yet this design is not simply an imitation of the text, but introduces its own symbolic dimensions. Blake seems to be making a pictorial allusion to the theme of a guardian angel presenting a human soul to God, as treated in the seventeenth-century emblem book *Amoris Divini Emblemata* by Otto von Veen (Vaenius) [10].[15]

This allusion completes the transformation in consciousness which is only implicit in the text: the black boy's emerging sense that despite his lessons in racial self-hatred ("I am black, but O! my soul is white"), he is equal and even superior to the English boy because he has had to suffer (ironically referred to as "bearing the beams of love"). Whereas the poem begins with the English boy "white as an angel" and the black boy in a fallen, damned condition ("bereav'd of light"), the design presents a near—but not total—reversal of roles. The black boy is now the angel who has absorbed and been refined by God's light and heat, and the white boy has, in a sense, been "bereav'd of light" in that he has not yet learned to bear the beams of love. Thus the design puts him in the position of the lost soul who has been rescued by his black "guardian angel." Even without the added dimension provided by its design, "The Little Black Boy" is a great poem, but it is a great fragment whose unity is part of a larger whole produced by its interaction with a design that has its own independent symbolic integrity.

The most pervasive kind of rivalry between text and design in Blake's illuminated books is simply the matter of conflicting aesthetic appeals. To open one of Blake's books is to be confronted with two equally compelling art forms, each clamoring for primary attention. Frye suggests that in some books this contest is clearly won by one art (text in *The Marriage of Heaven and Hell,* design in *Urizen*), but that in general Blake moves toward a balance of pictorial and poetic elements.[16] I suspect, however, that there are many readers like myself who find it difficult to read Blake's text in his illuminated books with any extended concentration. This difficulty must have been felt by contemporaries of Blake such as Dawson Turner, who despite what Blake considered "the Loss of some of the best things" asked for separate prints from the Lambeth books without their texts.[17] The difficulty arises in part from occasional illegibility and frequent smallness of print, from the distraction continually offered by rather striking designs, and from a tendency of readers to take the line of least interpretive resistance. Blake's pictures may contain "mythological and recondite meaning, where more is meant than meets the eye" (*DC,* E 522), but they are also clear and distinct pictures *of* something. His text makes fewer concessions to the "corporeal eye" and is thus most readily grasped, as a text, in a form where it can be underlined, annotated, and easily read. The total effect is rather like that of one of those medieval illuminated bibles, a *biblia pauperum* which provides us visionary paupers and illiterates with something to feed our imaginations.

Northrop Frye has remarked that the independence of Blake's designs from his words is rather surprising in view of the prevailing conventions within which he worked. The tradition of historical painting, Frye argues, tended to dictate a slavish fidelity to the text, and the naïve allegories of the emblem books were generally "an attempt to simplify the verbal meaning."[18] Blake's departures from these traditions have too often been explained, however, by recourse to value judgments and odious comparisons.[19] Not all the allegories were naïve, and history painting had its masterpieces. Blake's departures from traditional ways of connecting poetry and painting cannot, I would suggest, be understood simply as an improvement in the quality of his use of the two modes of expression. In the eighteenth century the idea of relating the "sister arts" of painting and poetry had become grafted to aesthetic concepts which were in many ways alien to Blake's philosophy of art. In order to understand his stylistic departures from these conventions we need to compare the assumptions that lay behind them with Blake's own understanding of the purposes of art, and of the nature of composite art in particular.

II. BLAKE AND THE TRADITION OF THE SISTER ARTS

It is probably an exaggeration of Blake's originality and uniqueness to say that his composite art has "scarcely a parallel in modern culture."[20] Blake seems so original because—to invoke Eliot's paradox in "Tradition and the Individual Talent"—he is so deeply traditional. His art is not reducible to the conventions of manuscript illuminations, the emblem, the *impresa,* the book of icons, or other forms of book illustration, because he is capable of using any and all of these forms when it suits his purpose. But he does not seem particularly eclectic in the loose sense: there are important aspects of the tradition of the sister arts that he conspicuously avoids, both in relations between text and design and in the formal qualities of his poems and pictures taken separately. Jean Hagstrum is certainly right to see in Blake "a theoretical commitment to the values of pictorialism, broadly conceived,"[21] but this could be said with equal force of Keats or Hogarth. The question is, what unique modification did Blake give to the tradition of the sister arts, and at what point was he likely to depart from it?

As illustrated books, of course, nothing like Blake's illuminated poems had been seen since the Middle Ages.[22] Although book illustration had become a minor industry in the eighteenth century, it was essentially a business of assembling work by different hands (printer, engraver, painter, and writer) into a final product which reflected the division of labor that went into it. The free interpenetration of pictorial and typographic form so characteristic of Blake's books is technically impossible in a medium which separates the work of the printer from that of the engraver. Blake's books unite the labors of the craftsman and the artist: he invents both the text and its illustrations (often at the same time), cuts both into the copper plate as parts of one total design, and prints them on his own press, retouching and adding final color by hand. In one sense, then, there is almost something perverse about discussing the "relations" between the constituent parts of an art form which is so obviously unified in both conception and execution.

Blake could hardly have been unaware, however, that his age was obsessed with the idea of unity in general, and with the goal of uniting the arts of painting and poetry in particular. The eighteenth century was, after all, the age that discovered that art could be spelled with a capital "A," and Abbé Batteux could entitle his 1746 treatise *Les beaux arts réduits à un même principe.*[23] As he set about uniting his two art forms in a single composite form, then, Blake must have meditated on the kinds of "unity" he did and did not want to achieve. It seems evident, for instance, that he had an instinctive antipathy to abstract notions of unity, systems based on the assumption that "One Law" governs the multiplicity of phenomena. If "One Law for the Lion & Ox is oppression," it seems reasonable to suppose that one law for painting and poetry is oppression too.

The problem is only aggravated when that one law or "même principe" is called "nature," and is defined as a reality external to and independent of human consciousness. Blake's rejection of an art based in the imitation of nature transcends the usual boundaries which divide artistic movements of the eighteenth and nineteenth centuries. Wordsworth and Pope get equally bad marks for "following nature," despite the fact that they mean radically different things by the word. In Blake's view the reliance on nature encouraged a tendency to evaluate art not in terms of its imaginative or visionary coherence, but in terms of its correspondence to the general idea of what is "out there." It did not matter to him whether the "there" was defined as the Lockean "ratio of five senses" or a Platonic realm of abstract forms to be apprehended through memory and reason. The problem with both concepts was that they split the perceiver from an "objective" world outside himself, and they encouraged, not just technical verisimilitude in art ("fac-simile representations of merely mortal and perishing substance"; *DC*, K 576), but conventionality and a tame correctness.

The doctrine of nature as the source, end, and test of art also had important consequences for the understanding of the relationship between the arts. If painting and poetry were imitations of the same thing, they ought to be reducible to their common origin. *Ut pictura poesis* ("as a painting, so also a poem") became, in eighteenth-century aesthetics, not a casual comparison but a commandment for poets and painters.[24] The dominance of this principle had, I would suggest, three major consequences for the practice of poetry and painting: (1) It encouraged a sense of *translatability*, a conviction that differences in mediums, like those of language, are superficial distinctions. It can hardly be an accident that an age believing so firmly in the possibility of translation turned book illustration and literary painting into a light industry. (2) It encouraged a belief in the *transferability* of techniques from one medium to the other; painting was not merely similar to poetry, it was supposed to borrow techniques from its sister art. (3) Where differences between the two arts were acknowledged, the issue of unity was resurrected in the notion of *complementarity*, the idea that the coupling of the two arts would provide a fuller imitation of the total reality. Blake had, I would suggest, a highly critical attitude toward these notions of the sister arts, and thus a basic foundation for the understanding of his style is an analysis of the way he confronts the prevailing conventions in his own stylistic choices, sometimes rejecting, sometimes assimilating and transforming traditional notions for his own purposes. . . .

[*Ed. note:* In the next several pages (not reprinted here) Mitchell discusses in detail Blake's response to the consequences just listed.]

III. THE UNITY OF BLAKE'S COMPOSITE ART

The tradition of the sister arts as modified in the eighteenth century is useful for showing the kinds of things Blake was reacting against as he set about uniting the verbal and graphic arts. But it also sets the stage for an understanding of the positive principles which animate his stylistic choices. Blake would probably not have been impressed by Lessing's attack on the excesses of *ut pictura poesis*, because it only tried to reaffirm the obvious differences between the sister arts rather than to discover a new basis for their unification, and it did not question the basic doctrine of nature as a source, end, and test of art. In Blake's view the attempt to make poetry visual and to make pictures "speak" and tell a story was inherently flawed, not just because it ignored fundamental differences between the two art forms, but because it presumed the independent reality of space and time and treated them as the irreducible foundations of existence. As we have seen, Blake considers space and time, like the sexes, to be contraries whose reconciliation occurs not when one becomes like the other, but when they approach a condition in which these categories cease to function. In the simplest terms, his poetry is designed to invalidate the idea of objective time, his painting to invalidate the idea of objective space. To state this positively, his poetry affirms the power of the human imagination to create and organize time in its own image, and his painting affirms the centrality of the human body as the structural principle of space. The essential unity of his arts, then, is to be seen in the parallel engagements of imagination and body with their respective mediums, and in their convergence in the more comprehensive idea of the "Human Form Divine." For Blake, in the final analysis the body and the imagination are separable principles only in a fallen world of limited perception, and the business of art is to dramatize their unification: "The Eternal Body of Man is The Imagination. . . . It manifests itself in his Works of Art" (*Laocoön*, E 271).

Blake's specific techniques for constructing his art forms as critiques of their own mediums are becoming increasingly clear. In the poetry he creates a world of process and metamorphosis in which the only stable, fixed term is the imagining and perceiving mind. Cause and effect, linear temporality, and other "objective" temporal structures for narrative are replaced, in the prophetic books, by an imaginative conflation of all time in the pregnant moment. The prophetic narrator-actor perceives "Present, Past & Future" simultaneously, and is able to see in any given moment the structure of all history: "Every Time less than a pulsation of the artery / Is equal in its period & value to Six Thousand Years" (*M* 28.62–63). Consequently, the narrative order of the poem need not refer to any incontingent, nonhuman temporal continuum. Most narrative structures employ what Blake would call "twofold vision": that is, the imaginative arrangement of episodes is constructed with reference to an implicitly objective time scheme. The narrative selects its moments and their order in terms of some imaginative rearrangement of the objective sequence: *in medias res, ab ovum,* or *recherche du temps perdu.* All of these selective principles assume, however, that there is an order of nonhuman, "natural," or "real" time which flows onward independent of any human, "subjective," or "imaginary" reorganization of its sequence. For Blake, this objective temporal understructure is an illusion which is to be dispelled by the form of his poetry, or adumbrated in the single mythic episode. The beginning, middle, and end of any action are all contained in the present, so the order of presentation is completely subject to the imagination of the narrator. Hostile critics have always recognized this quality in Blake's major prophecies when they indicted them for being "impossible to follow." That is precisely the point. Blake's prophecies go nowhere in time because time, as a linear, sequential phenomenon, has no place in their structure. *Jerusalem* is essentially a nonconsecutive series of epiphanies or visionary confrontations with the total structure of history (six thousand years) encapsulated in the poet's experience of the personal and historic moments in his own life. That is why Blake has Los, his alter ego, personify Time, Poetry, Prophecy, and the Imagination simultaneously. In this way Blake could dramatize the poet's management of fictive time and the prophet's quarrel with history as versions of the struggle of the individual with himself. It is also why Blake continues Milton's task of consolidating the forms of epic and prophecy in the embracing form of revelation.[25] The epic form provides the forward pressure, the sense of a journey through time and space (the "passage through / Eternal Death"). The prophetic strain emphasizes the visionary moment, continually asserting that the time is at hand, the journey really a dream ("the Sleep of Ulro") from which we can awake at any moment. The apocalyptic form provides windows into that awakened state which is found at the center (moment) and circumference (beginning and end) of time, the "awakening to Eternal Life." Blake's prophetic works stress these forms in different ways (*The Four Zoas* is more like a narrative epic, *Milton* a dramatic epic like *Paradise Regained*) which all tend to the final consummation in *Jerusalem*, an encyclopedic song "Of the Sleep of Ulro! and of the passage through / Eternal Death! and of the awaking to Eternal Life."

A similar consolidation of epic and prophetic styles can be observed in Blake's illuminated prints, in which the human figures of classical, Renaissance history (i.e., epic) painting, are placed in a Gothic (i.e., prophetic or apocalyptic) spatial setting.[26] Art historians have begun to recognize that this sort of hybrid style, far from making Blake a historical maverick, places him in the mainstream of experimental movements in late eighteenth-century art.[27] In historical terms, Blake's style must be defined (along with that of many of his contemporaries) as a kind of "Romantic classicism," an oxymoron which helps us to see that his art has affinities with Michelangelo, Raphael, and the mannerists in his treatment of the human figure, with Gothic illumination in his primitivism and anti-illusionism, and with contemporaries such as Flaxman in his stress on pure outline, Fuseli in his use of the terrific and exotic, Barry and Mortimer in their treatment of the mythic and heroic.

Historical terminology cannot explain, however, how and why these elements are transmuted into something unified and unique in Blake's pictorial style. His art is a curious compound of the representational and the abstract, the picture that imitates natural forms and the design that seems to delight in pure form for its own sake. The "flame-flowers" which are so characteristic of his early work, and which later inspired the arabesques of art nouveau, exemplify the interplay between representation and abstraction that informs all his work. Abstract linear forms such as the vortex or the circle provide the structural skeletons for a seemingly infinite range of representational appearances, and the postures of his human figures are repeated so systematically that they suggest a kind of pantomimic body-language, a repertoire of leitmotifs that can be repeated in widely differing contexts.[28] Blake provides a kind of emblem of the "life of forms" in his art in his picture of a serpent metamorphosing into a flame, then a leaf, and finally into the tendrils of a vine [11].

The effect of this sort of pictorial strategy is to undercut the representational appearance of particular forms and to endow them with an abstract, stylized existence independent of the natural images with which they are identified: serpent, flame, and vegetative form participate in one sinuous formal life. Blake frees his style, in this way, from the task of accurately representing nature ("fac-simile representations of merely mortal and perishing substances"; DC, E532), and develops a style which demonstrates that the appearances of nature are to some extent (but never completely) arbitrary, and subject to transformation by the imagination of the artist.

All art, of course, even that which claims only to provide a mirror image of external reality, transforms its subject matter in some way, through the imposition of some style or convention. But the very subject of Blake's art is this power to transform and reshape visual imagery, and, by implication, the ability of man to create his vision in general. This is what he means when he says that his art "copies Imagination" ("Men think they can Copy Nature as Correctly as I copy Imagination this they will find Impossible"; PA, E 563). The word "imagination" does not mean, I would suggest, a transcendent body of archetypal, quasiplatonic forms; it is rather the name of a process ("The Imagination is not a State: it is the Human Existence itself"; M 32:32, E 131). And this process is the activity by which symbolic form comes into being, not just the state of its finished existence. Blake's pictorial style embodies the interaction between imagination and spatial reality, then, just as his poetic form enacts the encounter between imagination and time.

The concrete symbol or icon of the imagination in Blake's pictures is, of course, the human body. The nonillusionistic, stylized character of the settings which surround the body is Blake's iconographic way of restating his central stylistic premise, that the shape and significance of spatial reality is not objective or given, but derives its form and meaning from the human consciousness that inhabits it. The environments of Blake's paintings thus serve as a kind of malleable setting for human form: there are no mathematically consistent perspectives, and very few landscapes or architectural backgrounds which would make any sense without the human figures they contain.[29] Pictorial space does not exist as a uniform, visually perceived container of forms, but rather as a kind of extension of the consciousness of the human figures it contains.

The essential unity of Blake's composite art, then, lies in the convergence of each art form upon the goal of affirming the centrality of the human form (as consciousness or imagination in the poetry, as body in the paintings) in the structure of reality. The coupling of Blake's two art forms is thus an enactment of his central metaphor, "The Eternal Body of Man is The Imagination. . . . It manifests itself in his Works of Art" (*Laocoön*, E 271). Blake's art is neither representational, imitating a world of objective "nature," nor allegorical, rendering an invisible, abstract, transcendent reality. It is, rather, an art of "Living Form," built upon the stylistic interplay between linear abstraction and concrete representation, the iconographic drama of the human body in pictorial space, and the poetic drama of the imagination in time, working to find the form and meaning of the moment, the individual life, and the total expanse of human history, "Six Thousand Years."

The consequences of this definition of Blake's art are perhaps more apparent in his poetry than his painting. Since Frye's *Fearful Symmetry* the nonallegorical nature of Blake's poetry has been regularly acknowledged,[30] and recent criticism has begun to explore the question of form in the major prophecies. *Jerusalem* is no longer treated simply as a quarry for Blakean "philosophy," but is being investigated as a poetic structure whose generic elements are just now coming into focus. The recognition of traditional structural topoi such as the epic quest, the descent into the underworld, the dream vision, the prophecy and apocalypse has become much more eclectic and pluralistic. We are now in a position to assimilate these structures into Blake's thoery of poetry as a critique of time, a project which may reveal that the major prophecies have formal and thematic intersections with works like *Tristram Shandy* as well as with the Bible and *Paradise Lost*.

It is generally acknowledged that the understanding of Blake's pictures has progressed more slowly, partly because art historians are not usually equipped to deal with the formidable complexities of Blake's verbal "system"; consequently the commentary on Blake's pictures has been mostly literary, i.e., concerned with the identification of imagery whose meaning is felt to reside primarily in the text, not in the formal treatment provided by the picture.[31] Our problem, then, is to go beyond the identification of Blake's symbolic figures to a grasp of his symbolic *style*, not just in a historical sense, but as a repertoire of specific formal devices, as a personal expression of the artist's ideology, and as a strategy for manipulating the visual field of the reader/spectator—a kind of visual rhetoric.

Notes

1. Frye, "Poetry and Design in William Blake," in *Discussions of William Blake*, ed. John Grant (Boston, 1961), p. 46; reprinted from *Journal of Aesthetics and Art Criticism*, X (Sept. 1951), 35–42. Jean Hagstrum, *William Blake: Poet and Painter* (Chicago, 1964), was, I believe, the first to refer to Blake's illuminated books as a "composite art."

2. *Problems of Art: Ten Philosophical Lectures* (New York, 1957), p. 86. Langer goes on to say that "every work has its being in only one order of art; compositions of different orders are not simply conjoined, but all except one will cease to appear as what they are."

3. I am employing here the conventional distinction between language as a system of arbitrary signs and pictorial representation as a system of more or less "natural" signs, containing intrinsic resemblances to what which is signified. Emblems and hieroglyphics thus occupy something of a middle ground between linguistic and pictorial representation. The key phrase in the distinction is "more or less," some kinds of pictorial representation being more explicitly verbal (and thus less "natural") than others. Further elaboration of this concept may be found in E. H. Gomrich, *Symbolic Images: Studies in the Art of the Renaissance* (London, 1972), p. 212, and Ronald Paulson, *Emblem and Expression* (Cambridge, Mass., 1965), p. 8.

4. Roland Barthes argues for the tendency of all symbolic forms to aspire to the condition of language: "it appears increasingly difficult to conceive a system of images and objects whose *signifieds* can exist independently of language: to perceive what a substance signifies is to fall back on the individuation of language: there is no meaning which is not designated, and the world of signifieds is none other than that of language" (*Elements of Semiology,* tr. Annette Lavers and Colin Smith [Boston, 1968], p. 10). Barthes' difficulty in conceiving of a system independent of language may, however, say as much about the linguistic bias of structuralism as it does about the actual nature of things. If Blake teaches us anything about symbolic systems, it is that there is an equally strong tendency for language to fall back into that which cannot be designated, the wordless realm of pure image and sound, and that this realm may have systematic features independent of language.

5. The widespread familarity of the St. Christopher image is suggested by H. C. Whaite in *Saint Christopher in English Medieval Wallpainting* (London, 1929). Whaite notes that despite the tendency to casually obliterate medieval paintings with whitewash in the eighteenth and nineteenth centuries, "it is surprising how much material has survived. Of the hundreds of paintings of St. Christopher which at one time adorned the walls of English churches, there are still over sixty known to exist in fair condition. In Keyser's list of 1883 one hundred and eighty representations of the subject are mentioned" (p. 13). The best general work on this theme is Ernst K. Stahl, *Die Legende vom Heil Riesen Christophorus in der Graphik des 15 und 16 Jahrhunderts* (Munich, 1920). Stahl cites Dürer, Cranach, Altdorfer, Schongauer, Bosch, and van Veen (whose work Blake definitely knew) among the artists who made prints of St. Christopher carrying the Christ-child.

6. *The Golden Legend,* tr. William Caxton, ed., Frederick S. Ellis (Hammersmith, 1892), pp. 645–48. Blake was probably familiar with Caxton's translation of this classic collection of saints' lives, perhaps learning of it during his apprenticeship among the antiquarians.

7. Whaite, *Saint Christopher,* p. 9.

8. Blake did not arrive at the term "Reprobate" for his wrathful prophet until writing *Milton,* but he certainly presents a clear image of the "just man raging in the wilds" in the Argument to the earlier *Marriage of Heaven and Hell.* I would not argue that he *meant* his readers to see the Bard of Experience as a "Reprobate" in 1794; but his later use of that term to describe the prophetic stance may have been an outgrowth of the St. Christopher legend.

9. Voragine, *The Golden Legend,* p. 645.

10. Commentary in Keynes' facsimile edition of *Songs of Innocence and of Experience* (London, 1967). Keynes' interpretation, like my association of the Bard with the Reprobate, involves an anachronism: we go forward in Blake's writing to find words adequate to pictures he conceived much earlier. I think this procedure is justified as long it is done consciously. It seems highly probable that Blake often developed graphic images long before he found the words adequate to describe them, and the act of anachronistic interpretation may have real value in tracing the process of Blake's imagination as it moves from vision to verbalization.

11. The distinction between "meaning" and "significance" here is drawn from E. D. Hirsch's *Validity in Interpretation* (New Haven, 1967), p. 8.

12. "Poetry and Design," p. 48. Frye's example of "syncopation" is the female figure harnessed to the moon at the bottom of plate 8 of *Jerusalem,* a figure which is not mentioned in the text until plate 63. Even more important than the physical distance, however, is the fact that the textual reference ("the Fairies lead the Moon along the Valley of Cherubim"; *J* 63:14) does not really explain the picture, but simply gives us a clue for further investigation.

13. Note, too, that all these metaphors can and perhaps should be reversed, since the scene of mass sexual resurrection comes before the more personalized encounter of devil and angel. This analysis, by the way, is the product of an exchange with John Grant in the footnotes of *Blake's Visionary Forms Dramatic,* ed. David Erdman and John Grant (Princeton, 1970), pp. 63–64 (hereafter cited as *VFD*).

14. The reclining figure is clearly a woman in copies C and D. The instrument held by the kneeling figure is only suggestively etched—perhaps a flute, shepherd's pipe, or lyre. The absence of conventional imagery to distinguish devil from angel (noted above) must be qualified in copies A and I, where, as Erdman notes (*TIB,* p. 98), the devil and angel *share* a halo. This humorous little touch may suggest that the conversion is, from another point of view, the transformation of the devil into an angel; similarly, the androgynous ambiguity of the devil's and angel's sexes stresses the major point of conversion, transformation, marriage of equals, rather than the superiority and victory of one point of view.

15. Hagstrum suggests that van Veen, among other well-known emblematists, "surely caught Blake's young eye in the engraver's shop where he worked and in the print shops he frequented as a boy" (*Poet and Painter,* pp. 50–51). The *Amoris Divini Emblemata* would probably have been more congenial to Blake's temperament than van Veen's emblems after Horace, or those on secular love. Mario Praz notes three editions of this work, two published in Antwerp (1615 and 1660) and one in Amsterdam (1711). See his *Studies in Seventeenth-Century Imagery,* rev. ed. (Rome, 1964), p. 526.

16. "Poetry and Design," p. 46.

17. Blake later complained, "Those I printed for M. Humphry are a selection from the different Books of such as could be Printed without the Writing, tho' to the Loss of some of the best things. For they when Printed perfect accompany Poetical Personifications & Acts, without which Poems they never could have been Executed" (Blake to Dawson Turner, 9 June 1818 [K 867]). It is interesting to note further that when Blake supplied these separate plates, the captions he inscribed on them were in no case quoted from the poems they were supposed to "illustrate," but were apparently written as Blake's latest responses to the independent symbolic meaning of the designs. Thus the title page of *Urizen* is inscribed not with a line about Urizen or the "primeval priest" but with a playful question evoked by the symmetrical quality of the design: "What is the way, the right or the left?"

18. Frye, "Poetry and Design," p. 45.

19. Rosemary Freeman, for instance, compares Wither's marigold emblem with Blake's sunflower, but she can only point to the superiority of Blake's poem, not the underlying difference in purpose. See her *English Emblem Books* (New York, 1970), pp. 24–29; reprinted from original edition (London, 1948).

20. Frye, "Poetry and Design," p. 46.

21. Much of the following section is the product of an exchange between Hagstrum and myself in *Blake's Visionary Forms Dramatic.* Professor Hagstrum's brief essay there, "Blake and the Sister Arts Tradition," was written partly in response to my claim in "Blake's Composite Art" that Blake was more critical than appreciative of the sister arts tradition. I have tried in the following pages to meet his objections and have altered my own views where appropriate. I should stress, however, that my debts to Professor Hagstrum's splendid scholarship far outweigh any disputes with his conclusions.

22. For an informative survey of the history of style and technique in this field, see David Bland, *The Illustration of Books* (London, 1951).

23. For a general study of the rise of aesthetics as a distinct discipline in the eighteenth century, see Paul O. Kristeller, "The Modern System of the Arts: A Study in the History of Aesthetics," *Journal of the History of Ideas* III (1951), 496–527. Useful recent studies include Lawrence Lipking, *The Ordering of the Arts in Eighteenth-Century England* (Princeton, 1970), and James S. Malek, *The Arts Compared* (Detroit, 1974). Malek notes that "comparative discussions of the arts, along with aesthetic speculation in general, gradually increased in popularity during the eighteenth century in Britain. In terms of total numbers of works produced, this branch of aesthetics achieved its most rapid growth between 1760 and 1790" (p. 154), precisely the period in which Blake was growing up.

24. Of the enormous body of literature on this subject, the most useful studies are Mario Praz, *Studies in Seventeenth-Century Imagery;* Robert J. Clements, *Picta Poesis: Literary and Humanistic Theory in Renaissance Emblem Books* (Rome, 1960); Jean Hagstrum, *The Sister Arts* (Chicago, 1958); Rensselaer Lee, *Ut Pictura Poesis: The Humanistic Theory of Painting* (New York, 1967), reprinted from *Art Bulletin* XXII (1940), 197–269; and Ralph Cohen, *The Art of Discrimination: Thomson's "The Seasons" and the Language of Criticism* (London, 1964). One obvious gap in our history of critical theory is the transformation of the idea of *ut pictura poesis* in the nineteenth and twentieth centuries. One of the few treatments of this subject is Roy Park's *"Ut Pictura Poesis: The Nineteenth Century Aftermath,"* *Journal of Aesthetics and Art Criticism* XXVII (1969), 155–64, which suggests that the critical, antipictorialist, and antivisual attitudes which I ascribe here to Blake are characteristic of Romantic criticism in general. Blake would surely have been aware of his friend Fuseli's sentiments in the matter: "From long bigotted deference to the old maxim that poetry is painting in speech, and painting dumb poetry, the two sisters, marked with features so different by nature, and the great masters of composition, her oracles, have been constantly confounded with each other by the herds of mediocrity and thoughtless imitation" (From the *Analytical Review* of 1794, quoted in *Encounters,* ed. John Dixon Hunt [London, 1971], p. 7).

25. The best recent work on this subject is that of Joseph A. Wittreich, Jr. See, for instance, his "Opening the Seals: Blake's Epics and the Milton Tradition," in *Blake's Sublime Allegory,* ed. Stuart Curran and Joseph A. Wittreich, Jr. (Madison, 1973), pp. 23–58.

26. In the sister arts tradition, history painting was considered the analogue of epic poetry, a comparison which Blake echoes when he writes in the margin of Reynolds' *Discourses,* "A History Painter Paints The Hero, & not Man in General" (E 641).

27. Robert Rosenblum's essay "Toward the *Tabula Rasa,"* in his *Transformations in Late Eighteenth-Century Art* (Princeton, 1967), does a great deal to demonstrate Blake's centrality.

28. Northrop Frye ("Poetry and Design," p. 48), was the first to suggest an analogy with Wagner's use of the leitmotif. Janet Warner's important essay "Blake's Use of Gesture," *VFD,* pp. 174–95, attempts to categorize the basic body positions.

29. On Blake's adventurous distortions of perspective, see Rosenblum, *Transformations,* pp. 189–91.

30. Allegory, that is, in the "corporeal" sense, as a kind of code whose "real meaning" lies behind the symbols rather than dwelling in their sensuous particulars. Blake obviously approves, on the other hand, of sublime allegory which "rouzes the faculties to act," stirring up the imagination of its readers.

31. Erdman (*VFD,* p. vii) notes that "in the reading of Blake's illuminations the advance has been slower and less steady," and Hazard Adams (*Blake Newsletter* VII: 3, no. 27 [Winter 1973–74], 69) traces this problem to excessive literariness of commentary on the pictures. A good primer on the thicket of methodological interference between literary criticism and art history is provided in *New Literary History* III (Spring 1972), an issue devoted to this subject; see especially Svetlana and Paul Alpers, *"Ut Pictura Noesis?* Criticism in Literary Studies and Art History," 437–58.

1. *Songs of Experience*, copy I. Frontispiece.

2. *Songs of Innocence*, copy Z. Frontispiece.

3. Albrecht Dürer, St. Christopher with head turned
back (1529).

4. *Christian Reading in His Book*, from Blake's designs for *Bunyan's Pilgrim's Progress*.

5. Drawing for the manuscript of *Vala*, or *The Four Zoas*, p. 66.

The terror answerd: I am Orc, wreath'd round the accursed tree:
The times are ended; shadows pass the morning gins to break
The fiery joy, that Urizen perverted to ten commands,
What night he led the starry hosts thro' the wide wilderness;
That stony law I stamp to dust: and scatter religion abroad
To the four winds as a torn book, & none shall gather the leaves;
But they shall rot on desart sands, & consume in bottomless deeps,
To make the desarts blossom, & the deeps shrink to their fountains,
And to renew the fiery joy, and burst the stony roof.
That pale religious letchery, seeking Virginity,
May find it in a harlot, and in coarse-clad honesty
The undefil'd tho' ravish'd in her cradle night and morn:
For every thing that lives is holy, life delights in life;
Because the soul of sweet delight can never be defil'd.
Fires inwrap the earthly globe, yet man is not consumd;
Amidst the lustful fires he walks: his feet become like brass,
His knees and thighs like silver, & his breast and head like gold.

6. *America*, copy N. Plate 8.

Thus wept the Angel voice & ... he wept the terrible blasts
Of trumpets, blew a loud alarm across the Atlantic deep.
No trumpets answer; no reply of clarions or of fifes,
Silent the Colonies remain and refuse the loud alarm.

On those vast shady hills between America & Albions shore;
Now barrd out by the Atlantic sea: calld Atlantean hills:
Because from their bright summits you may pass to the Golden world
An ancient palace, archetype of mighty Emperies,
Rears its immortal pinnacles, built in the forest of God
By Ariston the king of beauty for his stolen bride.

Here on their magic seats the thirteen Angels sat perturbd,
For clouds from the Atlantic hover oer the solemn roof.

7. *America*, copy N. Plate 10.

8. *The Marriage of Heaven and Hell*, copy C. Title page.

9. *Songs of Innocence*, copy I. Plate 10. "The Little Black Boy," second illustration.

10. Otto van Veen, *Amoris Divini Emblemata* (Antwerp, 1660). Emblem 13, guardian angel presenting the wayward soul to God.

11. *Jerusalem,* copy D. Plate 44 (detail).

Act [From *Poetic Form in Blake's "Milton"*]

SUSAN FOX

The body of Book I [of *Milton*] is composed of two sections, an account of the action to which the Bard's Song provides a prologue (13:45–24:47), and a vision of the providential workings of time and space liberated by that action (24:48 to the end). The action occurs simultaneously on various levels of existence. It has three distinguishable stages, a series, it would seem, of subactions, but Blake indicates repeatedly, by verbal echoes and by explicit references to the instant each event occurs, that the stages themselves are simultaneous. The three stages are defined by consolidations of major figures in the poem. In the first, the Bard enters Milton; in the second, Milton enters Blake; in the third, Los enters the union of Bard/Milton/Blake. Each consolidation at once inspires new vision and liberates the will to realize that vision.

The Bard's Song, with its implicit condemnation of weak pity and grasping love, has shaken its hearers even as the explicit judgment it describes shook the Assembly. The assembly of the Bard's generation is no wiser than the Assembly of Rintrah's; each questions the pronouncements of its sages, each is in need of purification. Challenged, the Bard claims divine authority even as the eternal in his Song "confirm'd [the judgment against Rintrah] with a thunderous oath" (11:27). His Song has had, he affirms, the very source Blake sought for his own song in its invocation:

> The Bard replied. I am Inspired! I know it is Truth! for I Sing
> According to the inspiration of the Poetic Genius
> Who is the eternal all-protecting Divine Humanity
> To whom be Glory & Power & Dominion Evermore Amen. . . .
> —(13:51–14:3)

The judgment in Palamabron's tent was met with Los's altering the poles of the world and the Assembly's uttering "a loud solemn universal groan . . . from the east & from the west & from the south / And from the north" (9:37–39); the Bard's judgment, too, causes the heavens to resound and the earth to shake:

> Then there was great murmuring in the Heavens of Albion
> Concerning Generation & the Vegetative power & concerning

> The Lamb the Saviour: Albion trembled to Italy Greece & Egypt
> To Tartary & Hindostan & China & to Great America
> Shaking the roots & fast foundations of the Earth in doubtfulness
> The loud voic'd Bard terrify'd took refuge in Miltons bosom. . . .
>   —(14:4–9)

On all levels of existence, then, there is fear and trembling—a trembling that exactly parallels its mythic precedent yet to be resolved. In that perilous atmosphere Milton alone, fortified by the Bard's presence within him, has the courage to act. The fleeing of the Bard into his bosom is a literalization of the idea that the Bard's Song inspired Milton; it is also a symbol of the failure of eternity to resolve the disputes of Eden, disputes that will only be resolved in time through the agency of Milton. The Bard's flight is thus both the symptom of disaster and its ultimate reversal—as the flames of Rintrah or the battles of Apocalypse are both destructive and renovative. The Reprobate Bard within him, Milton is himself now "Reprobate & form'd to destruction from the mothers womb" (7:37—38):

> Then Milton rose up from the heavens of Albion ardorous!
> The whole Assembly wept prophetic, seeing in Miltons face
> And in his lineaments divine the shades of Death & Ulro
> He took off the robe of the promise, & ungirded himself from the oath of
>   God. . . .
>   —(14:10–13)

Death is already apparent in him as he, like Los before him closed "from Eternity in Albions Cliffs" (10:10), rejects allegiance to the mundane god. The alliances that are to comprise the protagonist of *Milton* are thus suggested at the beginning of its action: Los, Rintrah, the Bard, Milton, and Blake himself have had, and have now, at the poem's moment, the same function on all their levels of reality. Each, inspired from without, sacrifices himself angrily to battle falsehood and preserve truth; each draws the disapproval of his peers and witnesses the devastation of life outside eternity. We have seen this sequence applied to all Reprobate figures but Blake (although it has been imputed to him by subtle similarities between himself and the Bard); his parallel course will be a principal subject of the body of *Milton*. He is the only one of the Reprobate who is solely a figure of our temporal life, the only one who does not descend into the Mundane Shell but, by an act of vision, ascends from it. Thus he will be, by the accident of his birth moment and by his deliberately cultivated receptivity to vision, the key to the redemption of all levels of reality. He is at the nadir; if he can ascend from it, humanity can ascend. It will take all the other Reprobate figures to help him make that ascent: he is their representative, their functional form, in this, the crucial level of reality.

As Rintrah bore the judgment of Satan and Los suffered his punishment, now Milton will sacrifice himself for the Elect sinner:

> And Milton said, I go to Eternal Death! The Nations still
> Follow after the detestable Gods of Priam; in pomp
> Of warlike selfhood, contradicting and blaspheming.
> When will the Resurrection come; to deliver the sleeping body
> From corruptibilty: O when Lord Jesus wilt thou come?
> Tarry no longer; for my soul lies at the gates of death.
> I will arise and look forth for the morning of the grave.
> I will go down to the sepulcher to see if morning breaks!
> I will go down to self annihilation and eternal death,
> Lest the Last Judgment come & find me unannihilate
> And I be siez'd & giv'n into the hands of my own Selfhood.
> The Lamb of God is seen thro' mists & shadows, hov'ring
> Over the sepulchers in clouds of Jehovah & winds of Elohim
> A disk of blood, distant; & heav'ns & earth's roll dark between
> What do I here before the Judgment? without my Emanation?
> With the daughters of memory, & not with the daughters of inspiration[?]
> I in my Selfhood am that Satan: I am that Evil One!
> He is my Spectre! in my obedience to loose him from my Hells
> To claim the Hells, my Furnaces, I go to Eternal Death.
>
> —(14:14–32)

This key speech sets the instant of the poem, the interim between death and resurrection, the moratorium ordered by Los in the Bard's Song. It is at once a declaration of personal intention and a plea for aid from without, its two contradictory impulses perfectly reflected in its shifting rhythms. Beginning and ending with the resolute "I go to Eternal Death," it is a kind of capsule of Blake's convictions of redemption. The progress of the speech is the progress of *Milton*. Its initial affirmation and brief summary of the conditions that make that affirmation imperative are spoken firmly, self-confidently; the beat of the lines is strong and, though not metrically regular, almost martial in its ringing control. The central portion of the speech is a traditional appeal for divine help, and its meeker rhythm is biblical in its lyrical regularity: "O when Lord Jesus wilt thou come? . . . I will arise and look forth for the morning of the grave. / I will go down to the sepulcher to see if morning breaks!" This is not, of course, merely a passive plea for outside control; it has, rather, the positive quality of John Milton's "They also serve who only stand and wait." Going down to the sepulcher is embracing Eternal Death; it is no evasion of responsibility, but a positive act of consciousness demanding enormous courage.

As salvation is a merger of external and internal responsibility, so is the evil that defies it. The last movement of Milton's speech is a confession: "I in my Selfhood am that Satan." The rhythm is once again the stirring, self-confident beat of the opening lines, but the tone has shifted from their asperity to a new and humbler determination. The evil of the opening lines has been recognized as an internal evil; the necessity to exorcise it is therefore even more profound. The second "I go to Eternal Death" has in its context a quieter and yet even more forceful tone than the first. It is as if in the beginning a decision is being made, but at the end it has been made. Decision, in this poem, is action; in the course of this one brief speech, Milton's sacrificial act is both conceived and executed. That course is the course of the entire poem, which begins in bardic anger, moves through a complicated dramatization of mutual responsibility for salvation, and ends in a series of intimate confessions that recapitulate the initial charges.

The next three lines emphasize the identity of decision and act: "And Milton said. I go to Eternal Death! Eternity shudder'd / For he took the outside course, among the graves of the dead / A mournful shade. Eternity shuddered at the image of eternal death. . . ." It is perhaps too subtle to rely on Blake's punctuation for such an important point, yet the punctuation of this quotation of Milton's speech suggests that it is the opening "I go to Eternal Death!" that causes such consternation in eternity: the concluding statement is followed by a quiet period, not an exclamation point. Thus Milton's taking the outside course would be simultaneous with the rest of his speech. A more reliable indication of this simultaneity is that as Milton descends, eternity shudders "at the image of eternal death"—just as, when he began to speak, eternity wept "seeing in Miltons face / And in his lineaments divine the shades of Death & Ulro." These are indeed subtle indications of the simultaneity of decision and action, but they are, I believe, substantial, and they will be supported by more explicit subsequent descriptions.

Milton's speech suggests two of Blake's principal arguments with his prophetic master. Frye cites the first: "But one is struck by the fact that Milton never sees beyond this sinister 'female will' [of Eve and Dalilah]. His vision of women takes in only the hostility and fear which it is quite right to assume toward the temptress who represents moral virtue, . . . but which is by no means the only way in which women can be visualized. There is no emanation in Milton; no Beatrice or Miranda; no vision of the spiritual nature of love."[1] However much one may disagree with this passage as a reading of John Milton, it is probably an accurate account of Blake's reading of Milton. The character Milton's existence in heaven without his emanation is an implicit criticism of the poet Milton's attitude toward women. It is, moreover, both a moral and a literary criticism: neither in his life nor in his writings did he, Blake implies, realize "the spiritual nature of love." It is not merely his attitude toward women Blake condemns here, of course; "Emanation" is, after all, not a Blakean translation of "wife," but a representation of all of a person's ideals and productions. Milton's ideals and productions are deficient not only in his alleged insensitivity to women, but in a perhaps more serious insensitivity to his own errors. Thus Blake has Milton return to

mortality to loose Satan from "my Hells . . . my Furnaces." He is to redeem
Satan, his spectre, from destruction even as Rintrah was forced to do in the
Bard's Song, but the action has an added dimension here: Milton calls them
his hells, his furnaces, not only because any of us condemns his enemy or that
portion of himself he deems his enemy, but because John Milton in his
greatest work consigned his Satan to hells of his own design. With God in
command and Satan in torment and humanity scheduled for redemption after
a mere female dream of history, the universe of *Paradise Lost* would be to
Blake static and unprogressive, unforgiving and uninspired. He would have
the Bard of that universe restore inspiration to it by recognizing, as Blake
implies in the epic invocation of this poem, that it is the universe of each
person's imagination, that all of its factions are vital and all must be preserved. So Milton descends to salvage the Elect portion of his own being.

The decision to descend is the first stage in the action of Book I, and
even as Milton makes the decision Death and Ulro are visible in him. The
second stage is the realization of that image. Milton descends, "taking the
outside course, among the graves of the dead / A mournful shade." At the
very start of the descent, "on the verge of Beulah," he enters into his Shadow,
"a mournful form double; hermaphroditic." S. Foster Damon, Milton O.
Percival, Frye, and Bloom have defined Blake's use of the word "hermaphroditic."[2] For now, we need only the sense of paradox the word invokes: outside
Eden, where males and females are truly one and indistinguishable, and
Beulah, where they are distinct but married, the masculine and feminine
portions of humanity are in a sterile state of ambiguity opposite both eternal
relationships. The senses of ambiguity and of opposition to eternal modes of
existence are crucial to Blake's conception of life in time. What Percival calls
the "checkmate and consequent sterility" of temporal sexuality is a kind of
demonic parody of the union Milton seeks with Ololon. Milton must reenter
the ambiguities of mortal existence in order to perfect his own marriage with
his emanation. What is unsatisfactory in eternity must be corrected in time,
subdued "from Particulars to Generals."

The hermaphroditic shadow is the very body of man, the universe of his
fallen perception. It reaches, the poet emphasizes, from the edge of eternity
through Ulro to Generation, "Albions land: / Which is this earth of vegetation on which now I write" (14:40–41). All existence outside eternity is a
mere shadow of eternity, horrible in its opacity and yet still providential: it is
the tissue that binds the mortal remnants of Albion to eternity. Without it
the members of Albion would be annihilate.

Milton's descent divides his existence among the various levels of reality. In order to perceive the whole Milton now, we must combine multiple
perspectives on him:

> As when a man dreams, he reflects not that his body sleeps,
> Else he would wake; so seem'd he entering his Shadow: but

With him the Spirits of the Seven Angels of the Presence
Entering; they gave him still perceptions of his Sleeping Body;
Which now arose and walk'd with them in Eden, as an Eighth
Image Divine tho' darken'd; and tho walking as one walks
In sleep; and the Seven comforted and supported him.

Like as a Polypus that vegetates beneath the deep!
They saw his Shadow vegetated underneath the Couch
Of death: for when he entered into his Shadow: Himself:
His real and immortal Self: was as appeared to those
Who dwell in immortality, as One sleeping on a couch
Of gold; and those in immortality gave forth their Emanations
Like Females of sweet beauty, to guard him round & to feed
His lips with food of Eden in his cold and dim repose!
But to himself he seemd a wanderer lost in dreary night.

Onwards his Shadow kept its course among the Spectres; call'd
Satan, but swift as lightning passing them, startled the shades
Of Hell beheld him in a trail of light as of a comet
That travels into Chaos: so Milton went guarded within.
—(15:1–20)

Milton exists now, because of his decisions, in three forms. Because he entered into death, his eternal portion seems to the other eternals a corpse on a golden couch. The life which fled that corpse "vegetates beneath the deep," incarnate in this Generation. Because his entry into Generation is an act of mercy, he maintains even in this earthly life a providential sense of his eternal nature, a perception of his true humanity walking with the Seven Angels of the Presence. He has, then, a double awareness of himself, while the remaining immortals have a third vision of him and the mortal beings here on "this earth of vegetation" have yet a fourth. Only the Seven Angels themselves, presumably, comprehend all these visions.

The Seven Angels are crucial not only to the spatial perspectives of the poem, but also to the temporal "perspectives." They are the Seven Eyes of God of *The Four Zoas,* the watchers of the seven thousand years of fallen existence, the six named by the Bard plus the seventh, millennial guardian, Jesus. That they all watch and support Milton indicates that their reigns are complete, that fallen history is about to be consummated in Milton's great venture. The day of mourning is about to end.

The problem of perspective is not just a cosmic jigsaw puzzle, an intellectual game. It is a central issue to every human being:

The nature of infinity is this: That every thing has its
Own Vortex; and when once a traveller thro' Eternity
Has passd that Vortex, he percieves it roll backward behind
His path, into a globe itself infolding; like a sun:

Or like a moon, or like a universe of starry majesty,
While he keeps onwards in his wondrous journey on the earth
Or like a human form, a friend with whom he livd benevolent.
As the eye of man views both the east & west encompassing
Its vortex; and the north & south, with all their starry host;
Also the rising sun & setting moon he views surrounding
His corn-fields and his valleys of five hundred acres square.
Thus is the earth one infinite plane, and not as apparent
To the weak traveller confin'd beneath the moony shade.
Thus is the heaven a vortex passd already, and the earth
A vortex not yet pass'd by the traveller thro' Eternity.

—(15:21–35)

Each observer stands at the point at which two vortices meet. Wherever he looks, he sees a vortex passed, or one yet to be passed through; thus is his standing point an infinite plane, a featureless, endless platform for vision. How much he sees depends on how well he looks. If he looks well, if he sees with fourfold Edenic vision, he embraces what he "sees" as part of himself and there is no distance between perceiver and perceived. If he sees with a fallen eye, he establishes, by the very act of perceiving, his separateness from what he sees: he opens a vortex between perceiver and perceived.

Frye, Hazard Adams, Bloom, and Thomas R. Frosch all define the vortex, as it must be defined, in terms of perception.[3] Frye's useful example of a book as the apex of vision drawn from two reading eyes diagrams the concept neatly: "The book therefore has a vortex of existence opening into its mental reality within our minds. When Milton descends from eternity to time, he finds that he has to pass through the apex of his cone of eternal vision, which is like trying to see the book from the book's point of view. . . ." Frosch acknowledges the value of diagrams in first formulating a definition of the vortex, but pursues the definition beyond the diagram; examining the concept in terms of its constant movement, he suggests that the movement itself is a crucial factor in any definition: the relationship between observer and observed is never static.

The most serious problem with diagrams of the vortex is not just that they cannot comprehend the motion, the three-dimensionality of the device, but that they tend to isolate the vortex as a separate entity, to make it seem independent of both the perceiver and the perceived: perceiver A sees object C through vortex B. Actually, as the Book I passage states, A, B, and C are a continuum; the vortex is not only the mode of A's perception, but the perception itself: the globe, universe, or friend perceived *is* the vortex as it recedes from the observer, who is himself the apex of the figure. The vortex is thus a parody of the Edenic relationship of what in time we must call perceiver and perceived: what is unified in Eden is divided outside of it, and the vortex is at once the emblem and the means of that division. Outside Eden there is no objective reality except the vortex, which, because it is a function of perception, is not itself objective. It only appears objective to the fallen eye.

This may sound perversely abstract, but it is really only a formulation of a basic principle of *Milton* which we can see expressed concretely in the action of the poem. Milton, when he made his decision to descend, saw Jesus as "a disk of blood, distant" (14:27)—"a globe itself infolding; like a sun." On this side of the vortex he will meet Jesus in the clouds of Ololon, and will thus see him "like a human form, a friend with whom he lived benevolent." When Milton and Ololon are united, Milton will be one with Jesus, one with the object of his perception, and the vortex that seemed to divide them will disappear. Milton will be Jesus, and eternal.

The vortex is a condition of fallen humanity. It is formed, as we can see in *The Four Zoas,* of the tension between eternity and eternal death:

> Terrific ragd the Eternal Wheels of intellect terrific ragd
> The living creatures of the wheels in the Wars of Eternal life
> But perverse rolld the wheels of Urizen & Luvah back reversd
> Downward & outwards consuming in the wars of Eternal Death. . . .
> —(I,20:12–15)

The apex of these conflicting directions is the point at which eternity meets chaos; from it a vortex extends in either direction, a whirlpool created by the opposition of the forces. Standing at that apex one is in a providential calm, the space created by the eternals for Satan's salvation. Wherever he projects his vision he sees the vortex, whether as the starry universe or as his own "corn-fields and his valleys of five hundred acres square": all is vortex. The earth itself, the center of our fallen vision, is merely our vortex point; as such it is part of that "one infinite plane" that by its whirling motion seems a solid form, a cone. So consumed are we fallen beings with the delusions of our existence, however, that we do not recognize the infinity on which we stand.

When Milton left eternity he lost the Edenic vision which sees everything on its own infinite plane. That is why he appears even to himself in several guises, corpse, darkened angel, vegetated man, satanic comet. That is why, also, Albion appears to him to be on alien planes:

> First Milton saw Albion upon the Rock of Ages,
> Deadly pale outstretched and snowy cold, storm coverd;
> A Giant form of perfect beauty outstretched on the rock
> In solemn death: the Sea of Time & Space thunderd aloud
> Against the rock, which was inwrapped with the weeds of death
> Hovering over the cold bosom, in its vortex Milton bent down
> To the bosom of death, what was underneath soon seemed above.
> A cloudy heaven mingled with stormy seas in loudest ruin;
> But as a wintry globe descends percipitant thro' Beulah bursting,

> With thunders loud, and terrible: so Miltons shadow fell,
> Precipitant loud thundring into the Sea of Time & Space.
>
> —(15:36–46)

What seemed a stormy covering beneath him becomes, as Milton descends through the vortex in the bosom of fallen man, "a cloudy heaven mingled with stormy seas": "what was underneath soon seemd above." The passage through the vortex incarnates Milton, whose shadow, or earthly portion, can enter into the mortal being Blake. Thus yet another dimension of the vortex is established: it is the conical womb through which beings pass from eternity into time. That the womb is in the bosom of Albion reflects Los's giving birth in the Bard's Song: "a red / Round Globe sunk down from his Bosom into the Deep in pangs . . ." (3:29–30). We see now that Los's childbirth was not the anomaly it seemed early in the poem, but simply a fulfillment of this prototypic function of Albion, his parent power.

Milton's descent incarnates him in Blake:

> Then first I saw him in the Zenith as a falling star,
> Descending perpendicular, swift as the swallow or swift;
> And on my left foot falling on the tarsus, enterd there;
> But from my left foot a black cloud redounding spread over Europe.
>
> —(15:47–50)

Blake's perception of Milton is described in words that recall the immediately preceding description of Milton's perceiving Albion: "Then first I saw him" echoes "First Milton saw Albion," allying the two figures in their act of seeing even though, looking in different directions, they see different things. That he sees Milton "as a falling star" identifies Blake with the "shades of Hell" who "beheld him in a trail of light as of a comet" earlier on the plate, although the shades with their inimical perception see him only as a frightening phenomenon "That travels into Chaos," while Blake with his more human eye sees him travel to his foot like a small bird: how well one looks determines what one sees. Milton is a fiery comet or a graceful English bird depending on one's perspective.

Milton's entry into Blake's foot suggests an analogy with the division of Los in the Bard's Song: from Los's back "A blue fluid exuded in Sinews hardening in the Abyss" (3:35), just as now from the point of Milton's entry into Blake "a black cloud redounding spread over Europe." The key difference is that in the earlier event the imagery is all of separation, whereas here the principal action is of union. Los gave birth to the separate form of his emanation and his spectre divided from him; Milton is born into Blake and his spectre, too, the shadow into which he entered to be born, separates from him.

Entering into Blake produces a revelation for the immortal prophet:

Then Milton knew that the Three Heavens of Beulah were beheld
By him on earth in his bright pilgrimage of sixty years
In those three females whom his Wives, & those three whom his Daughters
Had represented and containd, that they might be resum'd
By giving up of Selfhood: & they distant view'd his journey
In their eternal spheres, now Human, tho' their Bodies remain clos'd
In the dark Ulro till the Judgment: also Milton knew: they and
Himself was Human, tho' now wandering thro Death's Vale
In conflict with those Female forms, which in blood & jealousy
Surrounded him, dividing & uniting without end or number.

He saw the Cruelties of Ulro, and he wrote them down
In iron tablets: and his Wives & Daughters names were chese
Rahab and Tirzah, & Mileah & Malah & Noah & Hoglah.
They sat rang'd round him as the rocks of Horeb round the land
Of Canaan: and they wrote in thunder smoke and fire
His dictate; and his body was the Rock Sinai; that body,
Which was on earth born to corruption: & the six Females
Are Hor & Peor & Bashan & Abarim & Lebanon & Hermon
Seven rocky masses terrible in the Desarts of Midian.

—(15:51–17:17)

As during his life, according to Blake, Milton struggled with his female forms (both human and spiritual, his wives and his gentler passions) and did not enter through them as he might have into visions of eternity, so he struggles now. In Ulro these forms are named after Blakean and biblical women of bad will; in eternity, we shall see, they are named Ololon. Significantly, their struggle with Milton is a form of union. They are "now Human, tho' their Bodies remain clos'd / In the dark Ulro," because their sexual threefold nature has been complemented by Milton's descent to them: together, they equal a single human entity; "they and / Himself was Human." A darkened fourfold being, this union holds potential not only for human perfection, but also for cosmic perfection: Milton and his female forms together are "Seven rocky masses terrible in the Desarts of Midian"; they are the earthly reflection of the Seven Angels of the Presence, ranged here in satanic opacity, to be sure, but nevertheless ranged together, waiting for apocalypse. Human perfection will be cosmic perfection.

Before Milton may realize the fruits of this new vision he must overcome the opposition of the fallen Zoas, who fear his prophesied approach. He appears within the Mundane Shell, the universe created that Albion not be annihilated. That Shell is a kind of demonic parody of "our Vegetated Earth," the worst of generated existence as Golgonooza is the best.[4] In its "twenty-seven folds of opakeness" (17:26), it is coextensive with Milton's shadow, which reaches from the verge of Beulah through all fallen reality. Horrid as it is, it is not interminable; it "finishes where the lark mounts"(17:27). Even "twenty-seven folds of opakeness" may be penetrated by a fragile bird of song. A true poet may rise in spirit from this vegetated earth through its grim ramifications to the inspired air of Beulah. Where he does so the Mundane Shell ceases to exist for him, spatially disappearing. *When* he does so, we shall see in Book II, the Mundane Shell disappears temporally also, for the mounting of the lark, the achievement of true inspiration, is the signal of apocalypse.

The eternals initially shuddered at Milton's descent because he "took the outside course, among the graves of the dead" (14:34). Now we learn that he had no other choice. "For travellers from Eternity, pass outward to Satan's seat, / But travellers to Eternity, pass inward to Golgonooza." As we shall see, the two paths are complementary, each essential to the completion of the other. Milton's journey outward will be realized in Blake's journey inward. Neither figure of this fallen existence, however, can make his journey without assistance from eternity. Thus Los, in the very next line, is called "the Vehicular terror"; for it is Los, the impaired but still eternal principle of imagination, who must convey these prophets along their way.

Milton's descent causes dissension among the fallen Zoas, who, because he appears within his shadow, assume that he is Satan. Los contends with his emanation, and Orc/Luvah with his; Urizen opposes Milton. The male/female contention and the contention with Urizen, who in another form is Milton's spectre Satan, are, as we shall see, dual aspects of the struggle Milton wages throughout the poem for full humanity, for apocalyptic wholeness.

The emanations see in Milton's coming the enhancement of their own power. Enitharmon rejoices that she will be freed from Los's protective bonds. The Shadowy Female, who is the spirit of the Mundane Shell, plans to lure him into worship of her false holiness: in a parody of art she will weave the garments of tyranny; in a parody of religion she will "take the Image of God" and "put on Holiness as a breastplate" (18:19–21). She will do so, appropriately, out of a parody of love, "To defend me from thy terrors O Orc! my only beloved" (18:25). Her love, like her art and her godhead, is born of fear and idolatry, the fatal distortions of love in the Mundane Shell.

Los and Orc seek to thwart their emanations, Los by putting out barriers to stop Milton from approaching, and Orc by trying to dissuade the Shadowy Female from luring him on:

> Orc answered. Take not the Human Form O loveliest. Take not
> Terror upon thee! Behold how I am & tremble lest thou also
> Consume in my Consummation; but thou maist take a Form
> Female & lovely, that cannot consume in Mans consummation
> Wherefore dost thou Create & Weave this Satan for a Covering[?]
> When thou attemptest to put on the Human Form, my wrath
> Burns to the top of heaven against thee in Jealousy & Fear.
> Then I rend thee asunder, then I howl over thy clay & ashes

> When wilt thou put on the Female Form as in times of old
> With a Garment of Pity & Compassion like the Garment of God
> His garments are long sufferings for the Children of Men
> Jerusalem is his Garment & not thy Covering Cherub O lovely
> Shadow of my delight who wanderest seeking for the prey.
>   —(18:26–38)

This passage is a kind of quarry for images that will later become significant. Orc offers the Shadowy Female "a Form / Female & lovely, that cannot consume in Mans consummation": a sanctuary like the Beulah created by Jesus for the emanations weary of Eden's strife (plate 30). Instead, the willful consort struggles by falsehood to become in herself a human fourfold. Hers is an ironic struggle, for it destroys its own objective: if she would only assume her rightful female form she would automatically reach fourfold perfection, because the feminine "Garment of Pity & Compassion" is truly "like the Garment of God"—an association that will be brought into clearer focus when Ololon herself assumes that garment later in the poem. The garment imagery culminates in this passage in a line that reveals both the way to perfection and the forces that obstruct it: "Jerusalem is his Garment & not thy Covering Cherub." The realization of the composite female in her rightful state completes the Divine Humanity. By contrast, the Covering Cherub is a kind of fraud, his very name reduced to a pun: whereas the true Garment of God glorifies and enhances him, the Cherub merely covers up his lineaments, obscuring him.[5]

The struggle of Orc and the Shadowy Female echoes the struggle of Los and Enitharmon, and amplifies the struggle of Milton and Ololon. All these struggles will be resolved only when Jealousy and Fear are put aside; it will be, ironically, for the lowliest of these couples to make that choice and redeem them all.[6]

As each level of the Mundane Shell she rules contains both heaven and hell, so does the Shadowy Female herself, in whose bosom are both "Jerusalem & Babylon shining gloriously" (18:41). The contention her dual nature causes creates a destruction we have seen before; as Los's wrath once "alter'd the poles of the world" (9:17), so does the wrath of Orc and his consort:

> Thus darkend the Shadowy Female tenfold & Orc tenfold
> Glowd on his rocky Couch against the darkness:loud thunders
> Told of the enormous conflict[.] Earthquake beneath: around;
> Rent the Immortal Females, limb from limb & joint from joint
> And moved the fast foundations of the Earth to wake the Dead. . . .
>   —(18:46–50)

Once again Blake has set the time of his poem: it is the instant before the resurrection, before the waking of the dead—the last moment of the millennium.

The battle of male and emanation yields to the battle of male and spectre. Urizen waylays Milton. In the poem's allegory of imagination Urizen stands for all the deadly snares to which inspiration is subject in time, snares Milton did not escape in his mortal span. He is thus the sum of Milton's earthly errors, and therefore an internal enemy. But he is also an external being, the regent of catastrophe, the bound form of our fallen universe; he thus represents the very condition Milton must enter to redeem those errors. Milton must assume his errors to redeem them; he struggles with Urizen now, embracing him in combat, as he earlier in the poem embraced his shadow to redeem it.

As Urizen pours icy waters upon Milton to freeze his imagination, Milton reaches for red clay, molding it with care

> Between his palms; and filling up the furrows of many years
> Beginning at the feet of Urizen, and on the bones
> Creating new flesh on the Demon cold, and building him,
> As with new clay a Human form in the Valley of Beth Peor.
> —(19:10–14)

What is happening here is that Milton is taking over the task of Los; he is completing the binding of Urizen, as the fallen Los could not complete it, by adding flesh to the bones Los fashioned ages before. Paradoxically, this further binding is ultimately a releasing; by completing the process Milton reverses it, for when he is finished Urizen will not be merely a stony parody writhing in the deep, but a reborn "Human form in the Valley of Beth Peor."

As Milton and Urizen engage in the struggle that is the central action of the poem, a struggle that at once begins and ends in Milton's self-recognition, Blake pulls back for the widest panorama he will offer of his fallen universe. We see now the effects of Los's wrath and Orc's fiery conflict—only now we are told explicitly for the first time in the poem of the prototype conflict, the original perversion:

> Four Universes round the Mundane Egg remain Chaotic
> One to the North, named Urthona: One to the South, named Urizen:
> One to the East, named Luvah: One to the West, named Tharmas
> They are the Four Zoa's that stood around the Throne Divine!
> But when Luvah assum'd the World of Urizen to the South:
> And Albion was slain upon his mountains, & in his tent;
> All fell towards the Center in dire ruin, sinking down.
> And in the South remains a burning fire, in the East a void.
> In the West, a world of raging waters; in the North a solid,
> Unfathomable! without end. But in the midst of these,
> Is built eternally the Universe of Los and Enitharmon:
> Towards which Milton went, but Urizen oppos'd his path.
> —(19:15–26)

The Bard said that "Albion was slain upon his Mountains / And in his Tent, thro envy of Living Form, even of the Divine Vision" (3:1–2); Leutha told us that the sin was Luvah's (13:8–9). Now we learn what that envy was, and how it operated; and we see its awful devastation.

The result of Luvah's action was a drastic reordering of the universe, the prototype of reorderings in succeeding generations when Los "Alter'd the poles of the world" (9:17), when the Bard finished his song (14:4–8), when Orc and his Shadowy Female struggled (18:46–50). In this prototypic reordering the Zoas have fallen from Eden, leaving as their ruins the formless elements of fallen existence, fire, waters, a solid, and a void. The scene is disastrous, and yet it does contain hope. At the center to which all the Zoas fell "Is built eternally the Universe of Los and Enitharmon," the Mundane Egg with which the passage began, and with which it now ends. That providential universe poised between eternity and chaos is the principal milieu of the poem, the ultimate battleground and crucial marriage bed. Perhaps that is why Blake's description of the fallen universe begins and ends with it.

The fall of the Zoas resulted from a contention among them, and produces the contentions we have been examining for two and a half plates. We have seen first the contention of Milton and his generated emanation Rahab/Tirzah, then the battles of Los and Orc with their emanations, and finally the wrestling of Milton and Urizen. Now we return to the original contention: Rahab and Tirzah, in league with Urizen and the Shadowy Female, send out their children to lure Milton to ruin:

> The Twofold form Hermaphroditic: and the Double-sexed;
> The Female-male & the Male-female, self-dividing stood
> Before him in their beauty, & in cruelties of holiness!
> —(19:32–34)

These sirens are "twofold" or "Double-sexed" because they are children of Generation and incapable of the threefold marriage of Beulah or of Eden's fourfold mental strife. They recall the hermaphroditic shadow Milton entered (14:37), and both Satan and the Shadowy Female with their "cruelties of holiness" (9:21–29 and 18:19–25). They are thus identified with the substance and the two regents of the Mundane Shell. Consequently, the lure they offer is to live this mortal life without inspiration, to realize eternal death.

Like the Shadowy Female, the hermaphrodites offer a delusion of godhead instead of the holiness of true humanity. Like her, they pretend to creativity. Tirzah, they claim, has the creative power of Los: "She ties the knot of nervous fibres into a white brain! / She ties the knot of bloody veins, into a red hot heart!" (19:55–56), even of Jesus: "She ties the knot of milky seed into two lovely Heavens / Two yet but one: each in the other sweet reflected! these / Are our Three Heavens beneath the shades of Beulah, land of rest!" (19:60–20:2). But whereas Los formed brain and heart to prevent extinction and Jesus created Beulah for a rest and a salvation, Tirzah forms only to rule. The body is for her only a vehicle of command, and her version of Beulah is a Bower of Bliss.

Thus Milton, embracing the shadow that is this mortal life, must resist its lures and transcend its delusions in order to redeem it. That is his struggle with the female will, his struggle with Urizen. Each facet of Milton's struggle contains the whole struggle; each is a battle of the fourfold with the twofold soul. Milton began the struggle when he entered into his shadow; it will not end until the last plate of the poem.

Notes

1. *Fearful Symmetry* (Princeton: Princeton University Press, 1947), p. 352.

2. S. Foster Damon, *William Blake: His Philosophy and Symbols* (New York: Houghton Mifflin, 1924), p. 412; M.O. Percival, *William Blake's Circle of Destiny* (New York, 1938), p. 280; *Fearful Symmetry*, p. 125; and *Blake's Apocalypse* (New York: Doubleday, 1963), pp. 282–283.

3. *Fearful Symmetry*, p. 350; Hazard Adams, *Blake and Yeats: The Contrary Vision* (Ithaca, N.Y.: Cornell University Press, 1955), pp. 104–110; *Apocalypse*, pp. 358–359; Thomas R. Frosch, *The Awakening of Albion: The Renovation of the Body in the Poetry of William Blake* (Ithaca, N.Y., and London: Cornell University Press, 1974), pp. 69–76. For the relation of Blake's conception of the vortex to Descartes', see Donald Ault, *Visionary Physics* (Chicago: University of Chicago Press, 1974), and Martin K. Nurmi, "Negative Sources in Blake," Rosenfeld, pp. 303–318, esp. pp. 307–312.

4. Nurmi defines Blake's vision of the Mundane Shell as "traceable partly to his reaction against a writer who used Newtonian principles to account for the creation: Thomas Burnet" (*op. cit.*, pp. 312–317).

5. For further analysis of Blake's use of garment imagery in *Milton* see Morton D. Paley, "The Figure of the Garment in *The Four Zoas, Milton,* and *Jerusalem,*" *Blake's Sublime Allegory* eds. S. Curran and J.A. Wittreich (Madison: University of Wisconsin Press, 1973), pp. 119–139, esp. pp. 131–135.

6. Morton D. Paley thinks the inclusion of Orc in *Milton* problematical, finding him, as energy principle, not fully compatible with the dominant imagination principle of the poem (*Energy and the Imagination: A Study of the Development of Blake's Thought* [Oxford: Clarendon Press, 1970], pp. 249–251). Paley suggests that Blake planned Orc's place in *Milton* when "he had not yet made his final disposition of the Orc symbol in *The Four Zoas.* He still hoped somehow to reconcile Orc's revolutionary energy with the regenerative Imagination symbolized by Jesus, Milton, and the inspired Los" (p. 249). Although I agree that Blake probably did greatly alter his attitude toward "revolutionary energy" as *Milton* developed (witness his suppression of the angry call to arms of the prose preface after the first two copies of the poem were engraved), I do not believe that there is "no place for Orc in this vision of regeneration": the anguished, passionate, destructive struggle of Orc seems to me an inescapable aspect, as I have defined it in the text, of the central struggles of the poem.

Spectre and Emanation
[From *The Continuing City*]

MORTON D. PALEY

While the identities of Los are separable for the purposes of discussion, they do not establish discrete significances on several levels of allegory but are rather fused into a single figure which has a palpable identity unified by its reference to Blake himself. The Los who struggles at his Furnaces to save Albion is Blake, labouring at *Jerusalem,* passionately addressing an England that will not hear, driven close to despair, yet hopeful of that signal of the morning when sleepers awake. The Los who struggles with his Spectre is Blake, too, the visionary artist in conflict with his workaday self. This conflict expands inward in reference to a deep psychic division at times; at other times it expands outward to take an ideological form. Enitharmon also exists in both quotidian and mythical aspects. "Enitharmon is a vegetated mortal Wife of Los: / His Emanation, yet his Wife till the sleep of Death is past" (*14*:13–14). She is at the same time Catherine Blake and the idealized counterpart that Jung calls the anima. Potentially, she embodies the fulfillment of creative impulse, but in the fallen world, divided from Los, she struggles with him for dominion. Los's endeavour to save Albion by visionary work is at the same time a quest to reintegrate his own Spectre and Emanation. This double enterprise refers to Blake both as an artist/poet and as a man.

Los's conflict with his Spectre begins on *6* and carries through the next four plates (including inserted *10*) until Los compels the Spectre to labours mighty in *11*. The conflict resumes intermittently until *91*, where Los divides the Spectre into a separate space, but the Spectre also has a benign aspect, as in *43/29–44/30* when he and Enitharmon appear as fugitives from Albion's fall and in *83* where he labours co-operatively with Los at the furnaces. In the end, *100,* only that positive aspect remains. So most of the content of the Urthona myth involves a war within the self, a war which is waged both for the emanation Enitharmon and between Los and Enitharmon. Like the Spectre Enitharmon attempts to assert dominion over Los; and like him, too, she is integrated into the harmony of *100.*

In addition to the Spectre's personal meaning as an aspect of Blake, he also has a more general meaning, one which is nevertheless appropriate to Los—and therefore to Blake himself. It is difficult to separate these two levels of significance here, as elsewhere in *Jerusalem,* but to the extent that we can do so, we can understand the Spectre's power as alternatively projected outwards into ideology and inward into paranoia and self-hatred. In both senses the meanings particularly concern William Blake as distinguished from the meaning of the more generalized Spectre of Albion.

"The Spectre is, in Giant Man; insane, and most deform'd," says Los when he feels his own Spectre rising upon him.[1] In Albion's Spectre that insanity takes the ideological form of the worship of authoritarian Reason; in Los's it manifests itself as an obsession with a God who damns His subject creatures irrevocably and without reason. The Spectre's God is thus precisely the contrary—or, rather, the Negation—of Blake's "brother and friend" (4:18). The Spectre's great speech of *10* is an almost unbearably moving expression of the conviction of damnation:

> I said: now is my grief at worst: incapable of being
> Surpassed: but every moment it accumulates more & more
> It continues accumulating to eternity! the joys of God advance
> For he is Righteous: he is not a Being of Pity & Compassion
> He cannot feel Distress: he feeds on Sacrifice & Offering:
> Delighting in cries & tears & clothed in holiness & solitude
> But my griefs advance also, for ever & ever without end
> O that I could cease to be! Despair! I am Despair
> Created to be the great example of horror & agony: also my
> Prayer is vain I called for compassion: compassion mockd[,]
> Mercy & pity threw the grave stone over me & with lead
> And iron, bound it over me for ever: Life lives on my
> Consuming: & the Almighty hath made me his Contrary
> To be all evil, all reversed & for ever dead: knowing
> And seeing life, yet living not; how can I then behold
> And not tremble; how can I be beheld & not abhorrd
> —(10:44–59)

As I have suggested elsewhere, there is a model for this speech in the tragic life of William Cowper, a poet whose work Blake admired and whose example he had reason to dread.[2]

Blake's interest in Cowper was extraordinary. Cowper's letters were, wrote Blake to Thomas Butts, "Perhaps, or rather Certainly, the very best letters that ever were published."[3] He executed at least a dozen finished pictures on Cowperian subjects in various media, including six engravings for William Hayley's *Life and Posthumous Writings of William Cowper,*[4] two miniatures in water-colour and one larger pen, ink, and wash portrait after Romney, an idealized tempera portrait, two tempera illustrations to *The Task* (*Winter* and *Evening*), and a frieze of the bridge at Olney.[5] In his *Notebook*

Blake wrote an epitaph for Cowper (E. 498) in which he accused Hayley of ignoring Cowper's inspiration:

> You see him spend his Soul in Prophecy
> Do you believe it a confounded lie

And he had a vision of the insane Cowper which he recorded in a copy of Dr. J. G. Spurzheim's *Observations on the Deranged Manifestations of the Mind, or Insanity* (London, 1817): "Cowper came to me and said, 'O that I were insane, always. I will never rest. Cannot you make me truly insane? I will never rest till I am so. Oh! that in the bosom of God I was hid. You retain health and yet are as mad as any of us all—over us all—mad as a refuge from unbelief—from Bacon Newton & Locke.' "[6]

In having Cowper call him "mad as any of us all," Blake is ironically acknowledging the views of spiritual enemies like Hayley, who wrote of Blake to Lady Hesketh: "I have ever wished to befriend Him from a Motive, that, I know, our dear angelic friend Cowper *would approve,* because this poor man with an admirable quickness of apprehension, & with uncommon powers of mind, has *often appeared to me on the verge of Insanity.*"[7] Cowper's words to Blake might be termed a visionary corrective of the conventional idea of madness. For Blake, Cowper had been mad in the wrong sense: his "madness" lay not in his Evangelical Christianity but in the beliefs expressed in his "Lines Written on a Window Shutter," first published in 1801:

> Me miserable! how could I escape
> Infinite wrath and infinite despair!
> Whom Death, Earth, Heaven, and Hell consigned to ruin.
> Whose friend was God, but God swore not to aid me![8]

Therefore Blake imagines Cowper as asking plaintively "Can you not make me truly insane?"—insane enough to believe, with Blake, that all could be saved. Blake's vision of Cowper was probably prompted by a flurry of controversy about Cowper's insanity that occurred after the publication of Cowper's account of his first period of madness, including his attempts at suicide, as *Memoir of the Early Life of William Cowper, Esq.*[9] in 1816. Some of the details of Cowper's insanity had, however, been known earlier. *The Examiner* used Cowper as an example of "The Folly and Danger of Methodism" in 1808—a year before it attacked Blake as "an unfortunate lunatic."[10] In any event, Blake would already have been familiar with the *Memoir* and with other suppressed writings concerning Cowper's madness. When Blake was working with Hayley on the *Life and Posthumous Writings,* he had ample opportunity to see these manuscript materials. This is evident in Hayley's letter to Cowper's nephew John Johnson ("Johnny of Norfolk")[11] dated 1 October 1801: "We want you as a faithful Coadjutor in the Turret more than I can express. / I say *we;* for the warmhearted indefatigable Blake works daily by my side, on the intended decorations of our Biography."[12] Johnny of Norfolk came twice to Sussex to give Hayley materials for the *Life*.[13] Evidently these included Johnny's transcripts of the *Memoir* and of a diary of 1796 in which Cowper had recorded his certainty of damnation; Johnny had, moreover, kept one notebook in which he had recorded Cowper's visions and voices and another in which he recounted his life with Cowper.[14] Hayley must have seen all or most of this material, for he quotes from the manuscript of the *Memoir* in the *Life* (I. 24–5) and shows familiarity with the two notebooks elsewhere. Blake himself became at least a friendly acquaintance of John Johnson, painting his portrait in miniature as well as executing for him the two *Task* temperas and the frieze of Olney Bridge.[15] There was probably ample opportunity for Blake to learn about Cowper directly from Johnson as well as through Hayley, and there is much to suggest that Blake drew upon this knowledge in creating the speech of the Spectre in *Jerusalem 10.*

"O that I could cease to be!" cries the Spectre. "Despair! I am Despair. . . ." In Cowper's *Memoir,* his despair is a reiterated theme: "Being assured of this [having sinned against the Holy Ghost], with the most rooted conviction, I gave myself to despair."[16] [And] "After five months' continual expectation, that the divine vengeance would plunge me into the bottomless pit, I became so familiar with despair, as to have contracted a sort of hardiness and indifference as to the event."[17] The "speaker" of Cowper's great poem "The Castaway" (first published in Hayley's *Life*) "wag'd with death a lasting strife, / Supported by despair of life."[18] Cowper wrote in his diary "My Despair is infinite, my entanglements are infinite, my doom is sure"; and, in a letter to Hayley, "Perfect Despair, the most perfect, that ever possess'd any Mind, has had possession of mine, you know how long."[19]— "O that I could cease to be! Despair! I am Despair. . . ." Furthermore, the Spectre resembles Cowper in viewing his destruction as predestined. The Spectre says, "The Almighty hath made me his contrary / To be all evil, all reversed & for ever dead. . . ." The Castaway is a "Destined wretch"; "Hatred and vengeance" are Cowper's "eternal portion"; he is "Pre-ordained to fall."[20] Cowper compares himself to Abiram, one of the Levite leaders who was swallowed by the earth for rebelling against Moses:

> *Him* the vindictive rod of angry justice
> Sent quick and howling to the centre headlong;
> *I*, fed with judgment, in a fleshly tomb, am
> Buried above ground.[21]

And like Cowper, the Spectre expresses his condition by an image of immolation, saying "Mercy & pity threw the grave stone over me & with lead / And iron, bound it over me for ever. . . ." The Spectre appropriates not only Cowper's belief that he had been condemned by a God without mercy but also the terrible pathos of his tone, the same sense of desolation and abandonment: "Such was not the mercy I expected from Thee, nor that horror and overwhelming misery should be the only means of deliverance left me in a moment so important! Farewell to the remembrance of Thee. For ever, I must now suffer thy wrath, but forget that I ever heard thy name."[22]

> So spoke the Spectre shuddring, & dark tears ran down his shadowy face
> Which Los wiped off, but comfort none could give! or beam of hope
> —(10:60–1)

To create the suffering Spectre of *Jerusalem 10,* Blake must have drawn upon deep-rooted fears of his own that were dramatically opposed to his conscious beliefs. Blake believed in a God of infinite mercy and explicitly repudiated predestination,[23] but he too experienced despair, as he recorded in his Notebook: "Tuesday Jan^ry. 20. 1807 between Two & Seven in the Evening—Despair" (E. 672). Although Blake was not tempted to believe in Cowper's God, his own despair enabled him to conceive of what such a God might be. Other personal characteristics of Blake's also go to make up the Spectre in different parts of *Jerusalem.* If we consider some of these characteristics as Blake himself described them, we will appreciate the extent to which Los's Spectre is built of aspects of Blake himself.

> And my Angels have told me that seeing such visions I could not subsist on the
>   Earth,
> But by my conjunction with Flaxman, who knows how to forgive Nervous Fear.[24]

> . . . My Abstract folly hurries me often away while I am at work, carrying me over Mountains & Valleys . . . in a Land of Abstraction where Spectres of the Dead wander.[25]

> When I look, each one starts! when I speak, I offend;
> Then I'm silent & passive & lose every Friend.[26]

> . . . It affronted my foolish Pride [of his encounter with Schofield].[27]

These Verses were written by a very Envious Man[28]

> I have entirely reduced that Spectrous Fiend to his station, whose annoyance has been the ruin of my labours for the last passed twenty years of my life. He is the enemy of conjugal love and is the Jupiter of the Greeks, an iron-hearted tyrant, the ruiner of ancient Greece.[29]

Drawing upon these qualities which he feared and disliked in himself, Blake created a Spectre whose characteristics include anxiety, hostility—both passive and active—envy, pride, and black melancholy. Of another Spectral emotion, sexual jealousy, Blake says nothing with reference to himself; but it is often a theme in his other poetry and particularly in some of the very personal *Notebook* poems, to a degree that makes one suspect that Blake too had experienced the jealous rage that sometimes characterizes the Spectre of Los. In projecting these fearsome qualities into a *doppelgänger*, Blake achieves the goal of giving Los—in this respect his ego—the possibility of controlling them, and consequently of freeing his own artistic energies.

At the very end of 5 the Spectre begins to divide from Los,[30] and this division with its attendant conflict is in Chapter 1 the main subject of 6–10; it is then taken up once more on 17. Descending upon Los in the 6 design in the form of a bat,[31] the Spectre goes on in the text of 7 to tempt Los to suspect Albion:

> He drinks thee up like water! like wine he pours thee
> Into his tuns: thy Daughters are trodden in his vintage
> He makes thy Sons the trampling of his bulls, they are plow'd
> And harrowd for his profit, lo! thy stolen Emanation
> Is his garden of pleasure! all the Spectres of his Sons mock thee
> Look how they scorn thy once admired palaces! now in ruins
> Because of Albion! because of deceit and friendship! . . .
> —(11–17)

This is a paranoid fantasy on the level of some of those that Blake himself experienced in the bitter years following the *Grave* disaster of 1805–6; compare Blake's *Notebook* accusation of Hayley, who "when he could not act upon my wife / Hired a Villain to bereave my Life."[32] The Spectre displays the cleverness of a psychopath, trying "To lure Los: by tears, by arguments of science & by terrors" (7:6), but unlike the double in Poe's "William Wilson," this *doppelgänger*[33] does not succeed in its destructive intent. The construction of Blake's myth tends towards integration, not schizoid bifurcation. The Los in Blake declares to his Spectre: "I know thy deceit & thy revenges. . . . I will compell thee to assist me in my terrible labours" (8:7, 15). He also recognizes that the Spectre is indeed part of himself—"Thou art my Pride & Self-righteousness"—much as Prospero recognizes Caliban ("This thing of darkness I / Acknowledge mine").[34] Now the Spectre becomes Blake as working engraver, guided by Imagination, labouring with Los at the Furnaces to perfect the Spaces of Erin, in response to Los's magnificent command:

> Take thou this Hammer & in patience heave the thundering Bellows
> Take thou these Tongs: strike thou alternate with me: labour obedient[.]
> —(8:39–40)

Throughout most of the rest of *Jerusalem* the Spectre of Urthona is under Los's control but remains always incipiently a threat. In 17 the emphasis is on the Spectre's division; however, he does Los's bidding. In 33/37 Los feels his Spectre rising within him, though the later appearance of the Spectre in Chapter 2 is in a benign aspect, in *43/29:28–83* to *44/30:1*–15. But as *Jerusalem* begins to approach its apocalyptic climax, the Spectre makes one more attempt to usurp Los's personality and function. In *88* the Spectre creates division between Los and Enitharmon. Then in *91* he asserts his power over the natural universe:

> The Spectre builded stupendous Works, taking the Starry Heavens
> Like to a curtain & folding them according to his will
>
> —(32–3)

The reference here is to the God of Psalm 104:2 "Who coverest thyself with light as with a garment: who stretchest out the heavens like a curtain. . . ." Blake is not impressed by such prestidigitation, any more than he is by the act that follows:

> . . . forming Leviathan
> And Behemoth: the War by Sea enormous & the War
> By Land astounding . . .
>
> —(38–40)

Now the Spectre is the God of Job, trying to impress his audience with his ability to create monsters. Blake's satirical view of such endeavour may be found in *Job* design 15 and in the Spiritual Portraits of Pitt and Nelson.[35] Los's response is to show up the emptiness of Spectral power by destroying its illusory achievements. The topos for this confrontation is the battle of sacred and profane magicians—Moses vs. Pharaoh's sorcerers, Paul vs. Simon Magus. "Los reads the Stars of Albion" for the same reason that the wise characters in Shakespeare accept natural (but not judicial) astrology: the stars and their influences relate us to a larger order of things.[36] "The Spectre reads the Voids / Between the Stars" in a vain attempt to measure quantitatively distances that Blake regards as unreal. So the Hammer of Los destroys the Spectre's works, including "the Smaragdine Table of Hermes." "Blake rejected this document," as Damon says, "and with it all occultism" because "it was the magician trying to be the mystic."[37] After beating down the Spectre's works, Los beats down the Spectre himself, until it becomes evident that it is his own Faustian will that he is hammering, "with many blows, / Of strict severity self-subduing."

In consequence of this last victory over the Spectre, Nature assumes a frail, evanescent, Shelleyan beauty:

> Then he sent forth the Spectre all his pyramids were grains
> Of sand & his pillars: dust on the flys wing: & his starry
> Heavens; a moth of gold & silver mocking his anxious grasp
>
> —(47–9)

The Spectre, being part of Los's identity, is not to be destroyed; he is "divided . . . into a separate space" where his powers contribute to the workings of that composite being whom Blake sometimes calls Urthona. When Albion awakens in 95, he compels the Zoas Urizen, Tharmas, and Luvah to their tasks; but one he does not need to compel: "Urthona he beheld mighty labouring at / His Anvil, in the Great Spectre Los unwearied labouring & weeping" (17–18). The integration of his Spectre with his imaginative self enables Los/Blake to actualize his powers in redemptive work.

The other division of Los is from his emanation[38] Enitharmon, who divides from him in 6 and continues divided and divisive through 93, to become part of a harmonious existence only in 100. In part, this is a more personal particularization of the sexual myth of Vala-Albion-Jerusalem. It too is triadic but involves two males and a female, with the Spectre representing the unfulfilled sexual drive that Los fears and that he feels he must control. This triadic situation is also the subject of the Notebook poem "My Spectre around me night & day,"[39] in which the first person speaker would correspond to Los divided from his Spectre and from Enitharmon. In "My Spectre around me," which Damon describes as "a poem analyzing an unhappy marriage,"[40] it is the Emanation and not the Spectre who plays the adversary role, burning for victory while savagely envisaging the death of the male speaker. The Spectre is the speaker's unleashed desire, tracking the Emanation "On the hungry craving wind," leaving the remainder of the divided self protected from entrapment by the female. This ambivalent view of sexuality is also found in Jerusalem 17, where once more the Spectre is the vehicle of aggressive male desire. Here Los "Dare not approach the Daughters [of Albion] openly lest he be consumed / In the fires of their beauty & perfection" (7–8). The Daughters are Siren figures who "wooe Los continually to subdue his strength"; instead of yielding, "he continually / Shews them his Spectre." As in the Notebook poems where the unabashed display of desire frightens away the love object,[41] "Shuddring they flee . . . / Subdued by the Spectre of the Living & terrified by undisguised desire" (14–15). Thus Los achieves an immunity from seduction but only at the cost of delegating his sexuality to the Spectre. At the same time he attempts through most of Jerusalem to regain his lost Emanation, an enterprise which the jealous Spectre opposes.

The separation of Los and Enitharmon is a theme in several parts of Jerusalem; it begins in 5 and persists unresolved throughout, until the great synthesis of 100. As previously in The Book of Urizen and The Four Zoas, Los in effect gives birth to Enitharmon in a travesty of the creation of Eve:

> And Enitharmon like a faint rainbow waved before him
> Filling with Fibres from his loins which reddend with desire
> Into a Globe of blood beneath his bosom trembling in darkness
> Of Albions clouds. he fed it, with his tears & bitter groans
> Hiding his Spectre in invisibility from the timorous Shade

> Till it became a separated cloud of beauty grace & love
> Among the darkness of his Furnaces dividing asunder till
> She separated stood before him a lovely Female weeping
> Even Enitharmon separated outside, & his Loins closed
> And heal'd after the separation: his pains he soon forgot:
> Lured by her beauty outside of himself in shadowy grief.
> Two Wills they had; Two Intellects: & not as in times of old.
>
> —(86:50–61)

This male fantasy of giving birth is painful yet reassuring, at least from the perspective of Los's creator. Although the unfallen Urthona may be thought of as androgynous, like the beings of Aristophanes' myth in Plato's *Symposium*, unlike them he is an androgynous *male*. His "Vehicular form," Los, is scarcely distinguishable from him—even their names become interchanged at times—but the manifestation of his Emanation is a lapse from a higher state of being. She is "like a faint rainbow" because she embodies the delusive beauty of the phenomenal world, once more a lapse from unity, as in the refraction of light.

There are passages concerned with the division of Enitharmon from Los in *6, 14, 17,* and *22,* but their longest conflict occurs in *86–8,* where they contend about how to weave the "wild fibres" that emanate from him, fibres of which she herself is made. The fibres are ambivalent: positive, they are woven in "the golden Looms of Cathedron sending fibres of love / From Golgonooza with sweet visions for Jerusalem, wanderer" (86:40–1). Negative, they "shoot in veins / Of blood thro all my [Los's] nervous limbs. soon overgrown in roots / I shall be closed from thy sight" (87:5–7). Fibres are basic life-stuff which can be used for regenerative purposes, as in the new ending which Blake wrote for Night VIIa of *The Four Zoas.* There Enitharmon asks Los to "fabricate forms sublime"[42] for the ravening, bodiless spectres, and he agrees. Working together, Los and Enitharmon become the powers of generation in a benign sense, creating bodies which sense may reach and apprehend, vehicles of joy. More particularly, they are William and Catherine Blake making the illuminated books. It is such happily productive activity that Los proposes to Enitharmon in *87:*

> sieze therefore in thy hand
> The small fibres as they shoot around me draw out in pity
> And let them run on the winds of thy bosom: I will fix them
> With pulsations, we will divide them into Sons & Daughters
> To live in thy Bosoms translucence as in an eternal morning
>
> —(7–11)

Behind this conception is a view of material existence that is also characteristic of *Milton* in contrast to the more pessimistic Lambeth Books, and which is expressed in *86:*

> Nor can any consummate bliss without being Generated
> On Earth; of those whose Emanations weave the loves
> Of Beulah for Jerusalem & Shiloh, in immortal Golgonooza
> —(42–4)

The achievement of such bliss, however, depends upon the harmonious collaboration of the powers embodied in Los and Enitharmon. This is not what happens in most of *Jerusalem*, with the exception of one very short section in *83:*71–4, where

> his Emanation
> Joy'd in the many weaving threads in bright Cathedrons Dome
> Weaving the Web of life for Jerusalem. the Web of life
> Down flowing into Entuthons Vales glistens with soft affections.

This magnificent image shows the positive valence of Enitharmon's weaving, but it is compressed into less than four lines. For the most part the situation is as in *87:*12–24, where Enitharmon opposes Los, declaring her intention to seize his Fibres and weave them as she wills, to create a body for Albion's Spectre. In the design on *85* we see her drawing the Fibres out of Los in the form of grape-vines emanating from his head, bowels, and loins.[43] In the text of *88* she weaves these Fibres into a husk of Moral Law for the natural man. Her goal is to create a religion in which God is a dependent child:

> That he who loves Jesus may loathe terrified Female love
> Till God himself become a Male subservient to the Female.
> —(20–1)

In that "Womans World" there is no place for Los, and without her "His rage or his mildness were vain, she scattered his love on the wind" (*88:*51).

The power struggle between Los and Enitharmon continues for the most part until *100,* the design which stands as an epitome of the regenerate world. In the *87* design they are shown as a pair of wilful children, evading the groping of their mother, the blind earth goddess Enion. In *92–3* occurs the last verbal exchange of this contentious pair. Enitharmon foresees her imminent disappearance as a separate identity when Albion awakens, for "My Looms will be no more & I annihilate vanish for ever" (*92:*11). This is indeed a partial truth, but it is because, Los answers, "Sexes must vanish & cease / To be, when Albion arises from his dread repose" (13–14)—part of the larger conception whereby in the regenerate world embracings will be comminglings from head to foot. Not comprehending this impending transformation, Enitharmon desperately clings to her individual existence. Her last speech is a complaint to her sons that "you forget all my Love! / The Mothers love of obedience is forgotten" (*93:*3–4). She speaks no more after *93:*16.

If it is the Los in Blake who urges Enitharmon/Catherine to collaborate in creative activity, it is the Spectre in him that continually interferes with such co-operation. The Spectre self is driven by an irresistible compulsion to absorb Enitharmon and at the same time to involve Los in paranoid delusion. In his very first speech, in 7, like Iago at Othello's ear, he urges Los to suspect Albion. In 10 he demands "Where is my lovely Enitharmon / O thou my enemy, where is my Great Sin?" (42–3). All appetite and dependence, the Spectre hates both himself and the object of his appetite and dependence. Los/Blake dreads this aspect of his own identity and he tries to guard Enitharmon from it: "he infolded her in his garments / Of wool: he hid her from the Spectre, in shame & confusion of / Face" (17:52–4). He exercises enormous psychic force to make the Spectre obey his conscious intention:

> that Enitharmon may not
> Be lost: & lest he should devour Enitharmon: Ah me!
> Piteous image of my soft desires & loves: O Enitharmon!
> I will compell my Spectre to obey: I will restore to thee thy Children.
> —(17:17–20)

Conversely, in 86:54 it is the Spectre that Los hides from Enitharmon, but the meaning is similar: the ego's control is ensured by the separation of desire from the object of desire. However, the ever-threatening Spectre succeeds in precipitating a crisis between Los and Enitharmon in 88. As their bickering continues, "A sullen smile broke from the Spectre in mockery & scorn / Knowing himself the author of their divisions & shrinkings . . ." (34–5). In this fine personal touch, we can sense Blake's satirical self-observation. As Blake wrote to Hayley, the Spectre is the enemy of conjugal love.

He is also the enemy of sexual joy. Guilt-obsessed, regarding Enitharmon as "my Great Sin," he engages in a demonic parody of Los's continual building of Golgonooza—"Continually building, continually destroying in Family feuds." He regards sexual love as a filthy, Yahoo activity: "For I will make their places of joy & love, excrementitious" (88:39). This sentence has been traced to Augustine's "Inter faeces et urinam nascimur."[44] Elaborating that statement in another way, Yeats, who may also have had Blake's words in mind, makes his Crazy Jane say that although Love's mansion is pitched in "The place of excrement," it is that very rending that makes a woman's love "sole or whole."[45] Crazy Jane's tragic sensibility unites what the Spectral self divides. Something like this happens—or almost happens—in The Four Zoas VIIa when Los embraces Enitharmon and the Spectre, and "Clouds would have folded round in Extacy & Love uniting,"[46] but at this point in Jerusalem Los himself is affected by the Spectre's sexual fantasies and becomes like Urizen, segregating sexual love from the rest of human existence, "dividing the Space of Love with brazen Compasses" (88:47).

An exception to the disharmony of Los, Enitharmon, and Spectre in

Jerusalem occurs in *43/29* and *44/30,* beginning when "two Immortal forms" tell the story of Albion's fall, rewritten from Night III of *The Four Zoas.* In *44:*1–2 these messengers are identified as "the Emanation of Los & his Spectre"; here "his Spectre is named Urthona" (4). In this benign aspect the Spectre and Emanation are suggestive of the Blakes' view of themselves amid the Hayley circle in Sussex, "Being not irritated by insult bearing insulting benevolences" (9). The Divine Hand bears them safely back to their humanity, "& Los put forth his hand & took them in / Into his Bosom" (16–17). This is also the subject of the *44* design, where Los extends his downturned palms to receive two figures which we last saw flying towards the upper right margin of *23.* Enitharmon has lepidopterous wings like those of the fairy mimes of the title-page; the Spectre's wings are once more batlike, but their effect is comical rather than threatening—a Fledermaus, not a Dracula. So positive is the view of the Spectre in *44/30* that we are told

> Therefore the Sons of Eden praise Urthona's Spectre in Songs
> Because he kept the Divine Vision in time of trouble.
>   —(14–15)

This high praise of the Spectre is repeated verbatim after Albion awakens in *95* and beholds "in the Great Spectre Los unwearied labouring & weeping" (18). There Los and the Spectre seem to have fused their identities. The Spectre is, then, capable of embodying positive value; although Los and his Spectre battle throughout much of *Jerusalem,* they are in harmonious relationship in *44/30,* in *95,* and in *100.*

Notes

1. *33/37:4.* This line occurs twice in *FZ*—5:38–9, 84:36–7.
2. "Cowper As Blake's Spectre," *Eighteenth-Century Studies,* I (1968), 236–52.
3. 11 September 1801, *Letters,* p. 52.
4. London: Joseph Johnson, vols. I and II, 1803; vol. III, 1804.
5. One of the two miniatures is in the Ashmolean Museum, the other in the collection of Mrs. Cowper Johnson; the pen, ink, and wash portrait is in the National Gallery of Art, Washington, D.C.; the tempera is in the Manchester City Art Gallery; *Winter* is in the Tate Gallery and *Evening* in a private collection; the picture of Olney Bridge was destroyed by fire.
6. *The Works of William Blake,* ed. Ellis and Yeats (London, Quaritch, 1893), I. 155. Some time after the editors saw this note "among the sheets of the Vala MS," the fragment of paper on which it had been written was lost.
7. 3 August 1805; *BR,* p. 164.
8. *Memoirs of the Life and Writings of W. Cowper, Esqr.,* ed. Samuel Greatheed (n.p., 1801), p. 33. Greatheed altered "Hell" to "all" and also made some less consequential emendations; I have rendered the text as it appears in *Complete Poetical Works,* p. 428.
9. Two editions were published in 1816: by E. Cox and by R. Edwards; the Edwards edition was reprinted with the corrections that same year, and it went into third and fourth printings in 1817 and 1818. There were also a Birmingham edition and three American

editions during those three years. See Norma Russell, *A Bibliography of William Cowper to 1837* (Oxford: The Clarendon Press, 1963), p. 195.

10. *Examiner,* 17 July 1808, 461; 17 September 1809, 605. Both articles are signed with a pointing hand.

11. On Johnson, see Morchard Bishop, *Blake's Hayley* (London: Victor Gollancz, 1951), pp. 217–24; and Gerald E. Bentley, Jr., "William Blake and Johnny of Norfolk," *Studies in Philology,* LIII (1956), 60–74.

12. Bentley, "Johnny of Norfolk," 64; *BR,* p. 82.

13. In spring 1801 and January 1802. See Maurice J. Quinlan, "Memoir of William Cowper," *Proceedings of the American Philosophical Society,* XCVII (1953), 363. Johnson wrote to Hayley disclaiming knowledge of the whereabouts of this manuscript (see Russell, *Bibliography,* p. 245n.), but even if he did not find it, another copy was in the possession of the Revd. Samuel Greatheed, who visited Felpham in 1803.

14. See Anon., "Cowper's Spiritual Diary," *The London Mercury,* XV (1927), 493–6; Hoxie Neale Fairchild, "Additional Notes on John Johnson's Diary," *PMLA,* XLIII (1928), 571–2; Robert E. Spiller, "A New Biographical source for William Cowper," *PMLA,* XLII (1927), 946–62.

15. Butlin (*Catalogue,* 1978, pp. 142–3) dates the miniature 1802 and the *Task* pictures *c.* 1821.

16. *Memoir* (London: R. Edwards, 2nd printing, 1816), p. 66.

17. Ibid., p. 72.

18. *Complete Poetical Works,* p. 431. Cf. *Memoir:* "Already overwhelmed with despair, I was not yet sunk into the bottom of the gulf" (p. 63).

19. 20 June 1797. *The Unpublished and Uncollected Letters of William Cowper,* ed. Thomas Wright (London: C. J. Farncombe, 1925), p. 82.

20. *Complete Poetical Works,* pp. 431, 290; John Johnson's diary entry for 5 August 1798 (Cambridge University Library, Add. MSS 5993).

21. "Lines Written During a Period of Insanity," *Complete Poetical Works,* p. 290. Cowper may have recognized the irony of Abiram's name, which in Hebrew means "My father is the Exalted One." See Num. 16:31; *Dictionary of the Bible,* ed. James Hastings (New York: Scribner, 1963), I. 46.

22. "Spiritual Diary," p. 496.

23. See Blake's annotation to Swedenborg's *Divine Providence,* E. 599–600.

24. Letter to John Flaxman, 12 September 1800, *The Letters of William Blake,* ed. Geoffrey Keynes (Cambridge, Mass.: Harvard University Press, 2d ed. 1968), p. 38.

25. Letter to Thomas Butts, 11 September 1801, *Letters,* p. 51.

26. Letter to Thomas Butts, 16 August 1803, *Letters,* p. 74.

27. Ibid., p. 73.

28. "Florentine Ingratitude," E. 504.

29. Letter to William Hayley, 23 October 1804, *Letters,* p. 106.

30. But this may not be the first reference to the Spectre of Los in *Jerusalem.* Among the inscriptions on the proof of *I* in the collection of Sir Geoffrey Keynes, occurs the reversed writing: "Every Thing has its Vermin O Spectre of the Sleeping Dead!" (E. 143). Of course the line may apply to the Spectre of Albion as well.

31. David V. Erdman points out that in John Gabriel Stedman's *Narrative of a Five Years' Expedition against the Revolted Negroes at Surinam,* for which Blake executed sixteen engravings, there is an engraving of a bat by A. Smith entitled *The Vampire or Spectre of Guiana.* (See *Blake: Prophet against Empire* [Princeton: Princeton University Press, 1954], p. 234n.). Among meanings of "Spectre" found in the *OED* are: "an apparition, phantasm, or ghost, esp. one of a terrifying nature or aspect"; "an unreal object of thought; a phantasm of the brain"; "an object or source of dread or terror, imagined as an apparition," "one whose appearance is suggestive of an apparition or ghost," "a faint shadow or imitation *of* something," and "one of the images or

semblances supposed by the Epicurean school to emanate from corporal things" (with an example from Reid, 1785). In creating his symbolic names and terms, Blake liked to play along a wide scale of meanings, and I suspect that all those I have selected here are relevant conceptually.

32. "On H----ys Friendship," E. 497. On the psychological consequences of Blake's betrayal by Cromek, see Robert N. Essick and Morton D. Paley, *Robert Blair's The Grave, Illustrated by William Blake* (London: Scolar Press, 1982), pp. 18–35.

33. For some other literary comparisons, see E.J. Rose, "Blake and the Double: the Spectre as Doppelgänger," *Colby Library Quarterly*, XIII (1977), 127–39.

34. *The Tempest*, V.i. 275–6.

35. See *Energy and the Imagination*, pp. 171–99.

36. Cf. Blake's spirited defence of an imprisoned astrologer: "The Man who can Read the Stars often is oppressed by their Influence, no less than the Newtonian who reads Not & cannot Read is oppressed by his own Reasonings & Experiments." Letter to Richard Phillips, 14 October 1807, *Letters*, p. 128.

37. *Blake Dictionary A* (Providence: Brown University Press, 1965), p. 183.

38. Sloss and Wallis point out that the term "emanation" occurs nowhere earlier than in late passages of *The Four Zoas*. They suggest that "Blake first met the term and its equivalent 'Eon' in Jacob Bryant's *New System, or An Analysis of Ancient Mythology* (1774–6, vol. i, p. 18)." See *The Prophetic Writings of William Blake* (Oxford: Clarendon Press, 1925), II. 153.

39. E. 467–8.

40. *Blake Dictionary*, p. 381.

41. Such as "Never pain to tell thy love" (E. 458), and "I asked a thief to steal me a peach" (E. 459).

42. 98:22, E. 356. On this section of VIIa, see my *Energy and the Imagination* (Oxford: Clarendon Press, 1970), pp. 157–61; and Mary Lynn Johnson and Brian Wilkie, "The Spectrous Embrace in *The Four Zoas*, VIIa," *Blake*, XII (1978), 100–5.

43. The beauty of this design in copy E can be misleading. Damon sees it as depicting the work of the male and female, weaving the Vine of Friendship in Beulah, but his own observation that "they are separated and their faces turned from each other" (*William Blake*, p. 474) should guide us to the true meaning.

44. See Raymond Lister, *William Blake* (New York: F. Unger, 1969), p. 154.

45. "Crazy Jane Talks with the Bishop," *Collected Poems* (London: Macmillan, 1958), p. 295.

46. 86:14, E. 354.

[From "Striving with Systems":
Blake and the Politics of Difference]

STEVEN SHAVIRO

"I must Create a System, or be enslav'd by another Mans," cries Los at a crucial moment early in *Jerusalem,* "I will not Reason & Compare; my business is to Create" (10:20–21, E151).[1] The emphasis in these lines is upon "Create" rather than upon "System," but it is in the conjunction of the two terms that the problematic of Blake's text may best be situated. On the one hand, what might be called Blake's systematizing mania is a major stumbling block for any reader of the longer poems; *Jerusalem,* with its bewildering cast of metamorphosing characters and its discontinuities of place and action, can scarcely be read apart from the commentary which it has generated, that of the elaborate mapping so painstakingly worked out by S. Foster Damon, Northrop Frye, and their successors.[2] Yet on the other hand, as such systematizing critics themselves never tire of pointing out, Blake's elaborate constructions are themselves only means toward the end of liberating the poet and his readers from any such limitations of system or of perspective. Systematization must remain subordinated to the process of creation of which it is nevertheless the result and the symptom. In the long run, any completed system, including even Blake's own, must be destroyed in order to be freshly recreated.

This problematic may be stated in another and starker way by noting the contradiction between the two most commonly received images of the poet: that of Blake as systematizer, as sage and teacher, as essentially doctrinal poet, and that of Blake as dramatic poet and master of irony who rarely or never speaks *in propria persona.* These opposed conceptions intersect or interfere at the moments (such as Los's resolution to "Create") in which the systematizing compulsion is dramatized as such within Blake's text. At such moments, a prior knowledge of Blake's system in its totality is needed in order to approach a point prior to that system and from which the system as such is generated. The poem itself dramatizes, and thereby reflects back upon and limits, the process of its own systematization. The poem suggests that any System is an object of desire, and needs to be constructed; but such an insight is available to us only if we ignore its applicability to the overarching

From *boundary 2,* no. 10:3 (1982), 229–50. Used by permission.

Blakean System in which, e.g., the function of Los as figure of Imagination is first defined. Any such identification of the role of Los depends upon a previous conception of Blake's myth or System as a coherent and organized totality. This means that Blake criticism, like the systematizing movement within the poetry itself, is able to validate itself only to the extent that it already assumes what it then sets out to prove.

In consequence, there seem to be two alternatives for any reading of Blake. On the one hand, we may move within the familiar paradox of pre-knowledge and the hermeneutic circle. Blake is interpreted systematically because it has been assumed not only that Blake's works do in fact constitute a System, but even that the contents or broad outlines of the System (such as the identities and functions of the characters) are already known prior to the act of reading. This accounts for what Thomas Weiskel has called "the charmed circularity of Blakean hermeneutics,"[3] the maddeningly cultish, self-referential and self-congratulatory tone of all too much Blake criticism. Or else, if the *a priori* postulate of totalization and systematic coherence is abandoned, then the contradictory perspectives and ironic reversals of Blake's text are resolved into some form of infinite regress, in which any System refers back, in its contingency, to the act by which it was created, while creators and acts of creation are themselves determined and made possible only within the context of previously existing Systems. Blake's dramatic ironies are regulated and distributed by his overarching System; but that System is itself only produced as an effect in the course of an essentially ironic dramatic interplay.

These alternatives exist for every critic of Blake because they are already contradictory features of Blake's text itself. In exploring this problematic, my own commentary will therefore not resist the temptation to function, at the same time, as an allegory of the critical process itself. In Blake's poetic discourse as in the discourse of criticism and of critical theory, an infinitely ironizing movement disqualifies and subverts, while at the same time establishing the possibility and preconditions of, any systematization or totalization. It would be misguided and premature, however, merely to invert traditional criticism by postulating a reversed hierarchy, in which irony occupies the place of mastery. In Blake's poetry, it is not subversion by means of irony, but rather precisely the contradiction between an ironic and self-limiting rhetorical and dramatic stance, on the one hand, and the conceptual, totalizing thrust of a mythopoeic system, on the other, which most needs to be explored. I will argue that it is this gap between irony and representation, between production and conceptualization, between desire and mastery, which constitutes Blake's discourse; and I will suggest the consequences which such a view of the interplay of irony and totality in difference has for current critical debates.

At one point in *Jerusalem,* Los is described as "Striving with Systems to deliver individuals from those Systems" (11:5, E153). Let this phrase stand as an emblem for the contradictory determinations of Blake's poetry. For "with" must be read as meaning both "against" and "by means of," while "deliver" must be read as meaning both "rescue" and "aid in the birth of." Thus creating a System is conjoined with attacking, destroying, or evading a System; and an Individual is constituted both as one whose individuality is realized only in the process of being freed from the constrictions of a System, and as one who is only produced or defined as individual within and by virtue of such a System. Blake is deliberately not a systematic writer, in that he characteristically and repeatedly overloads the same words, overdetermines the same symbols, with both positive and negative connotations. The declaration of desire: "I must Create a System" must be grasped in its immediate dramatic context (Los's struggle with the Spectre), which is rendered ambiguous by the possible multivalency of the "I" as much as by that of "Create" and of "System." The question is to what extent the dramatic and contextualizing principle which differentially distributes such valorizations is itself subject to the interplay of contraries.

Insofar as Blake's mode of presentation is dramatic and differential, it is always suggesting opposing perspectives, "Contrary States of the Human Soul" (E7), Innocence and Experience, Heaven and Hell, Beulah and Generation. The problem of systematization in Blake's text is thus one regarding the logic of binary oppositions. How is it possible to move from the radical perspectivism of the contrary states of the soul to the total System in which each of these states has its proper place? For Blake's Contraries are not dialectical. "Without Contraries is no progression" (MHH, E34), but also "Negations are not Contraries" (J17:33, E160). Dialectical progression always implies the "Abstract objecting power" (J10:14, E151) of negation and comprehension, whereas Blake insists upon the positivity of both contraries, their active and continuing opposition. "Progression" thus has a very special meaning for Blake, implying the continuation of a lived tension of opposites, rather than any sublation or furthering resolution.

Such a refusal of dialectics marks Blake's rejection of the intellectualizing and conceptualizing procedures of rationalistic philosophy. Yet such a rejection paradoxically presents itself in the form of a conceptual or cognitive moment within Blake's own text. The doctrine of Contraries, as put forth in *The Marriage of Heaven and Hell,* is differential and anti-discursive in terms of its polemical content, but universalizing, conceptual, and systematic in terms of its form. It becomes necessary simultaneously to read Blake's text both in terms of its System, or conceptual unity, *and* in terms of its anti-conceptual differentiality, or ironic perspectivism and dramatic contextualizations. But such a double reading reveals a fundamental *dissymmetry* which precedes and organizes the strife of Contraries as equal and binary opposites. This dissymmetry arises from the fact that the alternate readings are not of equal status, but may instead be hierarchically articulated. The systematic approach, as a claim to totality and to truth, transcendentally compares and organizes the disparate perspectives. The differential approach is founded upon the insistence of minute particulars which resist such a sublimation. A tension is maintained because Blake prohibits any dialectical movement from one level to the other.

The strife of Contraries is thus necessarily articulated in language which is itself contradictory; but in this latter case the contradiction is not one of binary opposition between equals, but rather a sort of Russell's paradox, a conflict between two different levels of discourse, between content and form or between statement and meta-statement. Gregory Bateson has claimed that the double bind resulting from such a conflict is constitutive of schizophrenia,[4] and we shall see that the principle of authority in Blake's poetry, the Urizen figure on one hand and the creative and System-building figure on the other, is always schizophrenic in precisely this sense. But at the same time, it is this dissymmetrical contradiction which generates the active tension of equal and opposed Contraries. The "marriage" of Heaven and Hell indicates at once the equalizing reconciliation and the differential irreconcilability of the opposed states.

We are told, in a passage which cannot be attributed to any particular voice, that the Contraries "are always upon earth, & they should be enemies; whoever tries to reconcile them seeks to destroy existence" (E39). The rhetoric of this statement is quite interesting. First, the eternal existence of the Contraries is presented as a given fact (they "are always upon earth"). But second, the enmity of the Contraries is presented not as a fact, but as an imperative ("they should be enemies"). What is in question is not their existence, or the existence of the world, but the mode of their relationships. Then third, the reconciliation of the contraries is presented as an empty and illusory desire, a project as impossible as it is pernicious: "Religion is an endeavour to reconcile the two," but the words "endeavor," "tries," and "seeks" imply an exertion which goes contrary to fact (since the Contraries "are always upon earth," the world continues to exist, existence is not destroyed). The paradox of a conflict between incommensurable levels of discourse is here reproduced more concretely in the contrast between the imperative "should" and the less forceful wording of "tries" and "seeks." "Should" at once invokes a necessity and confesses (since it is conditional rather than indicative) that that necessity may not in fact be the case. The statement "they should be enemies" is at once the expression of a particular perspective (one of the Contraries) and a meta-statement which thereby surpasses that, or any other particular, perspective. But its hypothetical contrary ("they should be reconciled") is presented only in much weaker terms, which disqualify it from attaining legitimacy as a meta-statement.

Blake's text thus establishes a hierarchy of authority at the same time that it overtly denies the possibility of such a hierarchy. This is possible because of the circularity whereby the content of each Contrary reflects back upon the mode of being of the system of Contraries as such. "Attraction and

Repulsion, Reason and Energy, Love and Hate, are necessary to Human existence" (E34), but it is always also a question of whether Attraction and Repulsion are attracted to or repulsed from one another, of whether "the passive that obeys Reason" and "the active springing from Energy" are actively or passively opposed to one another, of whether the relationship between the class of men who love and the class of men who hate is one of love or of hatred. The discourse of *The Marriage* is consistently dramatic and ironic, limited to the perspectives of specific speakers (so that it is inaccurate simply to identify Blake's own voice with that of Hell and the Devil); but to the extent that that discourse refers back to and founds the very perspectivism or doctrine of Contraries, within which and by means of which it is itself situated, it validates itself as a transcendent principle of authority. Blake's logic thus at once remains within the ironic limits of perspective and context, and yet escapes beyond them. No dialectical reconciliation of the Contraries is permitted, and yet it is in an authoritative statement, one which would have to transcend the contradiction, that the Contraries are maintained *as* Contraries, as states defined in opposition to and by means of struggle with one another. The rhetorical strategy of exalting one Contrary over the other, insofar as it is that which founds both, while at the same time maintaining the Contraries in the strict equality of binary opposition, permits Blake to have things both ways, to establish a position of transcendence, free from the limitations of any given perspective, and yet to maintain opposed perspectives in their minute particularity, free of any dialectical subsumption or sublation. It is an authoritative voice which warns the reader that no voice is authoritative, that every statement has a context and a perspective and must be actively and positively opposed by another statement made in another context and from another perspective. The principle which grounds and articulates the system of contradictory perspectives is itself located within that system as one of its contradictory terms, and it is precisely this infinite regress of the principle of authority which founds the self-validating circularity of the system as a whole.

A similar hermeneutical problematic is at work in the Preface to *Milton* (E94). Once again, the structure of Blake's argument is that of a dissymmetrical binary opposition. The Bible is opposed to the classics, Inspiration to Memory, "Painters! . . . Sculptors! Architects!," the "Young Men of the New Age," to the "Ignorant Hirelings." The latter class of men is defined, in contrast to the former, as containing those "who would if they could, for ever depress Mental & prolong Corporeal War." The opposition between the inspired and the hirelings is thus an opposition between mental warfare and corporeal warfare, a strife between a non-dialectical strife in which the tension between Contraries is maintained, and a finite or concludable strife culminating in a violent suppression, in which one Contrary is destroyed or swallowed up in the victory of the other. Once again, the leap to meta-statements implies a dissymmetry in the relationship of Contraries, a dissymmetry which in turn produces the equality of opposing Contraries. The hirelings "would if they could" defeat the ideal of the inspired (mental warfare), and replace it exclusively with their own ideal (corporeal warfare). Yet their own ideal is itself only this formal condition, its own proper triumph over its adversary. The grammar of the phrase "would if they could" implies a condition not only contrary to fact but logically impossible; the hirelings do not depress and destroy mental warfare because they cannot, because the strife of Contraries always subsists. Mental warfare and corporeal warfare both continue to exist. This state of co-existence is precisely the principle of mental warfare, and in contradiction with that of corporeal warfare. Hence the co-existence of mental and corporeal warfare is in fact the triumph of the former over the latter, even though it is only the principle of the latter which would authorize such a one-sided resolution. It is this reversal which generates Blake's aggressively polemical stance, his speaking from the side of one of the Contraries, and his implication that that side of the opposition is original (artists working by inspiration) whereas the other side is derivative ("hirelings" act only for money, not out of inspiration or conviction), at the same time that he proclaims the mutual and eternal necessity, the strict equality, of those Contraries.

Thus Blake's system of Contraries is generated by a movement which is endlessly contradictory, inadmissible by the standards not only of formal logic but also of Hegelian dialectical logic. In Hegelian terms, both the overt doctrine of Contraries which are never reconciled or sublated, and its underlying and determining double bind structure, are instances of what Hegel calls "the wrong or negative infinity," an undialectical fluctuation between the finite (Blake's corporeal war) and the merely quantitative infinite (Blake's endless mental war), an opposition which "sets up with endless iteration the alternation between these two terms, each of which calls up the other."[5] Put more positively, the structure of Blake's argument reveals a differential and rhetorical movement which necessarily precedes and determines *any* argument based upon a logic of opposition (whether the argument be Blake's own, or—by anticipation—Hegel's). This unresolvable differential movement thereby also accounts for the polemic against Reason or philosophical logic which is so prominent a feature of Blake's text. Within the system of Contraries, Reason has precisely the same status as does corporeal war in the Preface to *Milton* or religion as an effort to reconcile the Contraries in *The Marriage:* it is the term which, as a meta-statement, would seek to put an end to the eternal strife of Contraries, and which is therefore itself suppressed in that proclamation, by the other Contrary, that neither Contrary may ever be subsumed or suppressed.

This generative differential movement exhibits in the first instance the rhetorical form of the chiasmus, since by virtue precisely of their dissymmetry the Contraries incessantly refer back to one another, taking one another's place without ever achieving any reconciliation or teleological subsumption, in that movement of endless circularity which founds even as it exceeds the possibility of the hermeneutic circle. But in the second instance, insofar as this movement is one of the infinite regress from statement to meta-statement, the closure presupposed in any systematization (whether it be that of Blake's own System, or that of the classificatory system of classical rhetoric), and implicit in the very notion of the hermeneutic circle, is itself disqualified and breached. The Contraries can be neither exhaustive nor mutually exclusive. The regress from statement to meta-statement continues; the differential movement which generates the doctrine of equal Contraries also goes beyond it, denying it the stability of a fixed law or final regulating term.

Blake's System, as the systematization of this untotalizable differential movement, is thus intrinsically incomplete. It is the positivity of this perpetual lack of closure which Blake privileges as Creation or as Imagination, the transcendent term nonetheless at the same time immanent to the System it founds and surpasses. If it is the Imagination which founds any systematization, it is also the Imagination which then goes beyond it, in the positive movement of the "wrong infinity" of the chiasmic-regressive figuration. Such a figuration, operating in accordance with the schizophrenic double bind structure of the meta-statement, at once enforces the closure of Blake's discourse, producing its systematic and conceptual coherence and its polemical force, and yet leaves it perpetually incomplete and open. Such a structure or movement has more than merely formalistic consequences, as I shall proceed to demonstrate by means of a detailed close reading of one brief poem, "The Tyger." But first, in order further to clarify the points which have been raised so far, I will hazard a brief comparison between the differential functioning of Blake's text and that of the (non-)concept of *differance* expounded by Jacques Derrida and his followers, in terms of their respective relations to the movement of dialectical logic.

Derrida remarks that "if there were a definition of differance, it would be precisely the limit, the interruption, the destruction of the Hegelian *relève* *{Aufhebung} wherever* it operates."[6] On one hand, the *Aufhebung* "is *the* concept of history and of teleology."[7] On the other hand, "except [for his] eschatology, . . . Hegel is *also* the thinker of irreducible difference."[8] Differance could be determined, therefore, as the inversion of the *Aufhebung* into mise en abîme, the movement of negativity always already suspended or interrupted, so that the totalizing and teleological negation of the negation is never realized. It is in terms of this suspension that Derrida neither accedes to nor simply steps beyond the logocentric enclosure. Yet it is because of this ambiguous positioning that Derrida's writing takes the form of a critique of philosophy, so that it necessarily becomes at times critical and polemical, that is to say, itself negative, itself carrying out the negative movement which it declares to have been suspended in the text to which it refers. Whenever deconstruction operates as ideology-critique, whenever the deconstructive reader critically isolates and denounces a logocentric moment in a given text, he or she thereby performs a movement of pure negation, simply surpassing the logocentric enclosure and for that very reason remaining trapped within it. In Derrida's own terms, *any* critical or polemical gesture (including especially that of the limitation/suspension/destruction of the *Aufhebung*), however inevitable, is itself nonetheless a totalizing and sublating movement, itself as much a part of the movement of the *Aufhebung* as that which it attacks and of which it is the negation. Hence the privileging of irony in Derrida and in other deconstructive critics, most notably Paul de Man. But conversely, insofar as differance "precedes" any origin or any metaphysical determination of Being, it is already operative in any given context, so that it should become impermissible to make the privileging and hierarchizing distinction, as Derrida does, between what a text "declares" and what it "describes,"[9] or to establish, as de Man does, a dialectic of "blindness and insight."[10]

While Derrida, in disqualifying all polemic, reintroduces the necessity of polemical error, Blake is freely polemical in such a way as to render the very issue of polemic and necessary error entirely irrelevant. Blake makes no attempt to suspend or limit the *Aufhebung,* but overtly performs the totalizing sublation in the very act of polemicizing against it. The *aporia* or ultimate undecidability of the text is not, in Blake, that which qualifies, limits, and "deconstructs" a teleological and totalizing movement. Rather, *aporia* and *Aufhebung* are dissymmetrically opposed and intricated metastatements, simultaneous effects of pure difference, of the non-cause which is the chiasmic-regressive figuration. Although there is an affirmative side to deconstruction, the deconstructive operation tends ultimately to express difference only negatively and critically, as the limitation or unmasterable contradiction subsisting within any teleological and totalizing project. Blake's text, however, expresses difference positively and affirmatively: not as that which compromises the totalizing project from within, but as that which, after the totalization has in fact been accomplished, still remains irreducibly exterior and prior to it. Deconstruction in effect grants priority to that which it at once opposes and declares to be inevitable and insurpassable, the ever-unsuccessful project of hermeneutical and cognitive mastery. But Blake's text can afford to be overtly polemical and overtly systematizing because it is ultimately not cognitive or hermeneutical at all, not even negatively. The Urizenic project of interpretative mastery, and its failure, are indeed inevitable consequences of the chiasmic-regressive figuration: this is the schizophrenia constituted by the double bind situation. But the figuration, as structure of pure difference, cannot be reduced merely to this cognitive aspect. Imagination is *not* ultimately undecidable: not because anything can be determined or decided, but precisely because there is finally nothing to decide. Imagination is fundamentally irreducible, in that it is not to be determined as any essence but also not to be negatively determined as the undeterminable or undecidable.

While deconstruction ironically privileges interpretation as infinite regress, for Blake the infinite regress is an affirmative movement of difference,
that which is always other than (rather than merely that which contradicts or
undoes) the will to closure and the will to interpretation. Deconstruction
finally remains (despite its disqualification of such terminology) a thought of
interiority and of internalization, of the ever-increasing internality of contradiction, which it represents as the contradiction of internality. Blake's discourse, on the other hand, remains open to exteriority: it can afford to be
unashamedly polemical because, in its differential play, its constant movement between incompatible levels of affirmation, another perspective always
arises elsewhere. The governing metaphor of deconstruction is always the
negative one of repression; the distinction between intent and content, or
between a given text's self-representation and that which it in fact represents
or reveals, is the one metaphysical binary opposition which never gets
"deconstructed." In Blake's discourse, however, the play of different perspectives is open and affirmative: they are juxtaposed so as to disrupt any project
of stable hierarchization, and the movement between them is not one of
repression and its undoing, of a psychoanalytic symptomatology, but one of
accumulation, of positive expansion, of the reproduction of the same differential nexus on a larger scale. . . .

[*Ed. note:* In the next several pages (not reprinted here) Shaviro discusses
Blake's poem "The Tyger."]

"Man must & will have Some Religion" (J52, E198): and if Imagination,
in its systematic functioning in Blake's work, seems to provide such a religion,
then in the humor of its minute particulars it ridicules any such ambition,
putting into question the subject "Man" no less than the predicate "Religion."
This fundamental ambiguity yet again instances the irreducible movement of
dissymmetrical difference. And again, to distribute these differences so that
either aspect of Imagination is privileged as the unconscious determinant or
hidden truth of the other is merely to deny the positivity of difference in the
very act of repeating it. The liberatory effect of Blake's discourse cannot be
reduced merely to its negative or critical aspect, its "deconstruction" of ideologies and of the totalizing drive which calls forth such ideologies. For it is by its
positive, affirmative force that Blake's discourse not only demolishes ideologies but also moves apart from the entire horizon of ideology and of meaning.
Similarly, Blake's political and cultural radicalism cannot be reduced to his
"apocalyptic humanism,"[11] to his active imaginative synthesis and creation of a
unique System. For the humanistic ideology which accompanies his myth of
Imagination is coordinated with a continuing project of hierarchization and
mastery. In part this is a consequence of Blake's historical position after the
triumph of the bourgeois ideals of the Enlightenment, but before industrial
capitalism had completed the proletarianization of the lower classes. On the

broadest historical level, Blake's discourse may be lodged in the contradiction between what the Enlightenment promised in the way of liberation and what the capitalism of which it was the harbinger actually produced. The contradictions of Blake's System are those of all modern humanism. The speaker of "The Tyger" imagines terrifying powers and ascribes them to God conceived as absolute Other; but the poet or reader, in reclaiming those powers for the human, necessarily arrogates to an idealized image of humanity the unapproachable prestige of that Otherness as well. That mastery which is the triumph of the Imagination is utterly dependent upon the very model and authority of religious totalitarianism which, in order to validate itself, it first has to destroy. The triumph of the Imagination in Blake's poetry is thus as sterile as it is magnificent. In thus circumscribing the ideological operation performed by the Age of Reason, Blake on the one hand foregrounds the unacknowledged limitations and exceptions to liberal humanism's claims of universality, while on the other hand suggesting that such limitations and exceptions are inevitable consequences of the very claim of universality itself.

Finally, the extravagance of humanistic claims for the Imagination is a symptom of an overwhelming despair and anxiety: a despair and anxiety born in the realization that the humanistic shifting of values from God to Man is on the one hand not enough of a change, since the same or equivalent structures of oppression persist, and too much of a change, since the attempt to ground within Man those hoped-for certainties whose religious sanction had been undermined by the Age of Reason is doomed to failure. "He who replies to words of Doubt / Doth put the Light of Knowledge out" ("Auguries of Innocence," 95–96, E483): what could be more desperate, or more despairing, than this dread of even the merest suggestion of scepticism? In its nostalgia for certainty and its disingenuous transformation of the textual, social, and political movement of difference into an intellectualized crisis of belief, the Blakean imaginative faith is as modernistic, that is to say as regressive and as much of a dead end, as is, for instance, T.S. Eliot's retreat into a more orthodox form of religious consolation.

But in its affirmation of difference, Blake's text does more than merely expose and delimit the contradictions experienced by later writers such as Eliot as crippling external constraints. "The Tyger" enacts a violent scene which conditions all interpretation and representation but cannot itself be interpreted or represented. This scene is not a scene and not an origin, and can only be constituted as such, or apprehended at all, by recourse to an act of interpretation or representation which it in advance disqualifies. Imagination as the movement of differentiality does not simply disqualify these acts of interpretation or representation, but also situates them in their difference from themselves and thus liberates the violent (im)possibility of the nonscene of non-origination as that which, in the positivity of its affirmation, is other than all interpretation and all representation. "The Tyger" is the production or reproduction—even as it is at the same time, to the contrary, the repression, representation, and interpretation—of that pre-originary anxiety which precedes repression. An anxiety which precedes repression is that movement which is not open to mastery or even to the failed attempt at mastery, even though it is that which calls forth repression or the (failed) project of mastery. To liberate that anxiety (despite the literal impossibility of such a liberation) is a political, no less than a literary, act, albeit one which lacks an author. Blake's discourse does not merely challenge liberal humanism, but also challenges, in reproducing it, the very fatality to which humanism is always subject, the inevitable process of identification whereby a challenge finds itself in solidarity with the totalization or indeed totalitarianism which it challenges. Blake's discourse affirms the positivity of alterity and of alteration within the problematic which Western civilization is still in the process of confronting, and which in our own time has been formulated most succinctly, perhaps, in the texts of Michel Foucault: "you may have killed God beneath the weight of all that you have said; but don't imagine that, with all that you are saying, you will make a man that will live longer than he."[12]

Notes

1. All quotations from William Blake are taken from *The Poetry and Prose of William Blake,* ed. David V. Erdman (Garden City, 1965), and identified by "E" and page number. For certain works I have also listed plate and line number, using the abbreviations M (*Milton*) and J (*Jerusalem*).

2. See especially S. Foster Damon, *William Blake: His Philosophy and Symbols* (New York, 1924, rpt. Gloucester, 1958); S. Foster Damon, *A Blake Dictionary* (Providence, 1965); Northrop Frye, *Fearful Symmetry: A Study of William Blake* (Princeton, 1947, 1969); Harold Bloom, *Blake's Apocalypse: A Study in Poetic Argument* (Garden City, 1963, rpt. Ithaca, 1970).

3. Thomas Weiskel, *The Romantic Sublime: Studies in the Structure and Psychology of Transcendence* (Baltimore, 1976), p. 65.

4. Gregory Bateson, "Toward a Theory of Schizophrenia," in *Steps to an Ecology of Mind* (New York, 1972), pp. 201–227.

5. *Hegel's Logic* (Encyclopedia Logic), trans. William Wallace (Oxford, 1975), p. 137. Maurice Blanchot suggests the importance for literature of this "wrong infinity" in "L'infini littéraire: l'Aleph," in *Le livre à venir* (Paris, 1959, 1971), pp. 139–44.

6. Jacques Derrida, *Positions,* trans. Alan Bass (Chicago, 1981), pp. 40–41.

7. Jacques Derrida, *Of Grammatology,* trans. Gayatri Chakravorty Spivak (Baltimore, 1976), p. 25.

8. Derrida, *Of Grammatology,* p. 26.

9. Cf. Derrida, *Of Grammatology, passim.,* e.g., p. 313.

10. Paul de Man, *Blindness and Insight: Essays in the Rhetoric of Contemporary Criticism* (New York, 1971), and especially "The Rhetoric of Blindness," pp. 102–41.

11. "Apocalyptic humanism" is Harold Bloom's phrase: see *Blake's Apocalypse, passim.*

12 Michel Foucault, *The Archeology of Knowledge,* trans. A. M. Sheridan Smith (New York, 1976), p. 211.

The Return to Logos
[From *William Blake and the Language of Adam*]

ROBERT N. ESSICK

Some of Blake's names have more than general phonetic ties to known languages, including homophonic relationships with specific words that indicate what the name represents in Blake's poetry. Thus the use of such names can function as a form of metalepsis, the substitution of a remote but original cause for present effects, both linguistic and extra-linguistic. Urizen is the best-known case in point, the creator of the fallen world whose name is the etymological ur-form of several terms particularly descriptive of that world. "Urizen" has been variously described as a pun on "your reason," the Greek "ourizein" (from which the English "horizon" is derived), "is risen" in the first line of *The Book of Urizen* chapter 1, "your eyes in," "ur reason," and "err-reason."[1] If we consider each conventional word or phrase as the source for "Urizen," we must either choose among them or take Blake's name for his arch-villain to be thoroughly overdetermined. But no matter what sparked the invention of the word, Urizen's role as a polysemous etymon, one of Blake's linguistic "Giant forms,"[2] is only strengthened by our discovery (or invention) of further punning plays upon his name. Blake sometimes provides his own clues as to how English words were derived from his reconstructed roots. One plate after introducing "Bowlahoola" in *Milton,* he points out one of its derivatives: "Bowlahoola is named Law. by mortals" (Pl. 24; E 120, K 509). This startling assertion is not explained or elaborated. Its primary justification would seem to lie in the body's natural laws governing our lives, but the presence of the letters of "Law" in the middle of "Bowlahoola" backs such conceptual extrapolations with etymological evidence. We are encouraged to find other homophones on the same plate, including "Golgonooza," the flute's "lula lula," and the "bellowing" furnaces, the last also associated with the stomach whose sounds echo through the passage.

The link between formulaic habits of composition and Blake's naming practices is particularly evident in the lists quoted from *The Four Zoas.* The second through the fourth names of the sons are familiar from *Visions of the*

Daughters of Albion. Their formulaic "-on" ending propels the onomasticon forward into "Antamon," first introduced in *Europe,* and then to the echoing nonce word "Ananton." The aural key changes to a play on initial and internal *o* sounds for the next three names. Such permutations, common to oral formulaic patterns, match in miniature the slow historical process of sound shifts. We are returned to the "-on" group by Mydon, whose presence as the only clearly Greek name in the list may have been motivated by the key phoneme alone. Names based on the "-on" radical form the largest family group among Blake's coinages, centred around the important figure of Enitharmon.[3] It is as though these words come from an ancient language in which all proper names end with the same sound, as is the case with sur-names in Armenian. Alternatively, all "-on" names suggest genetic descent from that single radical. This is precisely the way Bryant treats the same terminal morpheme, which he believed was "another title of the Sun among the Amonians," and its continuation through words such as "Amon," "Abelion," and "Abaddon."[4]

Place names, so important to eighteenth-century Celticists, play a par-ticularly prominent role in *Jerusalem.* Albion and his Emanation each join places and people into one name. Somewhat looser connections between these two types of proper nouns are suggested by wordplay: "O melancholy Magdalen [pronounced "Maudlen"] behold the morning over Malden break" (Pl. 65; E 217, K 700). Such lines accord with Bryant's guiding principle "that most ancient names, not only of places, but of persons, have a manifest analogy."[5] But Blake's major attempts at analogizing place names exceed even Bryant's generous methodology or the etymological speculations of Celticists who could find significance in the phonetic resemblance between "Babel" and a village in Norfolk. The most striking feature of Blake's align-ment of Jerusalem's "Gates" with the counties of Great Britain is the sheer arbitrariness of the system. Even a brief selection will indicate why most readers pass quickly over these passages:

> Of Reuben Norfolk, Suffolk, Essex. Simeon Lincoln, York Lancashire
> Levi. Middlesex Kent Surrey. Judah Somerset Glouster Wiltshire.[6]

Neither geographical parallels, as in transparent map overlays, nor phonetic conjunctions can explain the individual assignments. It is as though Blake found in incantatory naming a way to bring the absolutely arbitrary full circle back to the motivated and to construct a grammar of willed identifica-tions that could replace the poet's usual grammar of metaphor. We can perceive, at least with our fallen senses, no way in which Levi is "like" Middlesex. Yet language can bring them together in the temporality of their saying and the topography of their writing. Language serves as the vehicle for the imagining of a post-apocalyptic synchrony, a reconstruction of the geo-graphic schema through the reordering of the place names representing it. As

Blake wrote of "divine names" in *A Descriptive Catalogue*, "They ought to be the servants, and not the masters of man, or of society" (E 536, K571).

Blake's more exotic articulations have led us both back to the issue of origins and forward to how words are connected historically and, more immediately, in propositional and metonymic structures. Conversation is the primary interpersonal extension of these interverbal exchanges and is, in turn, an activity promoting change in both the language and its users. This social product of articulate performance, a formal characteristic of words as early as *An Island in the Moon* (*c.* 1784–5), becomes thematic in Blake's later poetry, particularly *Jerusalem.* The central linguistic concern moves away from what language is to what men can do with it—and what it does to them. As is so often the case with Blake's dramatizations of a concept, he implies an ideal condition by presenting it in a decayed or parodic form. Urizen's unsuccessful attempt in *The Four Zoas* to converse with animals is taken a step further in the image of fallen man "conversing with the Void" in *Milton.*[7] The phrase embraces two senses: a pointless attempt to gain a response from utter absence; but also the process of conversing by means of a differential semiotic, the same one we encountered with the Spectre's proclivity for reading "the Voids | Between the Stars" in *Jerusalem.* It is obvious that silent partners make poor conversationalists, but verbal interchange is also stopped if we become overly conscious of the empty matrix of grammar and treat words as anything less than articulated positivities. As Blake emphasizes in his ideas about artistic creation, abstract contemplation inhibits performance.

In more positive contexts, Blake builds upon, but expands far beyond, the celebration of everyday conversation of the sort we encountered with Herder and Humboldt.[8] In *A Vision of the Last Judgment*, Blake describes "Poetry Painting & Music" as the media for "conversing with Paradise" because they are the remnants of the original semiotic "which the flood did not Sweep away" (E 559, K 609). Blake's energetic annotating of books suggests that he perceived reading as yet another conversational mode. In his own rather mechanical way, Harris established this concept of conversing with the written word: "For what is Conversation between Man and Man?—'Tis a mutual intercourse of Speaking and Hearing. . . . The same may be said of a *Writer* and a Reader; as when anyone reads today or tomorrow, or here or in Italy, what Euclid wrote in Greece two thousand years ago" (*Hermes*, p. 398). Visionary dictation could also become dialogue: at the beginning of *Jerusalem*, Blake claims "to converse with" the Spirit of Jesus "daily, as man with man."[9] If Blake's media were indeed his muses, as I have argued in the previous chapter, then the give and take between an individual poet and the ancestral voices speaking through his language may have prompted Blake's sense of engaging in imaginary conversations which to him were, like all imaginative acts, as real as material objects. Given these psychological conditions, those "who converse in the spirit" believe they "converse with spirits," as Blake proclaims in his annotations to Lavater's *Aphorisms* (E 600, K 88).

At the same time that he expands the circumference of what constitutes conversation, Blake envisions an ideal form—we might call it "hyper-conversation"—by literalizing those very qualities Herder and Humboldt found so appealing in the activity. As Los tells us in *Jerusalem,*

> When in Eternity Man converses with Man they enter
> Into each others Bosom (which are Universes of delight)
> In mutual interchange. and first their Emanations meet
> Surrounded by their Children. if they embrace & comingle
> The Human Four-fold Forms mingle also in thunders of Intellect
> But if the Emanations mingle not; with storms & agitations
> Of earthquakes & consuming fires they roll apart in fear
> For Man cannot unite with Man but by their Emanations
> Which stand both Male & Female at the Gates of each Humanity
> —(Pl. 88; E 246, K 733)

In our world, the closest we can come to such interchanges is through language, for only words can flow freely back and forth between us, entering into and building our consciousness of self and of other selves. Conversely, that common experience is the foundation—again, the "rough basement"—for conversations in which male and female Emanations replace verbal mediation. Semiosis becomes not simply literal but physical, a triumph of the body over abstraction that reaches beyond even the powers of the signifier in Boehme's linguistic alchemy. In Los's eternity, verbal and sexual intercourse merge into a single engendering act at once biological and intellectual. The ancient dream of the union of words and things in the Adamic sign is reestablished in an ideal of conversation. Thus, much as we found in Humboldt's writings, linguistic motivation is transported from the structural inter-objectivity of the signifier/signified relationship to the phenomenal intersubjectivity of communication.

The family groups in Los's description lead us beyond the conversations of one person with another to larger social units. Here and elsewhere Blake would seem to be moving toward a conception of language as the social Logos, the creator of communities based on an actively shared linguistic competency. The traditional language in which Blake frames his sense of speech communities indicates the commonality between images of Christian brotherhood, established by the kerygmatic signs of the type pictured in *Christ Blessing* (Plate 8), and enthusiastic proposals by Humboldt and like-minded philologists about language as the cement of social constructs. When language fails as a medium of intercouse, as it does so disastrously in *Tiriel,* the social order also collapses. Blake's image of a restored community centres on the body of Christ as defined by St. Paul: "So we, being many, are one body in Christ, and every one members one of another" (Romans 12:5). Blake repeats this formula in his *Laocoön* inscriptions and extends it by equating "The Divine Body" of

Jesus with "The Eternal Body of Man" which "is The Imagination."[10] Although Blake never explicity adds language to this line of identities, it is implicit as one of the chief means of bodying forth the imagination. Further, this communal body preserves the structure of the propositions defining its linguistic outline, an articulated unity in which the members retain their distinct identities. Any attempt to organize this body politic according to abstract, differential schemata is tantamount to dismemberment:

> Till Brotherhood is changed into a Curse & a Flattery
> By Differences between Ideas, that Ideas themselves, (which are
> The Divine Members) may be slain in offerings for sin
> —(*Milton*, Pl. 35; E 135, K 525)

Blake's model of community, like Humboldt's, argues against those Urizenic reformers who would "seek the consummation of humanity in attainment of a general, abstractly conceived perfection, rather than in the development of a wealth of great individual forms."[11] Simply put, community in human form is an extended conversation manifesting itself as the social body, just as Christ in the body of Jesus is the Word incarnate. In *A Vision of the Last Judgment*, Blake resolves this synthesis of Jesus/conversation/community into an image strikingly like his painting of *The Virgin and Child in Egypt* (Plate 7): "I have seen when at a distance Multitudes of Men in Harmony appear like a single Infant sometimes in the Arms of a Female" (E 557, K 607).

As John Barrell has recently demonstrated, the social role of the artist was a major issue in late eighteenth- and early nineteenth-century England.[12] Blake participated directly in this debate through works such as the *Descriptive Catalogue* of 1809 and the *Public Address* of *c*.1810. Here and elsewhere he focuses on the public responsibilities of the pictorial artist, but these also apply to poets who place themselves in a tradition of social conscience extending back to the Bards of ancient Britain, to "Jesus & his Apostles & Disciples" who "were all Artists" (*Laocoön*, E 274, K 777), and to the prophets of the Old Testament. Such poets need not directly address social issues at every turn to contribute to the community, for "Art is the glory of a Nation" and "Genius and Inspiration are the great Origin and Bond of Society." Hence, "Nations are Destroy'd, or Flourish, in proportion as Their Poetry Painting and Music, are Destroy'd or Flourish!"[13]

The relationship any linguistic performance establishes with its audience must determine in large measure its immediate contribution to the community in which it was produced. This issue clearly concerned Blake, for he made ambitious statements about the public importance of his work. In the prospectus "To the Public" of 1793, he claims to have already "engaged the attention of many persons of eminence and fortune" and to have "been regularly enabled to bring before the Public works (he is not afraid to say) of equal magnitude and consequence with the production of any age or country"

(E 692, K 207). This bit of puffery is exceeded by Blake's indignant letter of 23 August 1799 to Dr. John Trusler. Blake points out to the man who had rejected one of his paintings that "What is Grand is necessarily obscure to Weak men. That which can be made Explicit to the Idiot is not worth my care" (E 702, K 793). This implication that his work will select its own audience by rejecting those incapable of understanding it would also seem relevant to the words Blake scratched into the upper corners of his address "To the Public" at the beginning of *Jerusalem,* "sheep" and "goats," in allusion to Christ's parable of their apocalyptic separation.[14] Yet, in the text below, Blake asks from his audience a far more sympathetic response: "[Dear] Reader, [forgive] what you do not approve, & [love] me for this energetic exertion of my talent."[15] This appeal accords with Friedrich Schlegel's defini-tion of an ideal writer/reader relationship in his *Lyceum* aphorisms of 1797: "The analytical writer observes the reader as he is; accordingly, he makes his calculation, sets his machine to make the appropriate effect on him. The synthetic writer constructs and creates his own reader; he does not imagine him as resting and dead, but lively and advancing toward him. He makes that which he had invented gradually take shape before the reader's eyes, or he tempts him to do the inventing for himself. He does not want to make a particular effect on him, but rather enters into a solemn relationship of innermost symphilosophy or sympoetry."[16]

Schlegel's "synthetic" writer is matched by Schleiermacher's ideal reader: "In interpretation it is essential that one be able to step out of one's own frame of mind into that of the author."[17] Los's description of conversa-tions in eternity, and Blake's invitation in *A Vision of the Last Judgment* to "Enter into" the images of his painting (E 560, K 611), are more dramatic expressions of this same hermeneutic, then evolving in Germany out of Boehme's beliefs in mystical identification with the Word and into the historicism of the Higher Criticism.[18] This shared model of reading requires a suspension of our independent and judgmental selves that repeats, in the reception of a text, the sacrifice of the Selfhood so important to Blake's dictation theory of textual production. The author and his readers ideally meet and converse together in and through a text which thereby becomes the motivation for a hermeneutic community whose members share a common language. The essential paradigm shifts from dyadic signification (signifier/signified) to triadic interchanges among author, text, and reader, as in the kerygmatic sign. The *telos* of motivation is not abandoned, but sought for in a different dimension of linguistic activity. This attempt to replicate the struc-ture of the Adamic sign in the larger phenomenon of reading is one way Blake hoped "to Restore what the Ancients calld the Golden Age."[19]

Have Blake's works created a hermeneutic community, even if far from golden? The question cannot be answered by any feature intrinsic to the language of his texts, but only by the history of their reception. If we look at Blake's own time, the answer is "no." The audience he imagined in his poetry bears little resemblance to the one he actually had, a disparity he recognized in the last year of his life with the admission that he "is not likely" to "get a Customer for" the beautifully hand-coloured copy of *Jerusalem*. In these circumstances it is difficult not to view Blake's claims about laying up "treasures in heaven" as a compensatory gesture, the invention of a transcendental audience to fill the absence of an earthly one.[20] His chief patrons for his paintings and prints, Thomas Butts and John Linnell, showed little beyond curiosity about Blake's writings and seem to have appreciated the illuminated books primarily as works of graphic art. Even the "Ancients," that group of young artists who gathered about Blake in his last years, were brought together through their admiration of the man and a few of his pictorial efforts, not his writings. The selectivity enacted by Blake's language, its tendencies toward a private idiom even while in pursuit of the kerygmatic and universal, thwarted its ability to become the nexus and medium of even a small community.

If we turn to the present and repeat my earlier question, the answer changes. I may be breaking scholarly decorum by using the reader as a way of making a point, but surely anyone who has read this far in this book must be a member of something very like a hermeneutic community generated by Blake's works. Within this sodality—even if small, academic, and inconsequential in the greater scheme of things—there is a shared language of images, verbal and pictorial, a dictionary, canonical texts, a wealth of commentaries, a pantheon of mythic figures, and sporadic gatherings to discuss common concerns. Blake has even made an impact outside this community of dedicated Blakeans. "The Tyger" is one of the best known lyrics in English; "And did those feet in ancient time" has been set to music and become one of the Church of England's most popular hymns. Blake's reputation as a visual artist is higher with the general museum-going public than with art historians. *The Ancient of Days* has become one of the most recognizable icons of Anglo-American culture. And "Urizenic," a modern extension of Blake's invented articulations, has almost entered the general lexicon.

The study of Blake's texts as culturally effective phenomena necessarily ends with the history of their modern audience. This does not, however, exhaust Blake's dramatization of the power of words over the world. His *Adam Naming the Beasts* led us to speculations, as old as Genesis and as modern as the philosophy of Martin Heidegger, on how being itself is constituted by semiotic activity. We must now return to a more detailed consideration of that theme, including its enactment in Blake's figural strategies, as a way of approaching his reconstitution of the relationship between meaning and being.

Several times in this book I have referred to Blake's "literalization of figuration"—that is, how he (or one of his characters) grants substantial being to what we would usually take to be only a figure of speech. The technique emerges out of conventional extensions of a key metaphor through several metonymically related images, as in Blake's own "King Edward the Third":

> . . . Our names are written equal
> In fame's wide trophied hall; 'tis ours to gild
> The letters, and to make them shine with gold
> That never tarnishes: . . .
>
> —(E 424, K 18)

The metaphor of writing in fame's hall is treated, in the images of the letters, as an actual event. But gilding and shining the letters of one's name relate metaphorically to the concept of fame, and thus each image becomes an alternative vehicle for the single guiding tenor. We can normalize the lines into a conceit and avoid the oddity of constructing a hall and its contents with a fictive reality equivalent to that of the king who speaks these lines. The distinction between the "real" referents of the language and the figures of rhetoric is maintained. That barrier becomes a little less certain in "The Human Abstract" and "a poison tree" of *Songs of Experience*. In the former, "Humility takes . . . root" and from it grows the tree of "Mystery" (E 27, K 217). The "Caterpiller and Fly," which we can imagine feeding on a tree, instead feed on its tenor, "Mystery." Our first attempt at rationalizing the lines might be to convert the insects into concepts, so that they operate in the same sphere as "Mystery," but this goal can also be accomplished by giving Blake's metaphorical tree the substantial presence of a real one which can indeed fall prey to insects. Our usual distinctions between literal and figural, the substantial and the conceptual, are further confounded by Blake's return of his by now fully realized tree to "the Human Brain" in the last line of the poem.[21] Have the tree and its inhabitants been an allegory all along, or are real trees productions of mental states? The first alternative reinstitutes the comforting distinction between thought and being, but the second is implied by Blake's famous dictum that "Mental Things are alone Real" (*A Vision of the Last Judgment*, E 565, K 617).

The sinister uses of literalization are particularly evident in *The Book of Urizen*. There the strategy dramatizes the aggrandizements of the differential structures defining Urizen's semiotic consciousness, as for example in the shift of his "web" from trope to material object and religious law.[22] But the process is not in itself restrictive. Everything depends on *what* is transformed from the figural to the literal, and whether the result is a prison or the realization of desires imagined in language. The technique is pervasive in *Jerusalem*, where it becomes most apparent in the hypostatization of simile:

> Then Mary burst forth into a Song! she flowed like a River of
> Many Streams in the arms of Joseph & gave forth her tears of joy
> Like many waters, and Emanating into gardens & palaces upon

> Euphrates & to forests & floods & animals wild & tame from
> Gihon to Hiddekel, & to corn fields & villages & inhabitants
> Upon Pison & Arnon & Jordan. And I heard the voice among
> The Reapers Saying, . . .[23]

Mary and her song and tears are posited as literal presences—that is, as signifieds within the referential matrix. The river and waters to which they are compared act in this context as second-order signifiers within the tropic matrix. Suddenly, with the word "Emanating," simile is carried beyond itself and the song and tears emanate into a well-populated landscape with known place names and figures capable of speech. The key verb takes Mary or her song as its subject, but the intervening terms of comparison make possible its objects. The figures of speech (song is "like" a river, tears are "like" many waters) are literalized back into the referential, giving their metonymic extensions through forests, floods, and villages the same status as signifieds, the same substantial being, as Mary and her song and tears. The process is a rhetorical analogue to Coleridge's stated method of composing "Kubla Khan" in a dream, one "in which all the images rose up before him as *things*," and to Blake's sense of his words becoming objects that "fly about the room."[24]

The underlying dynamic of literalization also finds expression in Blake's conversions of evanescent phenomena, particularly utterances, into more permanent objects. Los forges just such "condens'd thoughts" on *Jerusalem* Plate 9:

> I saw terrified; I took the sighs & tears, & bitter groans:
> I lifted them into my Furnaces; to form the spiritual sword.
> That lays open the hidden heart: I drew forth the pang
> Of sorrow red hot: I workd it on my resolute anvil: . . .
>
> —(E 152, K 628)

Paley has commented that these lines "make us uneasily aware of how (just barely) the imagery of the smithy accommodates the tenor."[25] Indeed, it may be wrong to treat such passages in terms of conventional metaphoric structures since Blake's language calls into question the very differences between the literal and the figural in which such structures are grounded, just as his basic principles of artistic creation tear down the usual barriers between execution and conception. Los's "sword" is intensely physical, but at the same time "spiritual." Blake's most characteristic tropologies are thus a peculiarly radical form of sortal transgression, for they cross the primary boundaries between the ontological, established by the language of reference, and the poetic, established by the language of tropes.[26] This feature of his rhetoric would seem to be the unacknowledged prompting for Karl Kroeber's observations on the anti-metaphorical thrust of *Jerusalem,* and for Geoffrey Hartman's recent comment that "we cannot be sure of the referentiality of [Blake's] figures—of the links between metaphor and concept, or between

literal and figurative in his poems."[27] I suspect that most of us share Hartman's uncertainty when confronted by texts that recognize his categorical
distinctions only to subvert and overwhelm them.

Steven Knapp has pointed out that, in late eighteenth-century discourse,
"the symbol must be saved by allegory from its innate gravitation toward the
literal."[28] This is precisely what Blake refuses to do. When, for example,
Reynolds in his *Discourses* declares that "to understand literally . . . metaphors
or ideas expressed in poetical language" is "absurd," Blake reacts sharply: "The
Ancients did not mean to Impose when they affirmd their belief in Vision &
Revelation Plato was in Earnest. . . . How very Anxious Reynolds is to Dis-
prove & Contemn Spiritual Perception."[29] In his own works, Blake not only
allows but encourages the tendency of the figural to create its own world and,
taking the process even a step further, pronounces that world to be the reality
hidden within the allegories of fallen time and space. We can also observe this
gravitational pull in Blake's visual art. His "Visionary Heads" convert the
imaginative recreation of a personality, historical or fictive, into the literality
of pencil portraits. As an illustrator of works by other poets, Blake habitually
takes metaphors, even if only implied by the text, as the basis for fully fleshed
human forms in his designs. Edward Young's personifications in *Night
Thoughts* become in Blake's illustrations of 1795–7 a world of men and women
who walk, soar, and even swim around the poem.[30] When criticized for similar
procedures in his designs for Robert Blair's *The Grave,* Blake defended himself
in his *Descriptive Catalogue* by pointing out that artists had for centuries been
"representing spirits with real bodies" and that "The Prophets describe what
they saw in Vision as real and existing men."[31] This last observation, like the
response to Reynolds, hints at how the literalization of the figural or imaginative delineates Blake's distinction between "allegory" and "Vision" in *A Vision
of the Last Judgment.*[32]

It is difficult to overemphasize the importance of the literalization of
figuration in Blake's later works, or to summarize adequately how it embodies his fundamental beliefs about the constitutive powers of semiosis. The
"Divine Revelation" of the Bible, so often rationalized into figural expression
by the exegetes of Blake's time, undergoes a similar transformation into
"Literal expression" in Blake's unfolding of Christ's textual garment at the
end of *Milton* (Pl. 42; E 143, K 534). Like Los, the figural has "kept the
Divine Vision in time of trouble" (*Jerusalem,* Pl. 44; E 193; K 655); its
literalization will again reveal its hidden truths. This apocalyptic movement
also enacts, within the secondary motivations of Blake's language, the movement from word to thing defining the primary motivation of the Logos and
Christ's incarnation. But the impact of language on being can be extended
well beyond these special cases. If language is the medium of thought, as
Schlegel, Coleridge, Humboldt, and others among Blake's contemporaries
argued, then it is also the medium of existence if we concur with Blake's
implied affirmative answers to his questions, "Where is the Existence Out of

Mind or Thought Where is it but in the Mind of a Fool."³³ We have already witnessed a foolish mind reifying itself into a world in *The Book of Urizen.* There the initial act of self-separation established difference as the enabling structure within language and its concomitant distinctions between subject and object, self and world. But Urizen's structuralist conception of the medium of being is not the only way to think language into its being. From Blake's compositional practices and ideas about articulation, conversation, and community evolves a phenomenological view of language with transactional events instead of difference as its essence. Rather than rigidly objectivist, grammatical, and spatial, this language is expansively subjectivist, instrumental, and temporal. If being were reconceived not on the basis of what language is as a structure but what it does as an event, then "being" would be returned to its etymological root as a present participle of a verb, a continual coming-into-being in which the verb substantive articulates a conversation between subject and object giving communal identity to both.³⁴ What if this language, the language of the poet and his figural explorations of the full range of the conceivable, were literalized into a world? What if that world could be as receptive to desire as language, and we could move bodily from heaven to earth, from earth to heaven, as easily as you have just done linguistically? *Jerusalem,* especially its concluding plates, provides some answers.

At the beginning of the ninety-sixth plate, Blake writes his last, half-hidden simile in *Jerusalem:* "As the Sun & Moon lead forward the Visions of Heaven & Earth | England who is Brittannia entered Albions bosom rejoicing" (E 255, K 743). The destiny of such tropes is indicated five lines later: "And the Divine Appearance [Jesus] was the likeness & similitude of Los." The figural productions of the linguistic imagination manifest themselves in the actual appearances of the incarnate Word. Accordingly, the personal relationship between Jesus and Los, as they "conversed as Man with Man" in "Eternity," is itself a simile. Our own conversations produce figures of comparison; those in eternity produce human figures of similitude. The difference between saying "Jesus is like Los" and "Jesus is a simile of Los" may seem trivial, but if we attend to the precise literal meaning of the latter, and to the difference between a statement of comparison ("is like") and a proposition of identity ("is a"), we can grasp something of the difference between our world and the alternative Blake constructs in *Jerusalem.* Most readers, particularly those who also feel compelled to write about the poem, tend to re-allegorize it to accommodate it to a language grounded in a disjunction between being (the signifier) and meaning (the signified). Albion's bow, "loud sounding," "Murmuring," and shooting "Arrows of Intellect" in the ninety-eighth plate (E 257, K 744–5), can be taken as a metaphor for speech without disrupting what it means, but its being *as a bow* is cast into the immateriality of the figural. Blake's language asks us to resist such conversions, however useful, and imagine a bow that is the literal incarnation of a speech act. Blake's "vision," a mode of seeing, hearing, and writing antithetical to allegory, demands nothing more nor less than a language of direct reference, just as we might describe a view before our eyes. What we perceive in Blake's words has been characterized by Hazard Adams as a "world *made into* words," and by Leonard Deen as "speech" that "transforms itself into act."[35] Each of these readers has described half of a chiasmus. At its crossing point, we find simple and reversible copular propositions where thoughts are things: "My Streets are my, Ideas of Imagination | . . . My Houses are Thoughts: my Inhabitants; Affections" (Pl. 34; E 180, K 665). As Deen suggests, language has been given the ontological status of "real" events. Yet the objects in this world made of words continue to behave as though they were parts of a language, as Adam's cogent phrase implies. Events in this world are limited only by Blake's generous sense of English syntax and grammar and his ability to form propositions. The medium of representation and the things represented operate on the same principles. This condition is achieved not, as in the schemes of ideal language projectors, by constructing a language isomorphic with its own prior reifications into fallen nature, but by reconstituting nature according to man's experience of language. Whatever can be imagined in language can be described as an occurrence in fact. Urizen and his historical allies, the rationalist grammarians and scientists, had turned their language and the world it invents into a prison house. Blake turns both into a poem.

Not surprisingly, the world of words in *Jerusalem* seems more than a little old. Some of its strangeness lessens if we keep in mind that transactions among persons and things accord with transactions among words. Language permits any noun to be substituted for any other in a proposition; it is only our sense of a "real" distinction between one thing and another that prohibits their interchange. Once free of such encumbrances, instituted by fallen perceptions, Blake explores a number of categorical transferrals. His many place/person conjunctions are his most obvious disruptions of conventional distinctions, but these are far less radical than his habit of interchanging time and space in ways perfectly acceptable to the rules of language yet resisted by our most basic ontological instincts. "Space" can be pluralized, so why not "time," or even "eternity"? Blake answers with "Times on times" as early as *The Book of Urizen; Jerusalem* expands multiple temporality into "Ages of Eternity."[36] Further, our ability to move through space is transferred to eternal time as we move "forward irresistible from Eternity to Eternity" (Pl. 98; E 257, K 745). The nature of this movement is not extrapolated from the spatial activity of things in our world, but from the movement of words in our conversations. That phenomenon must once again become our principal concern.

It will be helpful to recall Humboldt's sense of man's linguistic transactions before plunging into their apotheosis on the final two text plates of *Jerusalem*. His description of language as an interchange between the subjective and objective realms is especially pertinent:

In thinking, a subjective activity forms itself an object. For no type of imaginative representation may be considered a merely receptive apperception of an already existent object. The activity of the senses must be synthetically joined with the inner action of the spirit. From their connection the imaginative representation tears itself loose, becomes objective in relation to the subjective energy, and then returns to it, having first been perceived in its new, objective form. For this process language is indispensable. For while the spiritual endeavor expresses itself through the lips, its products return through the very ears of the speaker. The representation is therefore truly transformed into actual objectivity without therefore being withdrawn from subjectivity. Only language can accomplish this, and without this constant transformation and retransformation in which language plays the decisive part even in silence, no conceptualization and therefore no true thinking is possible.[37]

For Humboldt, language is itself a grand sortal transgression. As his student G. J. Adler points out, "the most general and characteristic function of language" is that "it constitutes, in the first place, the connecting link between the finite and infinite nature of man. In language . . . the subjective unites itself with the objective. By the act of speech the external world becomes converted into an internal one."[38] In one of his more speculative flights, Humboldt himself offers a vision of these semiotic transformations become a metaphysic: ". . . the language-creating energy in mankind will not rest until it has brought forth, whether in one place or everywhere, whatever accords most perfectly with its demands. . . . To express it in another way, one can see in language the striving of the archetypal idea of linguistic perfection to win existence in reality."[39] We have been tracing the pursuit of this same *telos* of language through *Jerusalem,* and have arrived at a vision of its consummation in a place/time Blake calls "Eternity" in the twenty-seventh line of the penultimate text plate. In the next line, Blake describes the eternal relationship between the Four Living Creatures—the four aspects of divine humanity—as linguistic performance: "And they conversed together in Visionary forms dramatic . . ." (E 257, K 746). The medium of this communal conversation, its articulated "forms," unites the signifying precision of vision with the action of drama. We have encountered this same combination in the kerygmatic signs of Christ and His followers and in Warburton's theories of the hieroglyphic combination of linguistics and kinesics by the Old Testament prophets.[40] Blake's own idea of poetic composition as a union of conception and execution, of the artist's vision and his labour, can also be described as a form both dramatic and visionary. Yet these important precedents, cultural and personal, capture neither the full ontological potency nor the conversational dynamic of language in eternity.

At the beginning of the second book of *Milton,* Blake equates "the breath of the Almighty," the "words of man to man | In the great Wars of Eternity," and the "fury of Poetic Inspiration" with "Mental forms Creating"

(Pl. 30; E 129, K 519). "Visionary forms dramatic" enact this same integration of human conversation, poetic composition, and divine Logos:

> And they conversed together in Visionary forms dramatic which bright
> Redounded from their Tongues in thunderous majesty, in Visions
> In new Expanses, creating exemplars of Memory and of Intellect
> Creating Space, Creating Time according to the wonders Divine
> Of Human Imagination, . . .
>
> —(E 257–8, K 746)

As the Living Creatures converse, their words are, like ours, "exemplars of Memory and of Intellect." Like the poet's, their words act "according to the wonders Divine | Of Human Imagination." And like God's, their words are continually "Creating Space, Creating Time." Humboldt's sense of language as an objectivity that is not withdrawn from subjectivity becomes in these lines the process in which *all* objectivity and subjectivity share their perpetual and participial coming-into-being.

The mediatory action of language, so important to Humboldt's theory of discourse, becomes an essential and literal event in Blake's eternity. When "England who is Brittannia entered Albions bosom" (Pl. 96; E 255, K 743), she follows the same course from objective and external to subjective and internal presence that Humboldt traces for words. As in language, the process is reversible. Urizen's self-reifications are a one-way avenue. The cohesive pluralism of the eternal and internal empties itself into a heterogeneous objectivity and becomes trapped in it, like a speech act without an auditor. In contrast, the Living Creatures "walked | To & fro in Eternity as One Man reflecting each in each & clearly seen | And seeing" (Pl. 98; E 258, K 746). This ideal conversation, with its back and forth movement and mutual understanding, varies "According to the subject of discourse." The senses and the things they perceive also function in accord with the perfected responsiveness of conversations in eternity; even "Time & Space | . . . vary according as the Organs of Perception vary." With this reification of discourse into a mode of perception, Blake returns us to a condition briefly glimpsed in *The Book of Urizen,* that time when "The will of the Immortal expanded | Or contracted his all flexible senses" (Pl. 3; E 71, K 223). This seamless intercourse between semiotic conception and ontological execution, and its absolute symmetry with desire, expands to become the movement of being in and out of time on the final text plate of *Jerusalem.* There Blake asks us to envision a world in which all "Forms"—not just words—are at will "going forth . . . | Into the Planetary lives of Years Months Days & Hours" (E 258, K 747). And from that exteriority all forms may return, like words heard and understood, into the interiority of Albion's "Bosom," there to awaken to the "Life of Immortality" Blake saw and heard in his linguistic imagination.

The alternative reality Blake conceives in *Jerusalem* is shaped by his experience of the medium of its execution. As so many philosophers of language from Herder to Humboldt insisted, that medium is profoundly human. Indeed, language is the activity that creates a being as human. Through the trope of personification, language can also be used to grant human qualities to the non-human or to the abstractions language itself produces. Blake takes such merely figural and provisional extensions to their radical conclusion. His projection of phenomenological linguistics into an ontology is the vehicle for the humanization of all being. At the same time, this language joins man to divinity. The "Words of the Mutual Covenant Divine" revealed to Blake near the end of *Jerusalem* are themselves the covenant, the medium establishing the mutuality of man and God (Pl. 98; E 258, K 749). This covenant calls forth, on the final text plate, the replacement of categorical difference with incommensurable and immutable identities.[41] Yet just as words acquire meaning through their participation in a community of other words, the articulated forms of eternity take on their identities by participating in a human community. "All Human Forms identified"—that is, all forms identified *as* human—"even Tree Metal Earth & Stone" (E 258, K 747). The human forms of these things in our world are the names we give them, the words by which they can be identified and made part of human subjectivity. In Blake's imagined world, the linguistic consciousness grounded in these words becomes the ground of being for the things they name. The generative power of language, available to Blake and to us through our ability to create propositions never before heard, has become the generation of ontological out of verbal identities.

The desire of language to win existence in reality has carried Blake's poem beyond the dream of the Adamic sign, even beyond the animating powers of the "ancient Poets" in *The Marriage of Heaven and Hell,* to a vision of language reclaiming its power as the Logos. The culminating act of this revivified language is to name the community of things it creates: "And I heard the Name of their Emanations they are named Jerusalem" (E 259, K 747). This is also the name of the community of words constituting Blake's poem. Thus we are returned, in the final sentence of the poem, to the simple yet necessary event of its author hearing the word "Jerusalem" before naming *Jerusalem.* The objective and communal presence of a single word has entered the consciousness of a poet who returns it to objective presence in a written text so that it may enter through the senses into the consciousness of readers whose shared linguistic experience creates the foundation for a community. In these common but miraculous acts lies the world imagined as the words of *Jerusalem.*

Notes

1. I take the last three possibilities from Hilton, *Literal Imagination* (Berkeley: University of California Press, 1983), p. 255. McGann, "Idea of an Indeterminate Text," *Studies in*

Romanticism 25 (1986), pp. 317–18, points out that Blake could have learned of the derivation of "horizon" from the Greek word for "*bound* or *terminate*" from a note in the Geddes Bible.

2. *Jerusalem,* Pl. 3; E 145, K 620.

3. De Luca, "Proper Names," *Blake Studies* 8:1 (1978), p. 10, notes a smaller family, also descending from Enitharmon, based on the "th" radical. Blake's interest in name families is most clearly indicated by his decompounding of "Enitharmon" to create the names of her parents, Enion and Tharmas. See also De Luca, "Proper Names," pp. 18–20, for an excellent analysis of the 4 name families in *Jerusalem.*

4. Bryant, *New System,* 1:16–18. Blake sometimes associates Enitharmon with the moon, another "-on" word that an imaginative etymologist like Bryant could consider a derivative from her name.

5. *New System* 3 vols., London, 1774–76, 1:xv. There are also numerous Biblical precedents for treating the same name as both a person and a place.

6. Pl. 16; E 160, K 637. Damon, *William Blake: His Philosophy and Symbols* (London: Constable, 1924), p. 442, comments that "this assignment of the various counties of Great Britain among the twelve Sons of Israel is not too important in the understanding of *Jerusalem.*" Paley, *Continuing City* (Oxford: Clarendon Press, 1983), pp. 269–70, sensibly concludes that "what the specific analogies are is less important than the fact that a general analogical relationship can be envisaged."

7. Pl. 5; E 99, K 484. Much the same passage appears in *Jerusalem,* with the phrase altered to "conversing with the ground" (Pl. 49; K 680). Oddly, Erdman takes this as an "error in copying *Milton*" (E 811) rather than a purposeful revision. Whether void or ground, the "conversing" is only a soliloquy.

8. This tradition continues in modern theological studies of language; see for example G. Ebeling, *God and Word* (Philadelphia: Fortress Press, 1966), 19: "It is not the concept of signification but far more profoundly the concept of answerability that points us to that which is fundamental in language."

9. Pl. 3; E 145, K 621. See also Blake's letter to Butts of 25 April 1803 in which he says he is returning to London so that he "may converse with [his] friends in Eternity" (E 728, K 822). Blake told H. C. Robinson that he "must have had conversations" with Socrates and Jesus (Bentley, *Blake Records* (Oxford: Clarendon Press, 1969), p. 310).

10. E 273, K 776. See also *Milton,* Pl. 3: "the Human Imagination | . . . is the Divine Body of the Lord Jesus" (E 96, K 482). At the beginning of *The Four Zoas,* Blake further identifies "The Universal Man" with "the Universal Brotherhood of Eden" (E 300, K 264). The importance of the human form throughout Blake's poetry is demonstrated by Frosch, *Awakening of Albion* (Ithaca: Cornell University Press, 1974). The body as an image of community is nicely summarized in Deen, *Conversing in Paradise* (Columbia: University of Missouri Press, 1983), pp. 8–13. See also M. Ferber, "Blake's Idea of Brotherhood," *PMLA* 93 (1978), 438–47.

11. Humboldt, *Observations on World History* (1814), in *Humanist without Portfolio,* trans. Marianne Cowan (Detroit: Wayne State University Press, 1963), p. 76.

12. Barrell, *Political Theory of Painting from Reynolds to Hazlitt* (New Haven: Yale University Press, 1986).

13. Advertisement to the Exhibition of 1809, E 528, K 561; *Jerusalem,* Pl. 3 (E 146, K 621).

14. *Jerusalem,* Pl. 3; E 145, K 620. In Matthew 25:33, the sheep are "on his right hand, but the goats on the left." These positions were preserved in Blake's copperplate, but are of course reversed in impressions from it.

15. E 145, K 621; the words in square brackets were partly deleted from the plate. For further observations on Blake's concept of his public that stress a personal poet/reader union, see M. Eaves, "Romantic Expressive Theory and Blake's Idea of the Audience," *PMLA* 95 (1980), 784–801.

16. *Dialogue on Poetry and Literary Aphorisms*, trans. E. Behler and Roman Struc (University Park: Pennsylvania State University Press, 1968), 131–2. For predecessors to Schlegel's idea of allowing the reader to do part of the "inventing," see my comments on Blair and Ossian in ch. 2.

17. "The Aphorisms of 1805 and 1809–10," in F. Schleiermacher, *Hermeneutics*, ed. H. Kimmerle, trans. J. Duke and J. Forstman (Missoula: Scholars Press, 1977), 42.

18. J. A. Ernesti's *Institutio interpretis Novi Testamenti* (Leyden: J. LeMair, 1762) is an important transition between Boehme and the Higher Criticism because it preserves the concept of sympathetic identification within a rationalist and historicist framework. For an impressive modern revision of this hermeneutic, one that stresses "a reading which is psychological and divinatory rather than grammatical and structuralist," see T. Rajan, "The Supplement of Reading," *New Literary History*, 17 (1986), 573–94. Rajan makes a distinction between a "hermeneutic" reading that tries to reconstruct an original meaning and a "heuristic" reading productive of new meanings. For Blake, this is a distinction without a difference because of his belief in the unity of origin and originality.

19. *Vision of the Last Judgment*, E 555, K 605.

20. Letter of 12 April 1827 to Cumberland, E 784, K 878; letter of 10 January 1803 (misdated 1802) to Butts, E 724, K 812.

21. P. J. Gallagher, "The Word Made Flesh: Blake's 'A Poison Tree' and the Book of Genesis," *Studies in Romanticism*, 16 (1977), 237–49, offers some similar observations on "a poison tree," finding that "tenor and vehicle are completely interconvertible, or rather the one becomes the other as the poem proceeds . . ." (p. 239).

22. Pl. 25; E 82, K 235 (see discussion in ch. 3).

23. Pl. 61; E 212, K 695. For a similar conversion of the human into a landscape by means of literalized simile, see *Four Zoas*, Night the Fifth, p. 61, lines 24–31 (E 341–2, K 308).

24. Prefatory note to "Kubla Khan," *Poetical Works of Coleridge*, 2 vols. ed. E. H. Coleridge (Oxford: Clarendon Press, 1912), 1:296; in Bentley, *Blake Records*, p. 547. Coleridge also claims for his opium-induced dream consciousness an Adamic unity of "things" and their "correspondent expressions."

25. *Continuing City*, p. 62.

26. For "sorts" in reference to lexical categories, see ch. 3 n. 92. For a similar, fundamental questioning of the literal/figural distinction (but without reference to ontological implications), see S. D. Ross, "Metaphor, the Semasic Field, and Inexhaustibility," *New Literary History*, 18 (1987), 517–33.

27. Kroeber, "Delivering *Jerusalem*," in Curran and Wittreich, *Blake's Sublime Allegory* (Madison: University of Wisconsin Press, 1973), pp. 347–67; Hartman, "Envoi: 'So Many Things,' " in Hilton and Vogler, *Unnam'd Forms* (Berkeley: University of California Press, 1986), p. 243.

28. *Personification and the Sublime* (1985), 22. See also G. L. Bruns, "The Problem of Figuration in Antiquity," in G. Shapiro and A. Sica, *Hermeneutics* (Amherst: University of Massachusetts Press, 1984), 148: ". . . recourse to the notion of figure, or to some equivalent concept such as allegory, symbol, or even catachresis, was for the ancients a way of normalizing the Scriptures. For once you have identified a scandal as a figure, you have already turned it into something you can deal with."

29. Reynolds, *Works*, 3 vols. (London: Cadell and Davies, 1798), 1:195; Blake's annotations, E 658, K 473.

30. For complete reproductions of the watercolours and engravings, see Grant, *et al.*, *Blake's Designs for Young's Night Thoughts*, 2 vols. (Oxford: Clarendon Press, 1980).

31. E 541, K 576. This response was probably prompted by Robert Hunt's review of *The Grave* illustrations; see R. N. Essick and M. D. Paley, *Robert Blair's The Grave* (1982), esp. pp. 26–7.

32. E 554, K 604. For the literality of vision, see discussion in chs. 2 and 3. For some brief suggestive comments on "vision" as "apostrophe . . . literalized," see G. Pechey, *"The Marriage of Heaven and Hell:* A Text and its Conjuncture," *Oxford Literary Review,* 3 (1979), 70–1.

33. *Vision of the Last Judgment,* E 565, K 617. See also *Jerusalem,* Pl. 71: ". . . in your own Bosom you bear your Heaven | And Earth, & all you behold, tho it appears Without it is Within" (E 225, K 709).

34. As this etymological excursion suggests, my route into Blake's ontological linguistics has been shaped by similar considerations in Heidegger's *Introduction to Metaphysics* (1959), *Being and Time* (1962), and *On the Way to Language* (1971). See also the discussion of *hayah,* "to be" in Hebrew, in Boman, *Hebrew Thought Compared with Greek,* p. 45: ". . . the meaning of *hayah* is as much 'become' as 'be'," sometimes one and sometimes the other. Sometimes it fluctuates between them, and at other times it encompasses both "becoming" and "being" and contains yet a third active motif; in this motif of *effecting* is apparently to be sought the "arch that spans the gap between 'becoming' and 'being.' "

35. Adams, "Blake and the Philosophy of Literary Symbolism," *New Literary History* 5 (1973), p. 137; Deen, *Conversing in Paradise,* p. 236. A similar perspective is suggested by Stempel's observation that "language and representation become one" at the end of *Jerusalem* ("Blake, Foucault, and the Classical Episteme," *PMLA* 96 (1981), p. 398) and by Paley's comment that "we sense" on Pl. 98 "the effort of the language to abandon its function as mediator and to become meaning itself" (*Continuing City,* p. 64).

36. *Book of Urizen,* Pl. 3 (E 70, K 222); *Jerusalem,* Pl. 96 (E 255, K 743). Taylor, "Semantic Structures and the Temporal Modes of Blake's Prophetic Verse," *Language and Style* 12 (1979), pp. 31–2, discusses the plural "times" as an example of how Blake is "playing with linguistic boundedness." That boundedness is in these examples a good deal more flexible than the fallen world of time and space.

37. Introduction to the study of Kawi, *Humanist without Portfolio,* p. 289.

38. *Wilhelm von Humboldt's Linguistic Studies* (1866), 16.

39. Introduction to the study of Kawi, *Humanist without Portfolio,* p. 258.

40. See discussion of Warburton in my ch. 2 and *Divine Legation of Moses,* 2:84–5, on the dual use of "significative *Action"* and *"Vision."* For some precedents in commentaries on Revelation, including the concept of "visionary theatre" in 17th-century works by John Lightfoot and David Pareus, see J. A. Wittreich, "Opening the Seals: Blake's Epics and the Milton Tradition," in Curran and Wittreich, *Blake's Sublime Allegory,* pp. 23–58; and Paley, *Continuing City,* pp. 285–7.

41. As Blake states in *A Vision of the Last Judgment,* "In Eternity one Thing never Changes into another Thing" (E 556, K 607).

Afterword

◆

The World-View of William Blake
in Relation to Cultural Policy

HAZARD ADAMS

I. THE PROBLEM OF THE TITLE

Blake would have thought the subject I have been assigned quite odd. I am sure he would have seen no connection between his "world-view" and "cultural policy," since to him "cultural policy" would have suggested something made by a king, a prime minister, or, perhaps worse, if that is possible, a committee or board of scholars. In other words, it would be an abstraction, and, for Blake, "to Generalize is to be an Idiot" (E641).[1] He remarks against Sir Joshua Reynolds: "Generalizing in Every thing the Man would soon be a Fool but a Cunning Fool" (E649). Furthermore, if Blake were to have reflected on the phrase "world-view" he would certainly have objected to it. For him, observation, or being a spectator, implied passivity of the imagination, and this attitude would have made him as suspicious of "views" as he was of landscape paintings and portraits. The point is not a trivial one, as I shall eventually try to show.

There is another more mundane problem to be gotten around. Blake was not in any of the usual senses a man of the world. Indeed, he seems to have had little experience of it except what he imagined (this was, of course, quite a lot) from his reading, especially the Bible and certain books of travel

From *Cultural Policy, Past, Present, and Future: The Proceedings of a Conference,* ed. Harold Coward (Calgary: Wilfred Laurier University Press for the Calgary Institute for the Humanities, 1990).

for which he made engravings. As far as we know, the longest trip he ever made was from Lambeth to Felpham on the southern English coast, a distance of some sixty miles. Except for the three years he spent there and a brief visit to a friend in Kent, he seems never to have left London. In most conventional ways he was isolated from the great world, impolitic, professionally unsuccessful, childless, and at least in his later years quite poor. He did not live in a world of politicians, political activists, theorists, or professors; and the concept of cultural policy had yet to be invented. In his day there were no ministers of health, education, or welfare, no national endowments for the humanities, or Canada councils. Hardly anyone had yet committed a social science. Such bodies as might have been thought in his time to further cultural life—the Church, the Royal Academy, the Royal Family—Blake viewed with either suspicion, resentment, or contempt, usually all three. He was in many ways an outsider, an embarrassment to a lady of class who had to sit beside him at a dinner, without formal education, and regarded as an artisan rather than an artist by many in the artistic establishment. His political views bordered on treason, if they were not in fact technically treasonous at the time. He had to stand trial in 1803 on what may or may not have been a false charge. He approved of the American and French Revolutions and spoke and wrote often in the tone of radical dissent, both political and religious.

II. ANTITHETICALITY

Blake was, it is probably fair to say, the first consciously antithetical artist. By this I mean that he conceived of his work as opposed to the usual oppositions embedded in the language of the culture. Among these were subject/object, body/soul, and the concepts of good and evil arising from them involving preservation of social, political, and cultural power in the patriarchal and class system of the time. The young W. B. Yeats, one of Blake's first conscientiously (but too often erring) interpreters, misunderstood Blake's antitheticality (a term I have actually taken from Yeats) and described him, in effect, as the first aesthetic artist, the first aesthete. But if aestheticism means a detached formalism, it is about as far as possible from Blake's conception of art. Nor was Blake's attitude anything like that of aesthetic subjectivism, represented later in its most extreme form by Walter Pater, another hero (at one time) of Yeats. Both the aesthete and the subjectivist would have been for Blake merely the other side of the coin from the objectivist. Blake's aim was to establish a position antithetical to this negation, in which each side exists by deploring the errors of its opposite. Thus they play roles familiar to readers of Blake's longer poems—the young, frustrated Orc and the old repressive Urizen. Their progress is but cyclical, that is, no progress at all.

Recently Tzvetan Todorov has observed, as have others, the curious embrace of or at least flirtation with tyrannical political systems by early twentieth-century intellectuals and their criticism of democracy: "We like to see our societies as ones in which both individuals and the collectivity have the right to set their own standards. Given which, the critique of existing norms is a crucial social task, and intellectuals have come to identify themselves with performing it. It is because the majority has chosen the path of democracy that intellectuals feel compelled to call it into question."[2] This phenomenon begins, I think, with romanticism and the revolutionary fervor and disillusion that followd it. Blake was never compelled to call democracy into question. For him democracy, though he did not have the word and imagined a more thorough form of it than anyone has seen on earth, was the antithetical dream of a classless, free society in the process of endless creation. Anything that contributed to it, including personal acts of charity and love, was what he conceived of as art.

Today Blake would have been vociferous in his criticism of the so-called democracies, not embracing some totalitarian form as an alternative but relentlessly pointing out where totalitarianism still lurked in political and social practices. There is a sense, of course, in which Blake must have appeared, in his own time, reactionary. He liked little that had happened in the fine arts since Raphael, and in various ways he was out of step with the contemporary. He had no sympathy with modern philosophy or the associationist psychology that for a while captured Wordsworth and Coleridge. But there is very little nostalgia in Blake, almost a principled flight from it to the future. As a result, his work has the opposite effect of that of his closest followers, the young "ancients" who gathered around him late in his life, the Pre-Raphaelites, and the early Yeats, who later detected in his own apprentice poetry a "slight, sentimental sensuality which is disagreeable."[3] Blake's complaints about the modernism of his own time were aimed at certain fundamental assumptions that to his eyes corrupted politics, religion, sexuality, and science. In spite of his own preferences in painting for Raphael and before, he did not seek a return to the past but sought a new future.

Almost all the modern intellectuals whom Todorov has in mind as reactionary critics of democracy imagined nostalgically some lost age or embraced (or at least admired for a time) some fascist or totalitarian idea or strong man. If Blake wished to return to something in the past (and he did, of course, speak of a golden age), it was the act of creation itself. And this was but to remind his readers that creation was in their power and not something imposed from above or beyond or the past by a distant god. Thus creation is, for Blake, actually removed from the past into potentiality and from surrounding space into the human mind.

Therefore, Blake's world-view, if that is what we are to call it, is always a projection outward of possibility rather than a "correspondence" to anything out there. This projection is an activity of what he calls imagination and is identical with his notion of religious activity, though he frequently uses the term "religious" in a derogatory sense to mean the very opposite— passive reception of the law of external authority paralleling the passive reception of sense data that he attacks in Locke's epistemology.

Blake's world-view can, therefore, be characterized as symbolical, though symbolizing nothing existent (that would be allegory in his language), but that which is yet to exist, desirable both individually and socially. This symbolized does not exist somewhere like a Platonic form or idea. Blake's symbols do not have objects to which they refer or previous ideas which they signify. They are radical possibilities *in themselves,* without attachment to things in themselves.[4] In this sense, Blake's world-view is not a view but is itself a sort of world, a world of language and design which does not copy nature, he declares, but projects a "vision." Blake's illuminated works are for spectators who can transcend the spectatorial, which in Blake is the spectral, condition. In his description of his painting "The Last Judgment," Blake wrote: "If the Spectator could Enter into these Images in his Imagination approaching them on the Fiery Chariot of his Contemplative Thought if he could Enter into Noahs Rainbow or into his bosom or could make a Friend & Companion of one of these Images of wonder which always intreats him to leave mortal things as he must know then would he arise from his Grave then would he meet the Lord in the Air & then he would be happy" (E560).

It is noteworthy that Blake called his designs "vision," not "fable" or "allegory." "Vision," emphasizing the painter's eye, means for Blake an active seeing of what is greater than nature or the object as it is opposed to the subject. In the passage I have quoted above, Blake hopes for an act of vision in the spectator that will make him more than a spectator, a visionary identifying himself with a world of possibility. That world is neither an epistemological object nor a phenomenological one. Rather it is an ethical projection, but not connected in any way with received moral law.

III. A VISIONARY WORLD

The archetypes of Blake's visionary world have been much discussed in recent decades, most illuminatingly by Northrop Frye in his monumental *Fearful Symmetry* and several of his subsequent essays: "Blake's Treatment of the Archetype," "Notes for a Commentary on *Milton,*" "The Road of Excess," and "The Keys to the Gates."[5] We know a great deal now about the interrelations of Urthona, Tharmas, Luvah, and Urizen, their fallen forms, their emanations, and the mental states inhabited by the giant Albion. There is no need to go over ground so eloquently treated. It is possible, however, to emphasize here some of the more general characteristics of Blake's visionary world or, as some have called it, mythology in order to see what is implied there for thinking about cultural policy.

I have divided this subject into four parts, and because Blake's visionary world is not a landscape or an external portrait but an imagining of mental activity, I begin with the problem of knowledge as Blake saw it.

a. *Against epistemology:* The term "epistemology" suggests the very thing Blake opposed most vehemently. It is a term that has come to be identified with the situational view of natural science established by Bacon, Newton, and Locke—an object situated vis à vis a subject or vice versa. The attitude of subject/object carried outside the realm of science, as Blake saw that it had been in his day, inevitably generated alienation of individuals from all that surrounded them, requiring measures to dominate that threatening other. Perhaps Blake's most powerful image of this figure is the hapless Urizen of *The Four Zoas,* who travels through such a universe and can find no foundation for it. Finally, he surrounds himself with books of arbitrary law as a fortress against chaos. This merely generates in that other outer world the repressed energy of Orc, who must be endlessly chained down or crucified in order to maintain control but whose moments of revolt establish a new negative force with its own pattern of alienation and fear—Urizen all over again. Blake's aim was to provide a contrary to this situation of negative opposition, which may be necessary to science as a fiction but which Blake nevertheless described in an unflattering way as a "cloven fiction."

b. *Contrary antithetical vision:* Obviously the contrary must be something not cloven in this way. At the same time it must not negate, that is, suppress that cloven opposite. Otherwise the cycle of alienation will continue with new terms playing the old roles. It cannot be a monolithic, seamless oneness. Rather it must maintain oppositions while it recasts their roles so that neither side can negate the other. This is one difference between a true contrary and a negation. There can be no "progression" in a situation of negation alone because it results either in continued suppression or in the cyclicity of the Orc/Urizen opposition. If, however, the negation is opposed by a contrary it can cease to be a negation because it is involved now in what Blake describes at the end of *Jerusalem* as conversations in "visionary forms dramatic" (E257). Establishment of a contrary requires, then, a sort of friendly opposition, yet clearly an opposition and tension. The heroic worker-artist Los in *Jerusalem* firmly asserts:

> I must Create a System, or be enslav'd by another Mans
> I will not Reason & Compare: my business is to Create.
> (E153)

Los's idea of system opposing system is not as precise as the whole poem seems to be and suggests that at this point in the poem Los may still be in error to some extent. *Jerusalem* is more like an antisystem, that is, antithetical to system as such, a true contrary that provides what system lacks or lacks what system imposes. As such, it isn't just an alternative system but *the* contrary. It would take too much space to show how *Jerusalem* antisystemically frustrates systematic analysis, though it would be instructive at this point. It is, however, possible to show that this contrary employs language in a way contrary to the view of language implicit in systems based on scientific epistemology. One can characterize this use of language as taking metaphor (in the sense of all tropes) seriously, that is to say, literally, or literarily.

c. *A vision of language, a language of vision:* For Blake it is language or languages (since there is for Blake a language of design) that constitute culture. Therefore, our view of language, a clear and distinct outline of what it is and can do, is critical to human life and will affect how society shapes itself. Blake's vision of language he offered relatively early in his career in *The Marriage of Heaven and Hell,* defining it, as was characteristic of his time, by imagining its origin in a symbolical story. In the story, he describes not just the invention of names by poets but the eventual hardening of language into "system." The "ancient poets animated all sensible objects with Gods or Geniuses" (E38), but gradually these gods became abstracted from their objects and under domination of an interpreting priesthood became objects of worship external to man, when they had originally been his invention and immediately experienceable. These original acts of naming were obviously metaphorical, so for Blake metaphor is fundamental to language and not something secondary or decorative added on to a system that has as its ideal form the pure abstraction from objects achieved in mathematics, where the trope has completely disappeared. Blake tells the story of language as if it were the history of a fall. If we read *Jerusalem* carefully, we discover that the fall was not the invention of abstraction but the suppression of metaphor in system, that is, the culture's failure to maintain the prolific contrariety of abstraction and trope. Concurrent with this was the failure to maintain the arts of life, which require the metaphor. Without it the arts can but copy a nature assumed to be already out there, for it is in the metaphor that two things unlike in nature are brought into "identity," a term I shall discuss at greater length in part IV. Without metaphor the arts must accept the cloven fiction of subject/object, identifying art with either one or the other, and cut themselves off from true making. In such a situation language cannot change. The world ceases to move, and we are all like Urizen or the frozen Satan of the *Divine Comedy,* the alien world of matter surrounding and imprisoning us. For Blake, the word "allegory," when he uses it in a derogatory way, means a language that has become abstracted from images so that it can no longer perform the metaphorical act of identifying things, cannot see the particular in a new way, but merely arbitrarily identifies words with phantasmal ideas as if the ideas had some power greater than and outside ourselves, but a distant power that can't really be given the body that the allegorical image pretends it has.

d. *Visionary religion:* Although Blake often used the word "religious" to indicate a tyrannical moral code imposed on people, often by those whose "desire . . . is weak enough to be restrained" (E34), he can be said to promulgate a visionary humanistic version of Christianity that is strongly dependent on his vision of language. In one of his late engraved works, "The Laocoön," done at a time when he had become more explicit in his writings about the meaning of Jesus, he speaks of the gods of Greece and Egypt as "mathematical diagrams" and cites as evidence Plato's works. In such states, Blake asserts, "All Visionary men are accounted Mad" (E274). This implies that Jesus represents the antithetical contrary to such gods. He is human, and he is as much a projection or part of the human mind as the abstract gods of Greece and Egypt (for good measure Blake adds Babylon). But the abstract gods are allegorical and empty inhumanity and would negate as seditious the contrary Jesus, who is crucified, as is the dying figure Luvah in the prophetic books.

Perhaps the most startling thing Blake does in "The Laocoön" is to identify his Jesus and Christianity itself with art. When Jesus advises giving to Caesar what is Caesar's, Blake believes that the coin implies empire and natural religion as well as worldly wealth or, simply, money. In citing Virgil's *Aeneid* vi, 848, where Anchises contrasts sculptors in bronze, pleaders of causes, and astronomers with the Romans, who are urged to guide the nations by their military authority, Blake identifies more than artists, as we think of them, with art and asserts that when art is degraded and imagination is denied war governs the nations. Clearly Blake was no admirer of Virgil, and he cites the *Aeneid* passage not only in "The Laocoön" but also in the little engraved essay "On Virgil," where art and war are explicitly opposed to each other. Art is, for Blake, creative activity of all kinds; creative activity can be symbolized by the metaphor, which puts things together that are normally (or passively) thought separate without violating individuality. This Blake describes in his poem on the poet Milton as "annihilation" of "selfhood." By the latter word he meant the radical separateness, aloneness, and consequent fear and desire to dominate the other that is the condition of the epistemological subject. Art is true charity. False charity is that which would not exist if there were "nobody poor." True charity searches for identity, which is the foundation of Blake's religious vision and the ethic that would be a ground for a Blakean cultural policy.

IV. Guiding Cultural Policy: A Blakean Ethic

Blake's poetry has as its fundamental contrariety the opposition of identity to the negation difference/indifference. Its fundamental trope is the synecdoche; the contrary and the trope are closely related. Blake does not actually use the terms "difference" and "indifference." Rather he uses "individuality" and "universality," which can stand politically for the extremes of anarchy and totalitarianism, which are caught in mutual negation. The contrary, "identity," is a word Blake employs tellingly at the end of *Jerusalem:*

> All Human Forms identified even Tree Metal Earth & Stone. all
> Human Forms identified. . . .
>
> (E258)

It is a mistake to think that identity for Blake meant some mystical indifference as much as it is a mistake to think that a metaphor declares an utter indifference of two things. To say that a metaphor is merely a comparison according to the apprehension of some common characteristics is equally a mistake, merely the other side of the same coin and an example of a naive imitation theory of language and art. Identity embodies the antithetical notion denying that we should make a choice. Since from the point of view of familiar logic and of science this seems absurd, we must either declare the idea mad or presume that it expresses not the "natural" view but some other equally as serious. I would describe that view as both artistic (in Blake's sense) and ethical. The ethical implication is that we are both individual and universal (and thus involved one in another) *at the same time,* which is what Blake meant by identity, modeled on the metaphor. In this sense, nature or at least ethical action should copy art, the basis of which is the metaphor. (Oscar Wilde's Vivian, though somewhat impertinently, had it right.) But this notion in Blake is not merely metaphorical, across entities; it is synecdochic, that is, it joins wholes and parts. Over and over in Blake we discover that part and whole are identical, with neither privileged.

A Blakean cultural policy would, first, have to take as its ground this notion as an ethical principle for individuals and a political ethic for states. It would have to be held in tension with its contrary, which tends, when not opposed, to move in the direction either of totalitarian indifference or anarchic individualism.

A second ground for a Blakean cultural policy would be the acceptance and maintenance of the contrariety of art and science. Contrariety means equality and creative opposition. If this existed, more would discover what many scientists already know, that the human artistic impulse toward making is what refurbishes the human scientific impulse toward understanding. Blake had terms for this: he called the first "prolific" and the second "devourer" and regarded them as necessary to human existence.

If the first ground is the ethical one for cultural policy, the second is the educational ground, and it appears to generate a principle for curriculum. At the base of such a curriculum would be study of the languages of man or what Ernst Cassirer called "symbolic forms." At one end of the base would be language as understood and practiced by Blake's mythic "ancient poets": the languages of myth and poetry in which tropes played their appropriate creative, identifying roles, not imitative ones. (In "The Laocoön" Blake wrote: "Israel delivered from Egypt is Art delivered from Nature & Imitation" [E274]). They would also include the nondiscursive languages of nonimitative visual design and music, which create new forms from old matter.

At the other end of the base would be number, the language of science, which generates antimythical structures that from one point of view look like copies of nature but can be regarded in a Blakean way as makings of nature that fictionally pretend to be copies.

An understanding of these foundations and an appreciation of their creative potentialities, limitations, and interrelations, both intellectual and political, are the Blakean ground for any workable cultural policy. Either alone creates an educational policy susceptible to tyranny. The hegemony of the antimythical creates the tyranny of technological alienation. The hegemony of myth creates the tyranny of superstition. Our age, as Blake prophesied, is an age of the former. The consequence is the alienation and perversion of myth, which has taken the destructive paranoical forms, among others, of Naziism, soviet genetics, religious fundamentalism, and corrupt nostalgias of concern to Todorov. This has been a negating response to the abstraction and technological madness that has been ruling us. Blake responded to it with a vociferous antitheticality, a broad defense of art, but he kept in mind the contrary, and therefore wrote: "What is the Life of Man but Art & Science" (E232).

POSTSCRIPT ON "THE LAOCOÖN"

Blake's own works are models of the antitheticality he advocated. He observed early in his career that one of the aims of art is to "rouze the faculties to act," a phrase containing a nice ambiguity when it is applied to education. He was not afraid of obscurity because "what it not too Explicit is the fittest for Instruction" (E702). Despite his opposition to allegory, which is usually associated with the didactic, Blake was not loath to identify his own work as didactic, though with a difference, and that difference can be described as its challenging nature. His late engraving of the Laocoön group is only one of his works that raises all sorts of challenges, "rouzing the faculties to act." The questions are about its parts but also about how its parts go together, if they do, causing us to reconsider our senses of parts and wholes.

Note first that Blake does not treat the statue he has "copied" as Laocoön at all. Indeed, the natural event that is supposedly depicted, Laocoön's agony, Blake treats as a sort of copy of art; for Blake describes the design as "י [Jah, for Jehovah] and his two sons Satan & Adam as they were copied from the Cherubim of Solomons Temple by three Rhodians & applied to Natural Fact or History of Ilium" (E273). These words are placed on the plate beneath the design as if they were the title. History itself (natural fact) finds

Art Degraded Imagination Denied War Governed the Nations

its shape in a copy of an artifact, rather than the other way around. The Rhodians, apparently chronicling an event, were copying art. On all sides of the central design, and woven around it are single words, phrases, and sentences, some of the words being in Hebrew. Some sentences are truncated as if urgently uttered; others seem added in as if suddenly generated by thinking on those already there, though temporal order either of composition or of reading is made impossible to determine. In his edition of Blake, cited below in note 1, David V. Erdman attempts to order these items thematically; there is nothing at all wrong with doing this, but it is as difficult to accomplish definitively as it is to detect conventional narrative pattern in the prophetic books. This is because Blake was determined to be, as Yeats called him, a "literal realist of the imagination" (actually Yeats said "too literal realist"). Blake took his conception of metaphor and synecdoche literally, so one discovers that one can begin with virtually any statement in "The Laocoön" and find, if one's faculties really are roused, that it leads to and implies, contains or is part of the others, and is a synecdoche of a whole that seems to be potentially limitless.[6] One can easily imagine an infinite accretion of elements that would threaten to burst the plate, the words flowing beyond its borders. It is as if the plate requires another dimension, which is perhaps the reason that there is an engraved figure (another art) and that the figure is based on a sculpture.

As for the choice of poor Laocoön and his two sons, Blake claims them to be copies of works of art in Solomon's Temple, these "Biblical" works symbolizing for Blake the "originality" or shaping and visionary quality of art above history and natural fact. Art is the form, in the sense of activity, into which an episode in the history of Ilium is put. Symbolically the original figures of the temple were shown to have been caught in the coils of the serpent of this world, nature, which for Blake always means objectivity, which is always locked together with its negation, subjectivity. As presented by the three Rhodians, Jehovah, Satan, and Adam become Laocoön and his two sons. You will recall that Laocoön made the right prediction but one nobody wanted to hear uttered. He and his sons became victims of epic events. Blake didn't think much of epics and here identifies them with "nature." They were poems which wrote "natural fact" or history in the pay of empire, to which Laocoön and his sons were sacrificed; one had to read epics "infernally" before they revealed their own errors, and this meant getting epics back to the sources of art, symbolized by Solomon's Temple. This is evidence in Blake of his own version of what we now call "deconstruction." Blake's deconstructions are unusual, however, and antithetical to deconstruction as it is usually presented because they are always toward making something. Though that something may never be quite fully accomplished, the act and the direction bear witness to an ethical effort that is always in process. So there is no external world in Blake to view, only finally a way of acting, not to be watched but to be performed.

Notes

1. All quotations from Blake's work are from *The Complete Poetry and Prose of William Blake,* ed. David V. Erdman, (Garden City: Anchor Press/Doubleday, revised edition, 1982), referred to in parentheses after quotations as "E."

2. *Times Literary Supplement,* June 17–23, 1988, p. 684.

3. *The Autobiography of William Butler Yeats* (New York: Macmillan, 1953), p. 196.

4. This matter I discuss at some length in *Philosophy of the Literary Symbolic* (Tallahassee: Florida State University Press, 1983), especially pp. 99–116.

5. *Fearful Symmetry: A Study of William Blake* (Princeton: Princeton University Press, 1947); "Notes for a Study of *Milton,*" *The Divine Vision,* ed. Vivian De Sola Pinto, (London: Victor Gollancz, 1957); "The Road of Excess" and "The Keys to the Gates," *The Stubborn Structure* (Ithaca: Cornell University Press, 1970).

6. I discuss this matter of what I call the "open synecdoche" at some length in "Synecdoche and Method," *Critical Paths: Blake and the Argument of Method,* ed. D. Miller, M. Bracher, and D. Ault, (Durham: Duke University Press, 1988), pp. 41–52.

Selected Bibliography

♦

CRITICISM AND BIOGRAPHY

Adams, Hazard. *William Blake: A Reading of the Shorter Poems.* Seattle: University of Washington Press, 1963.

Ault, Donald. *Visionary Physics: Blake's Response to Newton.* Chicago: University of Chicago Press, 1974.

Ault, Donald, Mark Bracher and Dan Miller, eds. *Critical Paths: Blake and the Argument of Method.* Durham and London: Duke University Press, 1987.

_____. *Narrative Unbound: Re-Visioning William Blake's The Four Zoas.* Barrytown: Station Hill Press, 1987.

Bentley, G. E., Jr. *Blake Books.* Oxford: Clarendon Press, 1977.

_____. *Blake Records.* Oxford: Clarendon Press, 1969. Supplement, 1988.

Bertholf, Robert J., and Annette S. Levitt. *William Blake and the Moderns.* Albany: State University of New York Press, 1982.

Bindman, David. *Blake as an Artist.* Oxford: Phaidon Press; New York: E. P. Dutton, 1977.

Bloom, Harold. *Blake's Apocalypse.* Garden City: Doubleday & Co., 1963.

Bracher, Mark. *Being Form'd: Thinking through Blake's "Milton."* Barrytown: Station Hill Press, 1984.

Bronowski, J. *William Blake and the Age of Revolution.* New York: Harper & Row, 1965.

Curran, Stuart, and Joseph Anthony Wittreich, Jr., eds. *Blake's Sublime Allegory.* Madison: University of Wisconsin Press, 1973.

Damon, S. Foster. *A Blake Dictionary: The Ideas and Symbols of William Blake.* Providence: Brown University Press, 1965.

_____. *William Blake: His Philosophy and Symbols.* Boston: Houghton Mifflin, 1924.

Damrosch, Leopold, Jr. *Symbol and Truth in Blake's Myth.* Princeton: Princeton University Press, 1980.

de Sola Pinto, Vivian, ed. *The Divine Vision: Studies in the Poetry and Art of William Blake.* London: V. Gollancz, 1957.

Doskow, Minna. *Structure and Meaning in William Blake's "Jerusalem."* Rutherford: Fairleigh Dickenson University Press, 1982.

Eaves, Morris. *William Blake's Theory of Art*. Princeton: Princeton University Press, 1982.

Erdman, David V. *Blake: Prophet against Empire: A Poet's Interpretation of the History of His Own Times*. Princeton: Princeton University Press, 1954. Rev. ed. 1977.

Erdman, David V., and John E. Grant, eds. *Blake's Visionary Forms Dramatic*. Princeton: Princeton University Press, 1970.

Essick, Robert N. *William Blake and the Language of Adam*. Oxford: Oxford University Press, 1989.

Essick, Robert N., and Donald Pearce, eds. *Blake in His Time*. Bloomington: Indiana University Press, 1978.

Fairchild, B. H. *Such Holy Song: Music as Idea, Form, and Image in the Poetry of William Blake*. Kent: Kent State University Press, 1980.

Fisher, Peter F. *The Valley of Vision: Blake as Prophet and Revolutionary*. Toronto: University of Toronto Press, 1961.

Fox, Susan. *Poetic Form in Blake's "Milton."* Princeton: Princeton University Press, 1976.

Frosch, Thomas R. *The Awakening of Albion: The Renovation of the Body in the Poetry of William Blake*. Ithaca: Cornell University Press, 1974.

Frye, Northrop. *Fearful Symmetry: A Study of William Blake*. Princeton: Princeton University Press, 1947.

———. *The Stubborn Structure*. Ithaca: Cornell University Press, 1970.

George, Diana Hume. *Blake and Freud*. Ithaca: Cornell University Press, 1980.

Gilchrist, Alexander. *Life of William Blake: "Pictor Ignotus."* 1863. Rev. 1880. Rev. with additional notes London: J. M. Dent & Sons, 1945.

Gleckner, Robert. *The Piper and the Bard: A Study of William Blake*. Detroit: Wayne State University Press, 1959.

Hagstrum, Jean H. *William Blake: Poet and Painter*. Chicago: University of Chicago Press, 1964.

Hilton, Nelson. *Literal Imagination: Blake's Vision of Words*. Berkeley: University of California Press, 1983.

Hirsch E. D. *Innocence and Experience: An Introduction to Blake*. New Haven: Yale University Press, 1964.

Hungerford, Edward B. *Shores of Darkness*. New York: Columbia University Press, 1941.

Keynes, Sir Geoffrey. *Blake Studies*. London: Rupert Hart-Davis, 1949. Rev. 1971.

Lister, Raymond. *Infernal Methods: A Study of William Blake's Art Techniques*. London: G. Bell & Sons, 1975.

Mitchell, W. J. T. *Blake's Composite Art: A Study of the Illuminated Poetry*. Princeton: Princeton University Press, 1978.

Ostriker, Alicia. *Vision and Verse in William Blake*. Wisconsin: University of Wisconsin Press, 1965.

Paley, Morton D. *Energy and the Imagination: A Study of the Development of Blake's Thought*. Oxford: Clarendon Press, 1970.

———. *The Continuing City: William Blake's "Jerusalem."* Oxford: The Clarendon Press, 1983.

Paley, Morton D., and Morris Eaves, eds. *Blake: An Illustrated Quarterly*.

Percival, Milton O. *William Blake's Circle of Destiny*. New York: Columbia University Press, 1938.

Rosenfeld, Alvin H., ed. *William Blake: Essays for S. Foster Damon*. Providence: Brown University Press, 1969.

Todd, Ruthven. *Tracks in the Snow*. London: Grey Walls Press, 1946.

Vogler, Thomas A., and Nelson Hilton, eds. *Unnam'd Forms: Blake and Textuality*. Berkeley: University of California Press, 1986.

Wilkie, Brian, and Mary Lynn Johnson. *Blake's "Four Zoas": The Design of a Dream*. Cambridge, Mass.: Harvard University Press, 1978.

Wilson, Mona. *Life of William Blake*. 1927. Rev. 1948; edited by Keynes, Oxford: Oxford University Press, 1971.

Wittreich, Joseph Anthony, Jr. *Angel of Apocalypse: Blake's Idea of Milton*. Madison: University of Wisconsin Press, 1975.

TEXTS AND DESIGNS

Bindman, David. *The Complete Graphic Works of William Blake*. New York: G. P. Putnam's Sons, 1978.

Binyon, Laurence. *The Engraved Designs of William Blake*. New York: Charles Scribner's Sons, 1926, 1967.

Butlin, Martin. *The Paintings and Drawings of William Blake*. New Haven: Yale University Press, 1981.

Damon, S. Foster. *Blake's Job: William Blake's Illustrations of the Book of Job*. Providence: Brown University Press, 1966.

Erdman, David V. *The Complete Poetry and Prose of William Blake*. Garden City: Anchor Press/Doubleday, Rev. ed., 1982.

―――. *The Illuminated Blake*. Garden City: Anchor Press/Doubleday, 1974.

Erdman, D. V., J. E. Grant, and M. J. Tolley, eds. *William Blake's Designs for Edward Young's "Night Thoughts": A Complete Edition*. Oxford: Clarendon Press, 1980.

Roe, Albert S. *Blake's Illustrations to the "Divine Comedy."* Princeton: Princeton University Press, 1953.

Tayler, Irene. *Blake's Illustrations to the Poems of Gray*. Princeton: Princeton University Press, 1971.

Index

♦